SINCERITY AND TRUTH

Sincerity and Truth

Essays on Arnauld, Bayle, and Toleration

JOHN KILCULLEN

CLARENDON PRESS · OXFORD
1988

Oxford University Press, Walton Street, Oxford OX2 6DP

Oxford New York Toronto
Delhi Bombay Calcutta Madras Karachi
Petaling Jaya Singapore Hong Kong Tokyo
Nairobi Dar es Salaam Cape Town
Melbourne Auckland

and associated companies in
Berlin Ibadan

Oxford is a trade mark of Oxford University Press

Published in the United States
by Oxford University Press, New York

© John Kilcullen 1988

British Library Cataloguing in Publication Data
Kilcullen, John
Sincerity and truth: essays on Arnauld
Bayle, and toleration
1. Toleration
I. Title
179'.9   BJ1431
ISBN 0-19-826691-X

Library of Congress Cataloging in Publication Data
Kilcullen, John, 1938–
Sincerity and truth.
Bibliography: p.
Includes index.
1. Arnauld, Antoine, 1612–1694. 2. Bayle,
Pierre, 1647–1706. 3. Toleration. 4. Ethics.
I. Title.
B1824.A864K57   1988   179'.9   87-28278
ISBN 0-19-826691-X

Processed by the Oxford Text System
Printed in Great Britain by
Biddles Ltd., Guildford and King's Lynn

PREFACE

I am grateful to the editor, *Philosophy Research Archives*, for permission to republish three essays originally printed in that journal: 'Antoine Arnauld against Philosophic Sin' (9 (1983), 595-638), 'Bayle on the Rights of Conscience' (11 (1985), 1-39) and 'Keeping an Open Mind' (7 (1981), no. 1440). I am grateful to Conal Condren, John Gascoigne and other members of the Sydney History of Ideas Group, to whom I read a draft of Essay I. The original version of Essay IV was discussed in a seminar at the Australian National University in 1971, and another version when I was a Visiting Fellow there in 1978. I am grateful for comments on it by Stanley Benn, Edward Curley, Barry Maund, Reginald Naulty, David Papineau, Frank Snare and Michael Tooley. I am grateful also to a reader for Oxford University Press, whose criticism of an earlier version of the book led to what I believe are considerable improvements. The thesis in which these essays originated was supervised by Stanley Benn, whose criticism, encouragement, example and friendship I will always remember.

R. J. K.
Macquarie University,
Sydney.

CONTENTS

NOTE ON REFERENCES

A cross-reference ('see above') is to another part of the same section or subsection of the same essay unless otherwise indicated.

References to the bible, and to works by Aristotle, Cicero, Augustine, Thomas Aquinas and other ancient and medieval authors use the traditional methods of citation by chapter and verse, book and chapter, question and article, etc. These divisions and subdivisions are indicated in most modern editions and translations. Generally such works are not listed in the Bibliography, but if references include page numbers the Bibliography gives the edition referred to. Since there are some differences between the Vulgate and other versions of the bible, bible references sometimes include '*Vg.*', or give alternative numbers.

Modern works (except for those of Arnauld and Bayle—see below) are referred to by author's name and (when necessary) short title. Full titles and publishing details are given in the Bibliography.

Numerals in brackets after a page number, or after 'a' or 'b' (indicating the left-hand or right-hand column of the page) give line numbers (measured with a marked slip of paper from the first line of text). For example, '76(23)–77(14)' means 'from line 23 on p. 76 to line 14 on p. 77'; '220 a63-b3' means 'from line 63 of the left-hand column to line 3 of the right-hand column on p. 220'. A numeral followed by a space (not by a comma or dash) is a page number. In '47 b46–48 a4','47' and '48' are page numbers. In '18 a11, b10, 15, 19 a3', '18' and '19' are page numbers, the rest line numbers; line 15 is in column b.

Arnauld

References to his *Œuvres* (Paris and Lausanne, 1775-83, repr. Brussels, 1967) will be given by the short titles listed below. In this list the date is the date of publication unless it is enclosed in square brackets, and then it is the date of composition of a writing not published in Arnauld's lifetime. (For dates I rely on the editors of the *Œuvres*; for the historical circumstances see the prefaces in this edition, and Jacques, *Les Années*, pp. 481-2, 660-6; on the edition see Jacques, 'L'édition'.) The volume is the volume of the *Œuvres* in which the work will be found:

Apology: *Apologie pour les saints Pères, défenseurs de la grace* (1650), vol. 18.

Commandment: *Hérésie impie contre le commandement d'aimer Dieu* (1690), vol. 31.

Denunciation 1: *Nouvelle hérésie dans la morale* (1689), vol. 31.

Denunciation 2 (3, etc.): *Seconde* [*Troisième,* etc.] *dénonciation du péché philosophique* (1690), vol. 31.

Difficulties: *Difficultés proposées à M. Steyaert* (1691-2), vol. 9.

Disquisition: *Disquisitio utrum, juxta Sanctum Thomam in sua Summa, amor beatificus sit liber ea libertate quam theologi vocant a necessitate* [1691], vol. 10.

Dissertation: *Dissertation théologique sur le commandement d'aimer Dieu* [1641] (printed 1657 as a note to the Latin edition of Pascal, *Provinciales*—the extant French text is a retranslation by another person), vol. 29.

Examen: *Examen de cette proposition: un philosophe ... peut ... faire une action véritablement bonne ...* [1693], vol. 10.

Excuse: *Sentiment de S. Thomas touchant l'ignorance qui excuse du péché en partie, ou totalement* [1693], vol. 10.

Ignorance: *Sentiment de S. Augustin sur les péchés d'ignorance* [1693], vol. 10.

Infidels: *Écrit sur les actions des infidèles* [1691], vol. 10.

Jansen: *Seconde apologie pour Jansénius* (1645), vol. 17.

Liberty: *De la liberté de l'homme* [1689], vol. 10.

Love: *Premier (Second) Écrit sur l'amour naturel de Dieu selon S. Thomas* [1693], vol. 10.

Necessity: *De la nécessité de la foi en Jésus Christ* [1641], vol. 10.

Bayle

His works are referred to by initials, as follows:

CG: *Critique générale de l'histoire du Calvinisme de Mr Maimbourg*, *OD*, vol. 2.

CP: *Commentaire philosophique sur ces paroles de Jésus-Christ, 'Contrain-les d'entrer'*, *OD*, vol. 2.

CPD: *Continuation des Pensées diverses*, *OD*, vol. 3.

DHC: *Dictionnaire historique et critique* (Paris, 1820).

EMT: *Entretiens de Maxime et de Thémiste*, *OD*, vol. 4.

HCD: *Historical and Critical Dictionary: Selections*, trans. R. H. Popkin (Indianapolis, 1965).

NL: *Nouvelles Lettres de l'auteur de la Critique générale de l'histoire du Calvinisme*, *OD*, vol. 2.

OD: *Œuvres diverses* (La Haye, 1727, repr. Hildesheim, 1966).

PD: *Pensées diverses à l'occasion de la comète*, *OD*, vol. 3.

RQP: *Réponse aux questions d'un provincial*, *OD*, vol. 3.

S: *Supplément du Commentaire philosophique*, *OD*, vol. 2.

Introduction

The four essays collected in this book are all in various ways concerned with problems arising from the fact that what we believe on subjects of the greatest importance may be mistaken. One response to this is to say: 'Do nothing until you are sure you are right.' But then we may never act at all. So another response is to say: 'Act decisively, and don't worry too much about the possibility of being wrong.' But other people wish to act on their beliefs too, which often seem mistaken. Do we act decisively to prevent them from doing what they think they should do, and make them do what we think they should? That would be one way of acting on our own beliefs. Or do we tell them to act on their beliefs, while we act on ours—except for the belief that they are wrong? Or do we adopt some more complicated policy of toleration? If so, what form should it take, and in particular how should we act toward people who are themselves intolerant? Almost nightly on the news we see the destructive results of decisive action based on religious or political convictions that would not stand up to academic examination. Among academics, on the other hand, there is often scepticism and inaction or merely conventional action. Somehow we need to work out how to combine being careful about being right with actually doing what ought to be done. I cannot say how to do this in detail, and I do not know how far I succeed in doing it, but I hope that these academic essays may be of some use to others who also make the attempt, and not merely a distraction from it.

The essays all arise in one way or another from reflection on Pierre Bayle's *Philosophical Commentary on the Words of the Gospel*, '*Compel them to come in*', one of the classics of the seventeenth-century debate about religious toleration. Christians believed

they had to be right in their religious and moral beliefs, un-
shakeable in their faith, courageous in acting on their faith: but
their beliefs disagreed, and Christendom was torn by cruel
wars. Bayle wrote the *Philosophical Commentary* to advocate religious toleration at a time when it seemed almost a lost cause.
Deeply committed to that cause, he was also an enemy to faulty
reasoning even on his own side of a question, a man of sharp
intelligence and in philosophy and theology very well informed.
His book is excellent, superior to Locke's better-known *Letters
on Toleration*. It is still, in my opinion, the best argument for
religious toleration, and by extension for toleration in other
spheres such as politics.

As a refutation of the Augustinian theories which in the
seventeenth century gave religious intolerance its motive, or
gave other motives a religious guise, Bayle's book does not
really succeed. To the followers of St Augustine some of Bayle's
premisses would have seemed false or arbitrary, including some
which today may seem trivial and self-evident. The Augustinians were not refuted: they died out without successfully
training later generations. Their failure may have been due
partly to difficulties raised by Bayle's arguments, and partly to
damage done to Augustine's general reputation in controversies
over predestination and the problem of evil, damage to which
in his other writings Bayle contributed. Mostly it was due to
causes unconnected with the intellectual merits of Augustine's
theories: the development of secular intellectual interests; the
military, political and other social causes working against Pres-
byterianism in England, against Jansenism in France, and
against Catholicism generally in Europe; the circumstances
that made the Jansenists defend freedom of thought and speech
within the Catholic Church; and so on.

To trace the causes which ended religious wars and overt
persecution in Europe is not, however, what I have set out to
do. My project is primarily philosophical: to analyse and assess
certain arguments for propositions connected with the ideas of
tolerance and the open society. But it is also historical, in the
first two essays especially. The arguments analysed are Bayle's,
and part of my concern is to assess them from the viewpoint of
some of his contemporaries, such as Arnauld. Although (as far
as I know) Arnauld never read the *Philosophical Commentary*, his

controversy with the Jesuits over 'philosophic sin' should give some idea of how Bayle's book would have seemed to a theologically conservative contemporary. I have not set out to write a comprehensive book on Bayle, or on Arnauld, or on toleration. My topic is toleration, primarily, but only as it can be treated by reflection on Bayle's writings; I am concerned with Bayle only as a writer on toleration, and I am concerned with Arnauld only in so far as what he wrote is relevant to Bayle on toleration. The book is in fact merely a collection of essays which I have thought worth bringing together because of the many connections between them.

Philosophical readers may feel some impatience with the details of Bayle's and Arnauld's arguments. I do not regard the history of ideas as an end in itself, but on the other hand I do not find it easy to think about a philosophical problem without some historical reference point. Much philosophical writing is a response to something written earlier (perhaps just recently): I am not doing anything very different, except that what I am responding to was written much earlier, in a different age and culture, but with some of our problems. For me the different setting is part of the interest. The details cannot be avoided if we are to feel the force of what these earlier writers still have to say.

I have put first the essay 'Arnauld against Philosophic Sin', to make it easier to see the contentiousness of some of Bayle's apparent truisms and to show the thinking of some of the people Bayle had to convince. 'Philosophic sin' is not a sin that only philosophers can commit. It is the sin that anyone commits who sins without reflecting that the act offends God's infinite goodness: a fairly common sort of sin these days. Arnauld argues that there can be no purely philosophic or moral sin because every wrong act is also a 'theological' sin, that is, an offence against God. He argues further that it is possible to sin damnably without thinking of God, even without knowing that the act is wrong at all; in fact, any act done without thought of God, even an act otherwise good, is a sin against God, because his law requires that we do each act consciously for love of God. On Arnauld's account, then, sincerity is not enough; it is necessary to do what is really right for what is really the right reason, love of God.

The second essay examines Bayle's arguments on the rights of conscience. He argues that a sincere act may be (indeed always is) morally good even if it is really wrong. Even if our conscience is in error we have a duty *and a moral right* to obey it, and the act is as good morally as it would have been if the error had been truth. Sometimes he says that this is true if the error itself is sincere (not the result of negligence, self-deception, or other moral fault), sometimes—and this is more consistent with his premises—he says that it is true in any case. He tries also to show that, notwithstanding one's moral right to attempt the act that conscience commands, others may have the right, and the duty, to prevent it, if necessary by force. In particular, conscientious persecutors should be restrained—to prove this is indeed the main point of the book. This means that those who think they ought to impose their faith by force ought to try, and others ought to stop them; but since the persecutors have a moral right to try to do what they wrongly think they ought to do, they should not be blamed for trying, and they should be stopped if possible by physical restraint rather than by threats. In his earliest writings on this subject Bayle argues from the premiss that if the orthodox have a right to use force then heretics do too, but later he argues that even if no one else claims a right, those who think they have it in some sense do have it. This smacks of relativism and incoherence, but I try to show that Bayle is not really guilty of those philosophic sins; and that he is not a sceptic, at least not in the strict sense of the term.

The third essay is a restatement in my own terms of Bayle's strongest argument, which I call the 'reciprocity' argument, and a discussion of what arguments of that type are worth. By a 'reciprocity' argument I mean an argument to show that we should renounce what would otherwise have been (or seemed) a right or liberty because if we claim it and exercise it others will too, with evil results, whereas if we renounce it and accept certain contrary duties others may do so too, with good results. Such arguments have certain limitations, which also affect some similar arguments, such as John Rawls's argument for liberty of conscience and David Richards's appeal to 'moral reciprocity' in international economic relations.

The fourth essay is concerned with the ethics of thinking. Rejecting widely held ideas of 'epistemological responsibility', I argue that we have a right to believe, assert and act on what seems true even if we can give no supporting reasons. This is part of what Bayle regards as the 'rights of conscience'. Although he emphasises the duty of examination, as one would expect a Protestant to do, he also defends those who refuse to examine because they are afraid of going wrong or think they lack time or talent, and says that their refusal to examine may even show love of truth. And he holds that we have a right to affirm and act on opinions for which we do not have conclusive evidence— that we have a duty and a right to act on whatever *seems* true, perhaps in the complete absence of evidence, or in the face of evidence to the contrary. These points seem to me to be right, and worth asserting against the more rigorous 'ethics of belief' which liberals sometimes invoke against opponents to the right and to the left.

The Conclusion is a discussion of certain aspects of Bayle's moral philosophy. It was an accidental encounter with Arnauld's essays on the views of Augustine and Thomas Aquinas on sins committed in ignorance that made me realize how contentious and arbitrary Bayle's moral theory would have seemed to some of his contemporaries. When I looked further into Arnauld's writings and read his attacks on Jesuit moral theory, I realized that on many points Bayle agreed with the Jesuits. Pierre Jurieu, Bayle's former friend and severest critic, remarked that Bayle 'must have learnt his abominable moral theory during the three years he spent with the Jesuits' as a student; though I suspect there were many Protestants from whom he could have learnt it. When I looked further still, I realized that Arnauld himself shared with Bayle and the Jesuits certain questionable assumptions about morality which were shared also by Augustine and later by Kant and by many other moral philosophers. In this tradition there is much emphasis on retribution and on free will: moral goodness and badness are identified with merit and demerit, with good and bad desert, with entitlement to reward and liability to punishment; praise and blame are thought of as kinds of reward and punishment; the source of merit and demerit is supposed to be the exercise of free will; free will (though Augustine had understood it differently) was regarded by Bayle, and by many in this tradition, as a 'power for opposites', an ability at the moment of choice to choose either way. In the Conclusion I argue against these items of Bayle's moral theory and consider what effect rejecting them has on his case for toleration.

Since I spend so much time explaining Arnauld's views, criticising Bayle's, emphasising the limitations of arguments for toleration and defending the closed mind, it may sometimes seem that I must have set out to encourage dogmatism and intolerance. That was not my intention, and I hope it will not be the result. My sympathies lie altogether on Bayle's side, but, following his example, I wish to test his arguments by criticism and consideration of alternatives.

ESSAY I

Arnauld against Philosophic Sin

INTRODUCTION

The reader may wish to know something of Antoine Arnauld and his times. His life was full of conflict, with the Jesuits, with the king of France and, though he was a zealous Catholic, with the pope.[1] The son of a wealthy lawyer, he never had to work for his living at anything he did not choose to do. As a priest he never seems to have had any pastoral or teaching responsibilities except those he chose to assume. By choice he was an almost full-time controversialist, whose extant writings fill some forty large volumes. Day by day he went into his study, sharpened his pen and attacked someone—or defended someone, or refuted an answer, or answered a pretended refutation, or wrote a *Premier Écrit pour la defense de la seconde lettre*. His writings are mostly in the style of some of the less well-known works of Hobbes and Locke, or of certain writings Marx and Engels left to the criticism of the mice.

To sympathise with the work of such an author one must have some interest in the controversies to which he devoted his life. In the Catholic Church in the sixteenth and seventeenth centuries there was much disagreement over questions of grace and freewill, especially between followers of the Spanish Jesuit Luis Molina (1536–1600) and those who considered themselves genuine followers of St Augustine. Controversy was especially acute in the University of Louvain in the Spanish Netherlands,

---

[1] For biography see Bayle, *DHC*, arts. 'Arnauld' and 'Arnauld, Antoine, docteur de Sorbonne' (vol. 2, pp. 389 ff. and 400 ff.), Carreyre, 'Arnauld, Antoine' (Baudrillart, vol. 4, cols. 447-84). For an account of the conflicts in the Catholic Church in France in Arnauld's lifetime see Whiteman, especially pp. 130-42. On the Jansenist movement see Sedgwick, Abercrombie, and Rex, *Pascal*.

and during Arnauld's lifetime (largely as a result of his own writings in defence of the Louvain theologian Cornelius Jansen) it spread into France, where those who called themselves followers of Augustine were usually called Jansenists.[2] In the Protestant Netherlands there was a similar disagreement between followers of Jacob Arminius (who like the Jesuits emphasized freewill) and followers of Calvin (who followed Augustine).[3] The Jansenists were accused by their Catholic opponents of being virtually Calvinists, which partly accounts for the zeal with which they attacked the Calvinists when they were not fighting the Jesuits. All these debates about grace and freewill were continuous with the controversies which arose when Luther and Calvin accused Catholics of Pelagianism, and indeed with medieval controversies in which Catholics had made the same accusation against one another.[4] All parties were eager or anxious readers of Augustine's writings against Pelagius.[5] Pelagius had taught that anyone who wishes can live a good life (meaning this as an encouragement to the good life). Augustine had answered that no one can live a good life, or even wish to do so, without special help from God, which he does not always give; his help is a grace—that is, it cannot be earned or deserved, but is given only to those whom God chooses from eternity (predestines) to receive it.

In Arnauld's time Christians of all varieties agreed that human beings cannot avoid evil and do good without grace,

[2] On controversies among Catholics over grace see Abercrombie, and Miel, ch. 1.

[3] See A. W. Harrison. Arminius seems to have been influenced by criticism of Calvin by the Jesuit Bellarmine (Harrison, p. 123). In turn Jansen 'followed closely the proceedings of the Synod of Dort' (Sedgwick, p. 48). At the Synod of Dort (1618-19) the Calvinists rejected the five propositions of the Arminian Remonstrance, which were, briefly: (1) God's decree of Predestination is in general terms—namely to save anyone who, through grace, believes and obeys; (2) Christ died for the forgiveness and redemption of all men (not only for the elect), though only those who believe actually obtain these benefits; (3) no one can do anything truly good without God's grace; (4) grace is not irresistible; (5) it is not certain that those who once have true faith can never fall away. (But it seems to me that something equivalent to Calvinist predestination will follow from (3), if God gives grace only to some and if he has decreed from eternity what graces he will give.) For the Arminian articles and the Synod of Dort see Schaff, *Creeds*, vol. 2, pp. 545 ff.

[4] See Oberman, *Forerunners*, pp. 123-40. Pelagius had no defenders or admitted followers. The accusation of virtual Pelagianism was made so often because no one wanted to be a Pelagian.

[5] Arnauld translated Augustine's *De correptione et gratia*, and seems to have regarded this as the best presentation of Augustine's doctrine. For an English translation see Schaff (ed.), *Select Library*, vol. 5, pp. 468 ff.

and all held some version of the doctrine of predestination. The controversies between Molinists and Jansenists, Arminians and Calvinists, were about the extent of God's help and its relation to human free choice. Neither Molinists nor Jansenists meant to deny either freewill or the need for grace, but each side accused the other of denying one or the other by implication. The Jesuits taught that God gives everyone grace sufficient for salvation, so that if we are not saved that is because we have chosen not to use God's help.[6] The Augustinians replied that since right choice is a good act, it also must be the effect of God's help; if we need help to do good, then we need help for the good act of choice. So both the good deed and the will to do it require God's help: 'It is God who worketh in you, both to will and to accomplish' (*Phil.* 2:13). This may seem to imply that those who receive all necessary grace cannot fail to do good, whether they want to or not. The Augustinians replied that indeed they will infallibly do good, but not 'whether they want to or not' because the first effect of grace is willingness to do good. But then if grace works infallibly those who in fact do not do good must get *less* than the grace they need. If no one needs or deserves help more or less than anyone else, how is it fair that some get less grace than others, and less than they need? This is the question that led the Jesuits to the doctrine of sufficient grace, that everyone gets all the grace needed for salvation. The Augustinians insisted that the question is inappropriate: God *is* fair, but we cannot demand to be shown how. Since experience shows that people are not equally good God must give grace unequally, and we must suppose that he has good reasons; but his reasons must remain incomprehensible to us.

Although these controversies were carried on with constant reference to the bible, it is worth noticing that the difficulties do not arise only from scripture texts. Questions of predestination, free will and grace arise for anyone who holds (a) that God's assistance is necessary for doing good, and (b) that choice of good is itself a good deed. On these premises the only consistent way of avoiding Augustine's conclusions is to

---

[6] Some Jesuits reconciled this with predestination by saying that 'predestination' means that God foresees that some will not use his help. Others said that God gives to those not predestined to salvation such help as he foresees they will not use. See Miel, pp. 51-2.

postulate also (c) sufficient grace for all, and (d) salvation for all. Kant's religion of pure reason seems to include all four points.[7]

  Their critics accused the Jesuits of being generally too ready to water down Christianity to make it acceptable to the powerful and worldly people they wanted to influence. The doctrine of sufficient grace seemed meant for people unwilling to be entirely dependent on God, inclined to believe that salvation must be within their own power of choice. Jesuit casuistry seemed to relax the demands of morality, countenancing acts which are really sins.[8] In their pastoral practice they seemed to grant absolution without proper evidence of repentance, and to allow people whose repentance was not genuine to receive holy communion. In his *Frequent Communion* Arnauld suggested that absolution and the reception of communion should be delayed until repentance was proved by the beginning of a better way of life, but the Jesuits were reluctant to refuse absolution or impose difficult conditions, especially since some of their penitents were kings and nobles whose exclusion from the sacraments might harm the cause of religion, and they took the view that frequent communion was needed to help establish a better way of life.[9] In their Chinese missions the Jesuits were accused by Dominicans and Franciscans of being too ready to compromise with Chinese religion, morality and customs,[10] and Arnauld and his allies publicised in France the controversies that broke out in China.

  Motives were of course mixed. The Jesuits enjoyed their influence, the Jansenists enjoyed the excitement and importance of the fight against it. Doctrinal conflicts got entangled with others. There was rivalry between the secular clergy and the Jesuits, and between the new Jesuit order and the older 'mendicant' orders, the Dominicans and Franciscans. In the universities many feared that the Jesuits would take the students and the jobs. Similar fears had motivated opposition to the mendicants when they were new orders, in the thirteenth century. Like the Jesuits, the mendicants had been close to the

----

  [7] See below, nn. 191 and 193.
  [8] See Pascal, *Provincial Letters*, which also describe the controversy over sufficient grace.
  [9] For a sympathetic account of the Jesuit attitude see Rex, *Pascal*, pp. 14 ff.
  [10] See Rowbotham, chs. 9 and 10, and Arnauld's *Œuvres*, vol. 32, pp. 213 ff.

papacy, and the pope had invoked his 'plenitude of power' to force the French bishops and the University of Paris to make room for them. This provoked or reinforced an attitude later called Gallicanism, the determination to limit the pope's right to intervene in French Church affairs.[11] Since the Great Schism, when there were several rival popes, Paris University had been a stronghold of 'conciliarist' theory, which held the subordination of the pope (at least in certain circumstances) to an ecumenical council.[12] The French kings were friendly to such theories, having had many disagreements with the popes. Gallicanism was at its height in Arnauld's lifetime, and the Jansenists allied themselves with it against the Jesuits. In the next century the alliance brought about the expulsion of the Jesuits from France,[13] but in Arnauld's time the political position of the Jansenists was always precarious, for two reasons. First, they were a section of 'the devout', who sometimes criticised the extravagant lives of king and court and their indifference to the suffering of the common people, and criticised French foreign policy, which sought to balance the power of the Spanish and Austrian Hapsburgs by aiding Dutch and German Protestants; the 'devout' party sometimes reminded the government of the Catholic League, which had been a vehicle of Spanish influence in France during the wars of religion in the second half of the previous century. Second, the Jansenists were accused of heresy, of being virtual Calvinists and of defying the authority of pope and bishops. When it suited the king or his ministers to be more devout than the devout, or more Catholic than the pope, they took action against the Jansenist and Calvinist heretics.

Antoine Arnauld was born in 1612, the twentieth child of a lawyer who had represented the University of Paris in 1594 in its attempts to prevent the establishment of the Jesuit order in France. His sister became abbess and reformer of the Cistercian convent of Port-Royal.[14] Eventually his mother, six of his sisters and five of his nieces became members of this convent. For many years he mostly lived in houses belonging to Port-Royal,

11 See Douie and Schleyer, and the article 'Gallicanism' in *New Catholic Encyclopaedia.* On Arnauld's Gallicanism see Sedgwick, pp. 156 ff.

12 On Conciliarism in the University of Paris see Skinner, vol. 2, pp. 42–7.

13 See Van Kley.

14 On Port-Royal see Sedgwick, pp. 14 ff.

with other gentlemen (including Pascal) not members of the
order but living a religious life without vows. The convent's
spiritual director was for a time Jean Duvergier de Hauranne,
abbé of Saint-Cyran, who became also Arnauld's spiritual
guide. Saint-Cyran had studied in Louvain and was friendly
with Cornelius Jansen. Jansen had been active in his university's attempts to prevent the Jesuits from teaching students
registered for Louvain degrees, but his main quarrel with the
Jesuits was theological. In 1640 he published a book entitled
Augustinus, intended to restate Augustine's doctrine of grace
and to show that the Jesuit doctrine was Pelagian.[15] By then
Saint-Cyran was being held in prison on the orders of Cardinal
Richelieu, the king's minister, perhaps because he was suspected of being the French translator of a pamphlet Jansen
had published criticising France's Protestant alliances, perhaps
because it was thought that his teaching on the kind of repentance required for absolution might trouble the king's conscience and strengthen the influence of the devout. When
Richelieu died Saint-Cyran was released from prison but died
soon after.

In 1641 Arnauld graduated as a Doctor of Theology from
the Sorbonne, the theology faculty of the University of Paris.
It was in this year that he wrote his penetrating objections to
Descartes's *Meditations*.[16] His main projects in these early years
were a book and other writings on frequent communion, in
which he supported Saint-Cyran's view that absolution and
communion should be delayed until genuine repentance was
evident,[17] others criticising the laxity of Jesuit moral theology[18]
and others defending Jansen's *Augustinus*.[19] For reasons presumably connected with those for which he had imprisoned
Saint-Cyran, Cardinal Richelieu had encouraged a well-known
preacher to preach a series of sermons against Jansen's book.

From 1649 there was controversy over five propositions put
forward by Jansen's critics as a summary of the contentious
points in his doctrine.[20] In 1653 the pope condemned these

---

[15] For a summary of the book see Abercrombie, pp. 126–53.

[16] The 'fourth objections' (Descartes, vol. 2, pp. 79 ff).

[17] See his *Œuvres*, vols. 27 and 28.

[18] Ibid., vol. 29.

[19] Ibid., vols. 15–17.

[20] They were, in brief, (1) that obedience to God's commands is sometimes
impossible; (2) that grace is irresistible; (3) that while moral liberty is inconsistent

propositions, and Arnauld and his friends accepted that they were, under some interpretation, heretical. But they denied the assertion made by some French bishops (at the suggestion of Richelieu's successor as the king's minister, Cardinal Mazarin)[21] that the Five Propositions were Jansen's. According to Arnauld only one was in Jansen's book, and in a non-heretical sense, and the others were not there at all. Prompted by Mazarin, the national Assembly of the Clergy demanded that all the clergy subscribe to a 'formulary' condemning the Five Propositions as heretical in the sense which they had in Jansen's book.[22] In 1657 the pope himself asserted that the propositions were in Jansen's book and had been condemned in Jansen's sense. Arnauld was willing to sign the formulary as it related to the 'question of right' (whether the propositions were heretical) but not as it related to the 'question of fact' (whether the propositions were in fact in Jansen's book in the sense condemned). He argued that the pope's doctrinal authority did not extend to questions of fact not an original part of Christian revelation.[23] In reaction to one of Arnauld's pamphlets on this matter the Sorbonne struck Arnauld's name off the list of its Doctors; Pascal's *Provincial Letters* were begun in an effort to ward off this action.[24]

The controversy over the Five Propositions and the formulary went on for years, and Arnauld wrote much on the subject.[25] The authorities would not accept subscription restricted to the question of right; they insisted on subscription 'pure and simple'. The nuns of Port-Royal were bullied, and those who would not sign were dispersed to other convents, put under surveillance and denied the sacraments. Arnauld went into hiding. In 1667 a new pope agreed that the Church

with constraint it is not inconsistent with other kinds of necessity; (4) that it is semi-Pelagian to say that we can choose whether to accept or refuse grace; (5) that it is semi-Pelagian to say that Christ died for all mankind. See Sedgwick, p. 68.

[21] See Sedgwick, pp. 65-71, and Rex, *Pascal*, pp. 41-2.

[22] Sedgwick, p. 73. The Assembly of the Clergy normally did not deal with doctrinal questions. It met every five years mainly to grant a 'donation' to the government in return for tax exemption.

[23] See Arnauld, *Œuvres*, vol. 10, pp. 705 ff. Some matters of fact, e.g. that Jesus rose from the dead, are part of Christian revelation, but not that certain statements are in a certain recent book.

[24] On the circumstances of the *Provincial Letters* see Cognet's introduction to his edition, and Rex, *Pascal*.

[25] See his *Œuvres*, vols. 19-22.

authorities should acquiesce tacitly in signature of the formulary with the explanation that it did not relate to the question of fact, provided the explanation remained secret. This shabby compromise was the 'peace of Clement IX'. The nuns of Port-Royal regained their liberty and Arnauld came out of hiding. For the next few years he left the enemies of Jansen mostly alone, and wrote against the Calvinists: on the *Perpetuity of Faith in the Eucharist* (arguing that the Catholic doctrine can be traced back to the early church), and on *The Overturning of Christian Morality by the Calvinists*.[26]

From this time Arnauld seems to have been on reasonably good terms with the pope, but after a while he came into conflict again with the government. Louis XIV clashed with certain bishops and then with the pope over the *régale*, the practice under which royal officials took charge of the revenues of vacant episcopal sees. The reputed Jansenism of the bishops protesting against this practice, the new rapport between the Jansenists and the papacy, and the king's wish to demonstrate his zeal against heresy at a time of conflict with the pope and at a time when French foreign policy was again troubling devout Catholics, led to a renewed attack on both Port-Royal and the Calvinists. In 1679 Louis XIV put the convent under various restrictions and forbade Arnauld to go near it. Arnauld left for the low countries, where he changed residence frequently, presumably as a precaution against arrest.[27] He continued to produce a stream of books and pamphlets. To this time belongs the controversy over philosophic sin which is the subject of the following essay, controversies with the Calvinists over political matters,[28] a philosophical correspondence with the young Leibniz, and controversy with

[26] Ibid., vols. 12–15, contain Arnauld's anti-Calvinist writings.

[27] In 1703 two of Arnauld's companions were arrested and returned to France. One escaped, the other was imprisoned for seven years until he signed the formulary, and died soon after release. See Sedgwick, p. 189.

[28] Arnauld was critical of the persecution of French Calvinists (Orcibal, *Louis XIV*, p. 73). Nevertheless, he wrote an *Apology for the Catholics* (*Œuvres*, vol. 14), defending 'new converts' against Calvinist accusations of insincerity and restating St Augustine's opinion that coercion in religious matters may sometimes do good. When William of Orange invaded England and drove out his wife's father, the Catholic James II, Arnauld wrote *A True Portrait of William Henry of Nassau, New Absalom, New Herod, New Cromwell, New Nero* (*Œuvres*, vol. 37).

Malebranche in the journal edited by Bayle.[29] He died in Brussels in 1694, at the age of 82.

* * *

Since the eighteenth century liberal and enlightened men and women have often put a higher value upon sincerity than on actually being right. The earliest exponent of this attitude seems to have been Pierre Bayle; as he said in his *Philosophical Commentary* (1686-7), 'it is enough to consult sincerely and in good faith the lights God has given us.'[30] This implies that a well-meant but objectively wrong act may not only be excused but even deserve praise and reward: 'An action done in consequence of a false persuasion is as good as if it had been done in consequence of a true persuasion.'[31] Bayle's premisses include propositions about invincible ignorance taught at the time in some scholastic courses in moral philosophy.[32] Some Jesuits taught (or were alleged to teach) that we cannot sin without knowing that we are sinning, which implies that if we act according to our consciences we do not sin; and that if we realise that the act is morally wrong but do not think of it as an offence against God's infinite goodness then it is a merely 'philosophic' or moral sin which cannot deserve eternal punishment. This is not the ethic of sincerity, since there is no suggestion that a well-meant wrong act may deserve praise, but it is a step in that direction.

The battle over philosophic sin was an episode in Arnauld's life-long war with the Jesuits. In 1689 he denounced as heresy

[29] Ibid., vols. 38-40. See Leibniz, *Correspondence*, Church, ch. 6, and Lennon, 'Commentary', pp. 793-809.

[30] Bayle, *CP*, p. 438.

[31] Ibid., p. 428. Benjamin Hoadly wrote, 'the favour of God ... equally follows every equal degree of sincerity'; William Law replied, 'then ... he that burns the Christian, if he be but in earnest, has the same title to a reward for it, as he that is burned for believing in Christ' (both quoted Sykes, pp. 142, 147).

[32] Bayle refers to the courses in scholastic philosophy, *CP*, pp. 524, 536. For a short time Bayle studied philosophy at the Jesuit college at Toulouse. Pierre Jurieu saw that Bayle's theory was like the Jesuits', and that it went further: 'Clearly the author of the *Critique générale* must have learnt his abominable moral theory during the three years he spent with the Jesuits of Toulouse ... Whoever compares what has been said about the philosophic sin of the Jesuits and the effects of good intention according to them will see a perfect resemblance between the doctrine of the pupil and that of his masters. Except that the disciple goes further than his masters. For I know of no Jesuit who has dared to say that a man who commits a parricide with a good intention does an act which is praiseworthy' (Jurieu, p. 6).

a thesis defended in a Jesuit college that some sins may be
merely philosophic; his ulterior purpose was to discredit the
underlying principle that no one can sin without knowing it.
The Jesuits replied that they had never taught such things,
at least not in any heretical sense, and Arnauld tried to show
that they had. Rome condemned the thesis[33] but not the
underlying principle,[34] and shortly afterwards also condemned
propositions held by Arnauld and other Jansenists, including
the proposition that invincible ignorance is not always an
excuse.[35]

   In this essay I will examine what Arnauld wrote about
philosophic sin, and also about another Jesuit heresy which
he denounced and Rome condemned at the same time,
concerning the love of God.[36] From what Arnauld maintains
about the love of God it follows that *all* the actions of mere
philosophers are theological sins, since all sins are theological
and all the actions of infidels, even their best, are sins—one
of the Jansenist propositions which Rome also condemned.[37]
My aim is primarily historical, to understand what was said;
but I will also notice some things that should or might have
been said, since criticism helps understanding, and since the
point of the history of thought is to stimulate thought.[38]

I.   WHAT IS PHILOSOPHIC SIN?

The theory Arnauld attacked ran as follows.[39] There is a
distinction between formal and material sins, and among
formal sins between the philosophic and the theological. A

---

[33] Denzinger, p. 479, no. 2291. The editor, Fr A. Schonmetzer, SJ, notes that the
Jesuit whose thesis occasioned the condemnation did not mean it in the sense into
which his Jansenist accusers twisted it, and refers the reader to H. Beylard, SJ, 'Le
péché philosophique'. Fr Beylard repeats what the Jesuits claimed they had meant
after Arnauld attacked them, without reference to what Arnauld then said to justify
his interpretation (see below, sect. 3). It is ironic that the Jesuits have treated this
condemnation just as the Jansenists treated the condemnation of the five propositions
attributed to Jansen, by denying that their authors meant their words in the sense
condemned. The teacher (the pope) is treated with profound respect, but rivalry
prevents the pupils' admitting they ever need to be corrected.

[34] Arnauld, letter to Pelisson, in *Œuvres*, vol. 3, p. 370.

[35] Denzinger, p. 480, no. 2302.

[36] Ibid., p. 479, no. 2290; and *Commandment*.

[37] Denzinger, p. 481, no. 2308.

[38] The modern discussions of philosophic sin known to me are by Deman, Beylard
and Ceyssens. Laporte's book is a general study I have found useful.

[39] Arnauld's clearest brief account of the theory is in a letter to Pelisson, *Œuvres*,

'formal' sin is a sin in the proper sense of the term. A 'material' sin is almost a sin: it would be one, except that it lacks some feature essential to sin in the strict sense. Only acts which deserve blame and punishment are sins in the proper sense. Now according to the Jesuits—and according to Arnauld this is their basic mistake—an act does not deserve blame and punishment unless we do it knowing that it is wrong. If it is wrong, but we do not at the time know that it is, then it is a merely material sin. There are two sorts of wrongness. An act may be wrong as being against natural morality, or it may be wrong as being against God's will. Since obedience to God's will is a precept of natural morality, and since God wills that we obey natural morality, an act wrong in either way will be wrong in both ways. But since formal sin requires that the person doing the act know that it is wrong, and since we may know that the act is wrong in one way without knowing that it is wrong in both, we can commit one species of formal sin without also committing the other. If we do something knowing that it is against God's will it is a theological sin; if we do it knowing that it is against natural morality but not that it is against God's will, it is a philosophic sin.[40]

On this theory only theological sin deserves damnation; in fact, the purpose of constructing the concept of theological sin is to define the kind of sin that incurs damnation. Sin

vol. 3, pp. 367-70. Arnauld began by attacking a thesis presented in the Jesuit college of Dijon in 1686; as the controversy went on he collected more material until in the end he had extracts from some twenty-five writers going back to 1660. (For earlier material see Ceyssens, p. 390.) The term 'philosophic sin' seems to have been used first in 1670 (see *Denunciation* 1, p. 49). Extracts from Jesuit writers directly relating to philosophic sin will be found in his *Denunciations*, pp. 3-4, 40-1, 48-53, 78, 307, 367-85 (all written before the controversy broke out), and pp. 5-6, 301-2 (written during the controversy, and perhaps a modification to avoid the attack). Note that the exposition of pp. 14-17 (quoted again pp. 70-9), although it is put into the mouth of a Jesuit, is Arnauld's own, based (he claims) on notes dictated by the professor of Dijon; see pp. 239-41. (In its first occurrence this exposition is not in quotation marks, in its second it is because it is a quotation of the first.) A Jesuit spokesman claimed that the Dijon professor's notes show that he taught the opposite of what Arnauld attributed to him (Beylard, pp. 675-6). The notes were never published.

[40] Another Jesuit, Fr Duffy, recognising only one kind of 'malice' (wrongness), namely violation of the law of God, classes all sins which are not theological as material. Arnauld regards this as another heresy deriving from the same principle, that sin requires knowledge of the wrongness of the act (*Denunciation* 2, pp. 152-7).

deserves eternal punishment only if it expresses or implies contempt toward God: only God is infinitely worthy of respect, only contempt toward a being infinitely worthy of respect is infinitely worthy of punishment, and eternal punishment is infinite in duration.[41] And only acts done knowingly against God's wishes show contempt of God. The notion of contempt, and the purpose of defining damnable sin, guide the specification of the kind of knowledge required to make sin theological. First, we must know or believe (even mistakenly) that the rule being broken was made by God. To disobey a rule God made without knowing he made it does not show contempt toward God,[42] but to disobey a rule believing God made it, though in fact he did not, does show contempt. Second, we must think of God as infinitely worthy of respect. If we think of him as an evil tyrant, or as like a human being only immortal, then—assuming that the evil of contempt is greater the more goodness the offender can see in the person offended—the contempt shown in disobeying him is not great enough to deserve eternal punishment. The sin must be against a person of infinite worth known as such, or known as the highest and infinite good, or under some similar description.[43] Third, we must know that God will in fact be offended, and offended gravely.[44] If we believe as the Epicureans did that the gods do not care what we do, or that God is easygoing, that he does not mind the occasional sin, then the contempt shown by the act is not great enough to justify eternal punishment. Fourth, we must act with full attention to all these thoughts. The scholastics distinguished actual from

[41] On arguments to show that sin deserves eternal punishment see M. M. Adams. See also Thomas Aquinas, *Summa*, 1–2, q.87 aa. 3–5.

[42] 'For a legislator to be personally and formally offended by one who breaks his law, the latter must have some knowledge of this legislator' (Jesuit thesis quoted *Denunciation* 5, p. 318).

[43] Cf: 'an offence against a person of infinite dignity known as such (*cognitae qua talis*)', 'against God under the description (*sub ratione*) of highest and infinite good' (Jesuit writers quoted *Denunciation* 2, pp. 49, 51).

[44] 'Just as a human act is never evil without knowledge of its badness, so it is never an offence against God if it is not recognised to be an offence against God'; 'a sin committed by someone invincibly ignorant of, or not adverting to, the fact that God exists, or that he is offended by sin, is not mortal'; 'if it were possible to prove ignorance of the penalty imposed by the law, it could not be inflicted on a man who could not have done the action had he known it was forbidden under such a penalty' (Jesuit writers quoted *Denunciation* 1, p. 16, *Denunciation* 2, p. 78, and *Denunciation* 5, p. 382).

habitual knowledge: if we are not actually thinking of something but could if the need arose, then our knowledge of it is habitual. Habitual knowledge that the act is against God's will is not enough for theological sin, since the act would not then imply actual contempt of God. Actual knowledge or advertence can have degrees, and lower degrees of advertence imply less contempt.[45] To sum up: to be a theological sin deserving of eternal punishment, an act must be done with full attention to the thought, 'this is against the will of God, who is infinitely worthy of respect, and it will gravely offend him', or something equivalent. An atheist cannot have such a thought, and a Christian or other theist may not actually think it. An atheist or a Christian not actually thinking of God commits a merely philosophic sin which does not deserve damnation, no matter how wrong the act.

To do something because it is against God's will is direct contempt; to do it for some good reason, although believing or suspecting that it is against God's will, is contempt by implication, since in that case God's will is taken too lightly. To take direct contempt as necessary to the nature of sin is the position of the fictional Jesuit of Pascal's satire: 'To show you we do not permit everything, know that for example we never suffer anyone to have the formal intention of sinning for the sole purpose of sinning, and that if anyone insists on not having any other end in evil than evil itself, we break with him.'[46] But the theory Arnauld attacks assumes that it is possible to offend God by not taking his wishes seriously enough, as outweighing otherwise good reasons. In view of his infinite worth God's will ought to be taken with absolute seriousness, as outweighing *any* reason to the contrary. So whatever may be the reasons for doing the act, whether it is done precisely because it will offend God or for some other reason, the conditions stated above are enough to make it a theological sin.

The analysis of sin as contempt against God goes back to Peter Abelard and Anselm and perhaps beyond. Anselm

[45] *Denunciation* 5, pp. 351(34-5), 369(18-21), 376(7-15).

[46] Pascal, *Provinciales*, p. 116. The point of the joke is that Thomists (as the Jesuits were supposed to be) held that no one can possibly choose an evil except as an apparent good; see Thomas Aquinas, *Summa*, 1-2, q.8 a.1.

argued that because sin offends God's infinite honour it requires an infinite reparation which can be paid only by God become man. Abelard argued that although sin cannot harm God he avenges the contempt: 'Our sin is contempt of the creator,' and 'all who offer equal contempt to him are later punished with equal punishment.' According to Thomas Aquinas evil acts deserve blame and punishment because they do not serve God's honour, and ignorance extenuates because 'there is less contempt and consequently less sin'. According to Bonaventure 'sin is measured according to the amount of wilfulness and contempt'.[47] The theory of philosophic sin carries this analysis through with apparent consistency.

Despite the notoriety Arnauld gave it, the Jesuits (if it is indeed their theory) were not primarily interested in philosophic sin. Their concern was to give a more restrictive definition of the sort of sin that deserves eternal punishment; philosophic sin is merely another category of sin not to be confused with damnable sin. If they had analysed it as they did theological sin perhaps they would have said this: an act is a philosophic sin, deserving moral blame and (finite) punishment, if it is done with full actual knowledge (or with full attention to the belief, true or false) that the act is immoral.

2. THE FIRST DENUNCIATION

Arnauld begins the first *Denunciation* by remarking on the novelty of this doctrine. To live in forgetfulness of God is the way to damnation, Christians have always thought, not a guarantee against it.[48] He relates this 'Philosophism' (to use the term he later coined for it) to another Jesuit novelty, sufficient grace,[49] meaning the doctrine that God gives everyone (atheists and pagans included) enough grace on every

[47] Anselm, *Cur deus homo*, I.11 (see also I.21); Peter Abelard, *Ethics*, pp. 5–7, 45; Thomas Aquinas, *Summa*, 1–2, q.21 a.4, q.76 a.4; Bonaventure, *In 2 Sent.*, d.22 a.2 q.3, d.42 a.1 q.1. Cf. Bayle, *CP*, pp. 422–5; *L'Encyclopédie*, vol. 3, p. 903.

[48] *Denunciation* 1, p. 4(28–38); cf. Pascal, *Provinciales*, pp. 59–60.

[49] Arnauld uses the term 'sufficient grace' sometimes for the grace that God is said to give all mankind, sometimes for the doctrine that he gives it. Similarly he uses 'philosophic sin' sometimes for the sin which is said to be merely philosophic, sometimes for the doctrine that such sins are possible; in the last *Denunciation* (p. 298) he introduced the term 'philosophism' for the doctrine.

occasion to keep his commandments and avoid sin. The doctrine of sufficient grace is meant to answer the complaint sinners could reasonably make if God punishes with damnation all who fail to keep his commandments, though they cannot be kept without grace which he does not always give. The answer is that he does always give it. But, Arnauld remarks, against this there is an objection from experience. If God always gives the grace needed to avoid sin, why do we see so much sin? One answer is that God helps those who do their best with their natural powers and the help already given: there is so much sin because people do not do their best. But this answer has been criticised as semi-Pelagian. So now, Arnauld says, instead of trying to vindicate God's justice against the complaints of sinners, the Jesuits are protecting sinners against God's justice by claiming that no one can be damned except for theological sin narrowly defined.[50] There is a lot of sin, but not much of it is damnable; God gives to all sufficient grace to avoid damnation.

Some readers took this to mean that philosophism is a further stage in the development of the doctrine of sufficient grace. Arnauld rejects this interpretation indignantly, suspecting perhaps that it is an attempt to deflect his attack from the principle he regards as the source of the new heresy, namely that no one can sin without knowing the wrongness of the act. He insists that philosophism rests on that principle, and even claims that philosophism and the doctrine of sufficient grace are logically incompatible.[51] But his logic is at fault. There is no inconsistency between the statements that God inflicts damnation only for theological sin and that he gives enough grace to avoid sin (however sin is defined). The proponents of sufficient grace meant that God gives enough grace to avoid damnable sin, and distinguished that from merely material sin even before the distinction between philosophic and theological sin was invented.[52] If they had meant that God gives enough grace to

---

[50] *Denunciation* 1, pp. 6–9.

[51] *Denunciation* 4, pp. 250–6. The claim of incompatibility is in the words of another writer which Arnauld quotes with apparent approval, p. 252(23–5).

[52] In some of his earlier writing against sufficient grace Arnauld did not take the distinction between formal and material sin seriously enough. For example, against Fr Lemoine's theory that no one sins without an inspiration of grace to pray for strength to resist the temptation, Arnauld argued at length that it is absurd to

avoid even material sin they might have had to abandon the doctrine because of the objection from experience, and might have put philosophism in its place, but even then the two doctrines would have been logically compatible—the doctrine of sufficient grace would have been abandoned not as incompatible with philosophism but as incompatible with experience. But since they meant damnable sin, and distinguished that from material sin, they already had an answer to the objection from experience, an answer which philosophism strengthens by asserting that even some formal sins are not damnable. Since in our experience formal sin, and in particular theological sin, seldom or never happens, it is quite possible to believe that enough grace to avoid damnable sin is always given. Philosophism thus complements the doctrine of sufficient grace by strengthening the answer to an objection against it, and the latter complements the former by vindicating God's justice in the occasional (or at least possible) cases in which God damns someone for theological sin. Philosophism rests on its own principle and is logically independent of the doctrine of sufficient grace, but the two are mutually consistent and complementary.

The principle which led to philosophism was developed by Jesuit theologians over a long time. They laid down that only a voluntary act can be sinful, and that an act is not voluntary and culpable unless we know not only what we are doing but also that it is evil; for example, for an idolater to sin in sacrificing his child to Moloch he must know not only that he is sacrificing his child to Moloch, but also that such an act is evil.[53] The Jesuits claim that this conception of the voluntary is Aristotle's, but Arnauld shows that Aristotle holds that, although not to know what one is doing may make the act involuntary and excuse it, not to know that such an act is evil—that is, ignorance of moral principle—is no excuse.[54]

suppose that atheists, Epicureans, etc. think of praying whenever they sin—did Caligula think of praying whenever he gave way to his passions? See *Apology*, bk. 8, esp. pp. 918-20. Lemoine meant that if they do not think of praying then they do not really and formally (and damnably) sin: if Caligula did not think of praying he did not sin.

[53] *Denunciation* 1, p. 9(20-32). Cf. *Denunciation* 2, p. 71(11-23).

[54] *Denunciation* 1, pp. 9(36)-10(18). Cf. Pascal, *Provinciales*, pp. 68-70. See Aristotle, *EN*, III.1, esp. 1110 b27-33. A position like Aristotle's is adopted by Govier, 'Conscientiousness', pp. 249-51, and Goldstick, p. 248.

Elsewhere Aristotle distinguishes weakness of will from hardened vice, and says that the weak are less wicked because they know better—the opposite of what the Jesuits would say.[55]

Arnauld argues that St Augustine would also reject the Jesuits' principle. Augustine says that those who sin through ignorance do not will to sin, but they will the wrong act, and for sin that is enough.[56] And (to anticipate one of the later *Denunciations*) Thomas Aquinas would also reject it. A Jesuit writer quotes words of St Thomas as meaning that we commit merely philosophic sin if we turn toward a created good without turning away from God.[57] But, Arnauld points out, St Thomas's statement is conditional, and leaves the question open whether the condition is ever realised. Elsewhere St Thomas says that in serious sin the two turnings necessarily go together,[58] whatever we intend;[59] that is, in willing a

[55] *Denunciation* 1, pp. 10–11. See Aristotle, *EN*, VII.8. Aristotle says that the weak are more curable, and that they are better because the first principle (reason) is preserved. But that they are more curable, and for that reason better, need not imply, as Arnauld assumes, that their acts are better.

[56] 'Those who sin through ignorance do their action only because they will it, though they sin without willing to sin. Thus a sin even of ignorance can be committed only by the will of the sinner, though by a will of the act and not of the sin (*voluntate facti, non peccati*). All the same, it is a sin, because for that it is enough to do what one is obliged not to do' (*Denunciation* 1, p. 11, a free translation of Augustine, *Retractations*, I.15 (*PL*, vol. 32, col. 609)). Cf. Thomas Aquinas, *Summa*, 1–2, q.76 a.1 ad 3, quoted *Excuse*, pp. 668–9.

[57] 'Écrit des Jésuites', appended to *Denunciation* 2, p. 163. 'If the turning toward a created and temporal good could be without a turning away from God, this turning would be disordered but not a mortal sin' (Thomas Aquinas, *Summa*, 2–2, q.20 a.3). See also *Denunciation* 2, p. 73(11–13). On Augustine on sin as 'turning' see Burnaby, pp. 184–6.

[58] *Denunciation* 2, p. 73. Arnauld refers to the following as places where St Thomas says that in *serious* sin the two turnings go together: *Summa*, 1–2, q.72 a.5, q.73 a.3 ad 2 and a.77 a.6 ad 1; 2–2, q.10 a.3 and q.39 a.1 ad 1; 3, q.86 a.4. In *venial* sin there is a turning towards creatures without a turning away from God; *Denunciation* 2, p. 81(40). See Thomas Aquinas, *Summa*, 1–2, q.72 a.5. Arnauld assumes that the seriousness of a sin depends on the objective importance of the law broken and not on the state of mind in which it is broken, which begs the question: perhaps a sin is serious precisely when it is done with the thought of God that makes it theological.

[59] *Denunciation* 2, p. 82; cf. p. 106, and *Denunciation* 5, pp. 346–7. Arnauld quotes St Thomas: 'The seriousness of a sin is from the turning away, which follows from the turning toward *per accidens*, that is apart from the intention of the sinner' (*Summa*, 1–2, q.77 a.6 ad 1); and see Boyle. St Thomas's words are not to the point: if someone takes something because he wants to use it, knowing that it belongs to someone else who does not want him to use it, what he intends is not the offence but the use; yet his knowing that the owner objects may well be what causes the offence. That the offence may be apart from the sinner's intention therefore does not imply that it

gravely sinful act for the sake of some creature we do turn
from God even if we do not intend to turn away. So St
Thomas, as Arnauld interprets him, agrees with Augustine
that one can sin against God without willing to do so, by
willing something else. This implies a rejection of the idea
that the essence of sin is contempt.[60] Some sins relate directly
to God, such as hatred and murmuring against God, and in
these the sin consists in contempt, but this is not true of all
sorts of sins.[61]

The principle underlying the thesis that sins committed
without thought of God do not deserve damnation (namely,
that a sin is not voluntary unless we know that it is a sin) is
thus contradicted by Aristotle, Augustine and Aquinas. Arnauld shows also that the thesis itself directly conflicts with
scripture. With reference to those who simply do not know
God he quotes or refers to the following:[62] *Ps.* 78/79: 6 ('Pour
out your anger on the people who have not known you'; cf.
Jer. 10:25); *Eph.* 4: 17 ('they are far from the life of God
because of the ignorance they are in'); *Eph.* 5: 6 ('It is for
these things that the anger of God has come upon the
unbelievers'); 1 *Thess.* 4: 4 ('not in following the promptings
of concupiscence with the pagans, who do not know God');
Rom. 2: 12 ('those who have sinned without the law will perish
without the law'); *Jn.* 5: 28 ('those who have done evil deeds
... will rise to their condemnation'); *Mt.* 25:32, 33, 46 (those
on the left 'will go to eternal punishment'); *Apoc./Rev.* 21: 8 ('As
for the cowardly, the faithless, the polluted, as for murderers,
fornicators, sorcerers, idolater and all liars, their lot shall be in
the lake that burns with fire and brimstone'; cf. 20:15). The
passages about judgement day envisage only two categories of
people, the just and the damned; so if philosophic sinners are
not damned they must be among the just called to eternal life,
although they may be murderers, fornicators etc. According to
does not require the sort of thought of God that makes it a theological sin.

[60] See above, sect. 1.

[61] *Denunciation* 2, pp. 82(19–21), 83(4–6). Arnauld agrees with the Jesuits that sin
deserves eternal punishment only because it is against God, but denies that to be
'against' God the sin must express or imply contempt; see *Denunciation* 2, p. 81(15–
20).

[62] *Denunciation* 1, pp. 17–21. I will quote only what seem to me the most relevant
words; Arnauld quotes more extensively and adds comments. For parallels see Pascal,
Provinciales, pp. 63 ff.

Apoc. 21:8 such sinners are sent to the lake that burns with fire, without any exception in favour of atheists.

As for those who know God but sin without thinking of him, Arnauld remarks that forgetfulness of God is one of the greatest sources of disorder in the lives of people in modern times. Too many are badly educated, without any sentiment of piety, without thought of God in the sins they commit to satisfy ambition, avarice, lust or some other dominant passion, negligent of their salvation, led like beasts only by what strikes the senses. We can see how to judge such lives from what scripture says of those Israelites who forgot God, for example from passages in the Psalms which characterise the wicked as forgetful of God (e.g. 'The memory of God is banished from all their thoughts', *Ps.* 9:10). There is no hint that this forgetfulness is a protection against God's anger—quite the opposite: 'Listen, you who forget God, lest he drag you off to punishment' (*Ps.* 49:22). Consider the story of Susanna and the elders (*Vg. Dan.* 13): 'Their minds were perverted and they turned away their eyes so as not to see heaven and not to remember God's judgements'; yet scripture regards them as notable sinners. In *Mt.* 25:41–6 Jesus says that eternal punishment will be inflicted for sins of omission ('I was hungry and you gave me no food' etc.); but worldly people commit sins of omission without thinking of God or thinking that he obliges them to almsgiving and the like, being preoccupied with their own good and thinking only of enriching themselves; philosophists would have to say that God cannot justly inflict eternal punishment for such sins.[63]

Scripture shows that people may sin even when they do what they think *pleases* God, which they therefore do not think offends him. Jesus foretold that the Jews will think they serve God in persecuting the disciples (*Jn.* 16:2), for which, according to Paul, God's anger has come upon them 'to the end' (1 *Thess.* 2:16—although other translations say 'at last'). Speaking of the town which will not listen to his disciples Jesus says that on judgment day 'Sodom and Gomorrah will be treated less rigorously than that town' (*Mt.* 10:15). Speaking of himself, Paul says that he has been a persecutor of the

---

[63] *Denunciation* 1, pp. 21–4.

Church, and that he did this out of religious zeal (1 *Tim.* 1: 12, *Gal.* 1:13–14, *Acts* 26:9). The Jesuits would have to say that Saul persecuting the Church and heretics waging wars of religion are only philosophic sinners.[64]

After pointing out these conflicts with passages from scripture, Augustine and Aristotle, Arnauld applies the doctrine to some examples from which he expects that any well-instructed Christian will see its impiety. Suppose a libertine is converted by some extraordinary grace and makes a general confession of the sins of his past life: in his childhood no one taught him to know and serve God, he fell in with bad companions who led him into debauchery, drunkenness and the like, he developed habits of swearing and blaspheming, he made love to married women, he took cruel vengeance for anything he took as an affront, he cheated tradesmen, there was no evil he would not have done if he had got the chance. His bad habits made him so blind and obdurate that he never felt the slightest remorse; he was wholly occupied in satisfying his passions and never thought of God.[65] The Jesuits would have to say that because he never thought of God all these were only philosophic sins which he need not confess.

The last section of the first *Denunciation*, which answers answers to criticisms of philosophic sin made earlier by others, will be dealt with more conveniently below together with the other *Denunciations*, which answer answers to the first. But before leaving the first let us notice some weaknesses in Arnauld's arguments so far. Philosophic or moral sin is a species of formal sin, and formal sin deserves blame and punishment—finite punishment, in the case of philosophic sin. Now it is possible to think of moral wrongdoing as the concern of every member of the moral community, so that (if it is to be blamed and punished) any member, including God, may and should blame it and punish it (finitely), without taking it as an offence against him- or herself personally.[66] So perhaps God physically destroyed Sodom and Gomorrah as a finite punishment, but did not sentence their inhabitants to hell

[64] Ibid., pp. 24–6.

[65] Ibid., pp. 29–32. Arnauld later gave a real-life example, *Denunciation* 5, pp. 309–15.

[66] According to one Jesuit, God detests philosophic sin as something intrinsically bad, not as something against himself (*Denunciation* 5, p. 381(29–32)).

eternally. If Arnauld's scripture passages are reconsidered with such a possibility in mind it will be found that most are simply irrelevant to the real point at issue, namely whether philosophic sin deserves to be punished *eternally*. There are two passages which do refer explicitly to eternal punishment, *Mt.* 25 and *Rev.* 20–1. To these there are two possible answers. First, for those who have heard these passages, at least while they have them in mind, there is no possibility of merely philosophic sin, so reference to this possibility was unnecessary.[67] Second, although *Rev.* 20–1 says that the devil will be punished eternally in the lake of fire, it does not say that each sinner sent to join him will be kept there eternally.[68]

The passages quoted to show that acts thought pleasing to God may really be sins requiring apology and forgiveness do not imply that such acts deserve blame or punishment, and the doctrine of philosophic sin does not imply that they do not require apology and forgiveness. When one person apologises and the other forgives there need be no implication on either side that the act deserved blame. If we do something wrong in ignorance, not to regret it when the error is discovered shows that we would have done the same even if we had known; regret shows that the act is against the general disposition of our will.[69] Apology expresses and forgiveness acknowledges the apologiser's general disposition, leaving it an open question whether the act deserves blame. As a moral

[67] In saying that fornicators and the like will not possess the kingdom of heaven (1 *Cor.* 6:9), 'the Apostle assumes that those who commit such crimes know that God has forbidden them; and in fact the Corinthians to whom he speaks know it well' (Jesuit writer quoted *Denunciation* 5, p. 376; cf. p. 372(3–9)).

[68] Cf. 'The fire prepared for the wicked is an everlasting fire; but it cannot be thence inferred that he who shall be cast into that fire ... shall endure ... so as to be eternally burnt' (Hobbes, p. 490; cf. pp. 646–9). According to one Jesuit writer, philosophic sinners may go to eternal punishment, 'but very likely they will not suffer the fire of the eternal flames for ever' (*Denunciation* 2, p. 80 ('eternal flames' reads 'infernal flames' on p. 167)). Arnauld comments that if the scripture text can be interpreted thus for philosophic sinners so it can for all sinners, which is to revive the ideas of Origen (*Denunciation* 2, pp. 85(12–8), 95(31)). Origen suggested that after punishment even the devil might repent and be reconciled with God. Augustine rejected Origen's suggestion (*De civitate dei*, XXI.23). On the revival of Origen's ideas, see Walker.

[69] 'The man who has done something owing to ignorance, and feels not the least vexation at his action, has not acted voluntarily, since he did not know what he was doing, nor yet involuntarily, since he is not pained. Of people, then, who act by reason of ignorance, he who regrets is thought an involuntary agent' (Aristotle, *EN*, III.1 (trans. W. D. Ross)).

virtue goodwill means a settled resolution to do what is right, without concern for praise or blame except as an index of right and wrong. This is an important point: a person of goodwill seeks not to avoid blame, nor even to avoid deserving blame, but to do what is objectively right; failure in this purpose, even if not blameworthy, will cause regret. The appropriate religious expression of this is to ask forgiveness of God. The doctrine of philosophic sin does not mean that an act is not *wrong* unless one thought so at the time, but that unless one thought so it is not a sin deserving blame or punishment. Its advocates can therefore say, without inconsistency, that a person who ignorantly does what is objectively wrong does not deserve blame but should ask God's forgiveness when the mistake is discovered.[70] The same considerations apply to the example of the penitent libertine: the proponents of the doctrine of philosophic sin need not say he has nothing to confess; if they do, it will not be because they think that his sins are merely philosophic, but because they think that the sole purpose of confession is to ward off blame and punishment.

As for Aristotle's opinion that some sorts of ignorance excuse but not ignorance of moral principle, let us ask why he thought so. In a passage which Arnauld does not consider, Aristotle says that we punish a person for not knowing what he should know and could know if he took care. But Aristotle imagines an objection: what if he is simply a careless sort of person? Can he be blamed for being the sort of person he is, or is that a matter of innate temperament? Perhaps one must be born with an eye, as it were, by which to judge rightly and choose what is truly good; and then no one will be responsible for moral blindness or for the carelessness and other vices which result from it. Aristotle answers that if we are not responsible for our vices then we can claim no credit for our virtues either, and that in fact we do seem to be causes or at least co-causes of our own characters.[71] This passage suggests a possible reason why he thought that ignorance of moral principle is no excuse: perhaps he thought that moral principles are among the things a person should know and

---

[70] Cf. Bayle, *DHC*, art. 'Ruffi', rem. A, vol. 12, pp. 649–50.
[71] Aristotle, *EN*, III.5.

could know with care, and that we are always to blame for carelessness and blindness in such matters. But if we disagree, Arnauld's objection from Aristotle will lose its force. Since no amount of care gives knowledge of the true God unless he reveals himself, it would seem implausible to equate ignorance of God with ignorance of moral principle, so that even invincible ignorance of God would be no excuse; but as we will see later, that is Arnauld's position.

3. THE OTHER DENUNCIATIONS

To sin while actually thinking, 'this will offend God who is infinitely worthy of respect' must be a rare event. According to Arnauld the Jesuits turned to the doctrine of philosophic sin because the doctrine of sufficient grace lay open to the objection that despite this sufficient grace almost everyone sins and incurs damnation. The new doctrine seems to go to the other extreme and saves almost everyone. In most of the remaining *Denunciations* Arnauld's main concern is to block attempts to show that it leaves plenty of room for damnation after all.

In reply to the *First Denunciation* and to earlier critics the Jesuits of Louvain made the following points. (1) If a philosophic sin is serious it is mortal and will be punished in hell—though perhaps not eternally, since the eternity of sensible punishment corresponds to an infinite malice, which philosophic sin lacks. (2) For theological sin full advertence to the infinite goodness of God is not required; habitual, obscure or general knowledge is enough. (3) Since God gives everyone, even those who have not heard the gospel, sufficient grace to attain such knowledge, they cannot be ignorant, except for a short time,[72] without being at fault in resisting grace, which makes their sins theological. From (2) and (3) it follows (4) that the supposition of merely philosophic sin is a bit metaphysical: it rarely happens.[73] The Jesuits of Paris

[72] 'For a short time' is the translation provided by the Jesuit author for the original *tantisper*. But as Ceyssens points out, p. 392, this translation would require *paulisper*. The original is obscure; it may mean that ignorance is inculpable *as long as* grace sufficient to dispel it is not given.

[73] For points 1–4 see 'Écrit des Jésuites' appended to *Denunciation* 2, pp. 160 ff., esp. pp. 167–8.

said (5) that it is quite metaphysical: merely philosophic sin has never happened and never will. According to them, (6) 'none of our writers has ever taught this doctrine', that is, that it does happen; the Jesuits who wrote about philosophic sin were arguing conditionally on a false supposition, that *if there were* any such thing as merely philosophic sin it would not deserve eternal punishment.[74] As a Jesuit professor of Anvers put it, (7) 'philosophic' and 'theological' sin are merely two formalities (distinguishable aspects) of every sin, not two kinds of sin capable of existing apart.[75]

Arnauld replied to these points as follows. To say (point 1) that philosophic sin may be mortal and deserve to be punished in hell, but not eternally, is out of harmony with the rest of the theory, which is an attempt to define the sin that deserves eternal punishment; in any case it does not remove the objection since it is a merely verbal concession.[76] The question is not whether the punishment is called hell but whether it is eternal. The restriction to sensible punishment suggests that the other element of the punishment, namely the pain of loss, might be eternal, which is a sop to those who say that all serious sin deserves eternal punishment; but this restriction is arbitrary. The reason given why eternal sensible punishment would be unjust, namely that infinite punishment is due only to infinite malice, applies equally to the pain of loss of God. In fact it applies more strongly, since that pain would be infinite not only in duration but also by reason of the good lost.[77]

Point 2 is another concession out of harmony with the rest of the theory, which assumes that punishment is due to contempt and that contempt requires awareness: how can obscure, habitual or general knowledge be enough? And the concession goes either not far enough or too far. Consider the Americans before they heard the gospel. Their beliefs about their own gods cannot count as even obscure and general knowledge of the true God, enough to make the malice of their sins infinite, since their gods are finite.[78] On the other

[74] *Denunciation* 3, pp. 208, 232; and *Denunciation* 4, p. 267.

[75] *Denunciation* 5, p. 301.

[76] *Denunciation* 2, pp. 76(23)–77(14), 81(1–6), 85(1–7).

[77] Ibid., pp. 89–97.

[78] Ibid., pp. 98(25)–99(25).

hand, if it is enough to have general and implicit knowledge of God under the concept of the good, at which every human action aims (that is, good in general, not precisely infinite good),[79] then merely philosophic sin is not rare (point 4) but impossible. The claim (point 6) that this is exactly what was meant will be dealt with below.

Point 3 assumes the theory of sufficient grace.[80] Consider the Americans again. Since most of them had no human means of knowing the true God,[81] point 3 must mean that God gave each of them a direct revelation of himself. This must have taken the form of thoughts in their minds 'loud' enough to hear.[82] God can reveal himself this way, but there is no reason to suppose that he gives and must give such thoughts to everyone to whom preachers are not sent; in fact the normal means by which God reveals himself is outward preaching.[83] The supposition that the Americans have all had such thoughts is refuted by experience: no missionary reports meeting Americans who had already heard in their own thoughts anything of the true God; missionaries do not claim to be reminding them of what they have already thought of, and would be laughed at if they did.[84] If God gives all the Americans grace sufficient for knowledge which none of them has, then the grace must be ill-adapted to their state, and given merely to make their ignorance culpable and their sins theological and damnable. This hardly makes God seem more amiable.[85]

But even if the Americans' ignorance is their own fault, that is irrelevant to the distinction between philosophic and theological sin. If the sinner does not know God then, even if this is his fault, his sins are merely philosophic, according to the definitions originally given.[86] Perhaps the definition could be changed to make fault relevant; philosophic sin might be defined as sin done in *non-culpable* ignorance of God.

[79] Ibid., pp. 99(26)–100(28).

[80] Ibid., p. 112(30).

[81] Ibid., pp. 106–11.

[82] Ibid., p. 114(3–6).

[83] Ibid., pp. 125–30, 139(32)–140(7), 146(1–14) See also *Infidels, passim*.

[84] *Denunciation* 2, pp. 130(31)–131(21), 133(12–35).

[85] Ibid., pp. 134–6. Cf. Bayle, *DHC*, art. 'Lugo', rem. G, vol. 9, p. 537; and see above, n.6.

[86] *Denunciation* 2, pp. 87–9, 143.

This is another concession out of harmony with the basic ideas of the theory,[87] and it leads to an anomaly. The fault would be itself a merely philosophic sin, since when the sinner first resists the grace which would give him knowledge of God he is not yet at fault in not knowing, and resists in non-culpable ignorance: but because of this philosophic sin, other sins which would otherwise have been also merely philosophic count as theological sins of infinite malice.[88]

Since points 2 and 3 fail, it does not follow (point 4) that merely philosophic sin is rare; the many sins of the Americans must have been, on Jesuit principles, merely philosophic and exempt from the punishment of hell. But whether such sins have been few or many is a side-issue. The essential point is that, if there is no sin without knowledge of the malice of the act, then merely philosophic sin is not just 'metaphysically' but 'effectively' possible: it can really happen (whether often or only sometimes) that someone may voluntarily do a gravely immoral act knowing that it is such and yet not incur eternal punishment. According to Arnauld this is heresy no matter how seldom such sins are supposed to happen, and its originating principle is the proposition that there is no sin without knowledge of the malice of the act.[89]

If it were true (points 5 and 7) that philosophical and theological sin are distinguishable but not separable aspects of every sin, Arnauld would have no complaint, as he said before the Jesuits of Paris and Anvers entered the controversy.[90] But it is not true. Since there are two kinds of wrongness, and since they can be known separately, then—if there is no sin without knowledge of the wrongness of the act—it must follow that the two kinds of sin can exist separately and that there can be a merely philosophic sin.[91] To escape this conclusion

[87] Ibid., pp. 101-3.

[88] Ibid., p. 105(21-8).

[89] *Denunciation* 3, p. 234(16-21); *Denunciation* 4, p. 268(2-11). On the definition of the heresy and its principle, see *Denunciation* 4, pp. 250-6, and *Denunciation* 5, pp. 349-55.

[90] *Denunciation* 2, p. 159(13-23).

[91] *Denunciation* 4, pp. 273(34)-274(7); cf. Arnauld's letter to Pelisson, *Œuvres*, vol. 3, pp. 367-70. Beylard, pp. 689-93, refers to various Jesuit writers who argued that there are two kinds of malice, against morality and against God. Arnauld did not dispute this, nor did he dispute that it is possible to know that an act is against morality without knowing that it is against God. His contention is that the first kind of malice is never found without the second, and that sin does not require knowledge

it might be said that God makes sure that, at the point of decision, no one ever is ignorant of himself or of the divine law;[92] this is the theory earlier rejected (see above, point 3) that God speaks directly to those to whom preachers are not sent. Or it might be suggested that those ignorant of God and his law will also be ignorant of natural morality; but missionaries tell of people ignorant of God who know of at least some moral laws.[93] If this suggestion were true, then it would follow from the principle that sin requires knowledge of the wrongness of the act that the Americans and others ignorant of God commit only material sins exempt from blame altogether, which Arnauld thinks is even more shocking than the idea that their sins are only philosophic.[94]

Against the claim (point 6) that no Jesuit writer ever taught that purely philosophic sin can really happen, that they were arguing hypothetically on a false supposition, Arnauld shows that the words of many of them cannot reasonably be taken that way. One says explicitly: *Peccatum pure philosophicum possibile est*.[95] If they had thought that every philosophic sin is also theological, they would not have said that philosophic sin is committed by those who do not know or think of God (whether through their own fault or not): if every sin belongs to both species, then philosophic sin is not committed by a restricted class of persons.[96]

Further, the possibility of merely philosophic sin is a legitimate inference[97] from common Jesuit doctrines of invincible ignorance and probabilism. The treatment of invincible ignorance in a book published in 1670 by an English Jesuit, Fr Terrill, is a thoroughgoing development of the principle behind the theory of philosophic sin, namely that formal sin requires

of the malice of the act; thus, even when the sinner does not know that his act is against God, there is no purely philosophic sin.

[92] *Denunciation* 4, p. 272(19-24); *Denunciation* 5, p. 331(1-13).

[93] *Denunciation* 4, pp. 274-5.

[94] Ibid., pp. 276(37-40), 296(4-5); cf. *Denunciation* 2, pp. 153-4, and *Denunciation* 5, pp. 314-313 (misprint for 315).

[95] *Denunciation* 5, p. 379 (but possible in what sense?); cf. pp. 380(31-5), 381(11-20), 368(19-33), 372(20-6).

[96] *Denunciation* 2, p. 302.

[97] By itself this would not show that they hold it, since people never grasp all the implications of their own views. But to show that philosophism is connected logically with other parts of their ethical system may help to confirm Arnauld's interpretation of what they say explicitly about it.

full awareness of the wrongness of the act.[98] According to Fr Terrill, ignorance which is inculpable (or involuntary or invincible) always excuses sin so that it is not formally sin and is not imputable or punishable. Ignorance is inculpable unless we actually have the thought that there is or might be something more to know, and also the thought that we have a duty to find out.[99] Whether such thoughts occur is outside our power; if the ignorance is culpable it is because the thoughts have occurred but we have neglected to act on them; its continuance ceases to be culpable when they go or the opportunity for acting on them passes.[100] Culpable ignorance is no excuse, but an act resulting from it is a sin only 'in its cause': there is no new formal, imputable sin in addition to the sin of neglecting to dispel one's ignorance, and no additional punishment is due.[101] Inadvertence is a species of ignorance and therefore subject to the same principles.[102]

Arnauld rejects this theory of ignorance as excuse, as we will see in section 4. What matters here is that those who hold it cannot deny that merely philosophic sin is possible. Assuming that the loophole provided by the doctrine of sufficient grace is by now closed, and that the Jesuits will not want to say that

[98] *Denunciation* 4, pp. 278–96. Arnauld gives a similar analysis of the remarks on ignorance of the Jesuits of Paris and of Anvers; see *Denunciation* 4, pp. 269–72, and *Denunciation* 5, pp. 316–17, 323.

[99] *Denunciation* 4, p. 285.

[100] Ibid., pp. 283–4.

[101] Ibid., pp. 290–91. This means, as Arnauld points out (p. 293), that someone ignorant through negligence that murder is wrong who commits six thousand murders will be liable to blame and punishment not as a murderer but only as one who neglected to inform himself of his duties—blame and punishment to which he would have been liable even if he had not actually committed any murder. The Jesuit General in 1690, Fr Gonzalez, criticised Terrill and others who explain sins of ignorance as if the whole sin were in the negligence; the resulting sin is imputed, he says, because the negligence was culpable, but what is imputed is that sin and not merely the negligence (Ceyssens, pp. 409–10, 425). Bayle held that if someone sins in culpable ignorance he deserves punishment for the sin which caused the ignorance, but not for the sin which results from it (*CP*, p. 508 (ch. 3)). According to Thomas Aquinas there are in such cases two punishable sins, but the punishment for the resulting sin may be greatly reduced because it is done in ignorance, even though the ignorance is culpable (*Summa*, 1-2, q.76 a.4 ad 2). See also St Bonaventure, *In 2 Sent.*, d.22 a.2 q.3 ad 5; and Taylor, *Ductor dubitantium*, pp. 137–9.

[102] *Denunciation* 4, p. 269(31), *Denunciation* 5, pp. 323–4. Arnauld argues that inadvertence is not a species of ignorance in *Ignorance*, p. 646. If it is regarded as a species of ignorance, culpable only if one thinks of overcoming it but neglects to do so, then inadvertence can never be culpable, since to think of adverting to something is to advert to it (*Denunciation* 5, p. 324).

the Americans commit only material sins, he argues that, on a theory of invincible ignorance which sets such strict requirements for the culpability of ignorance and inadvertence, the Americans will generally be blameless in not knowing or thinking of God and his law, and their sins in so far as they are theological will therefore be excused; if they do wrong knowing that the act is against natural law (which Arnauld thinks the Jesuits must admit is possible), this will be an instance of merely philosophic sin.[103]

Probabilism can be seen as an application of the doctrine of inculpable ignorance. The probabilist principle is that a wrong act is excused if the agent knows that some reputable casuist says that such acts are permissible; the casuist's authority makes the mistake inculpable. The notion of inculpable ignorance gets stretched a long way: the act is excused even if, suspecting that it is wrong but wanting to do it, we have deliberately gone looking for an authority who permits it, and even if we knew that this authority might be mistaken and that other authorities said that the act is wrong. If such studied ignorance counts as inculpable then, Arnauld asks, can the Americans be blamed for their ignorance of God and his law?[104]

It seems to me that Arnauld gets the better of this contest. He shows that the principle that sin requires knowledge of the wrongness of the act does imply the possibility of merely philosophic sin. Even if no Jesuit had drawn out the implication (and Arnauld shows that some had) he had the right to point it out and to press them either to own philosophism or disown the principle; instead they said irrelevantly that merely philosophic sin hardly ever happens because no one can for long be involuntarily ignorant of God—which, as Arnauld had shown, is in any case false.[105] But there is something to be said for the Jesuits. Arnauld seeks to discredit their principle by drawing out an implication he expected would shock

---

[103] *Denunciation* 4, pp. 272–3, 282–3, 294–6; *Denunciation* 5, pp. 316–19.

[104] *Denunciation* 5, pp. 357–65.

[105] See Beylard, pp. 694 and 696–7, and Deman, cols. 270–1. Arnauld had already argued against the claim that no one can for long be ignorant of God without personal fault; see above, answer to point 3. The reason why, according to Arnauld, no sin can be merely philosophic is not that ignorance of God not due to some personal fault does not happen, but that it does not excuse; see below, sect. 4.

Christian consciences, namely that there might be serious violations of morality which could not justly be punished in hell forever. Some seventeenth-century Christians did find this implication shocking, but it seems not to be of the essence of Christianity to find it so. The Jesuits, on the other hand, were moved by an idea which does seem essential to Christianity and to any other religion worth taking seriously, indeed to any religion that is not an influence for evil, namely that God is just. 'Can anyone be persuaded that a God so just and good punishes a man eternally for having done what he believed in conscience he ought to do—has there ever been such a tyranny? ... that he has already condemned us to the eternal flames for things we did not know displease him—is that like a fair master?'[106] Let us see how Arnauld himself answers such questions.

4. THE JUSTICE OF PUNISHING SINS WHICH ARE UNAVOIDABLE

According to Arnauld, the Jesuits were misled by merely human ideas of justice, 'although God has said so positively that his thoughts are not like our thoughts, and that his ways are as far from those of men as heaven is from earth'.[107] But he himself tries to show the justice of God's ways in humanly intelligible terms. His arguments are mostly Augustine's, using texts already collected for the same purpose in Jansen's *Augustinus*.[108] Translating Augustine into scholastic terminology, Jansen argued that invincible ignorance does not always (as most scholastics seem to suppose[109]) excuse sin: invincible ignorance of fact or of positive law (including positive divine

[106] The Jesuits of Paris, quoted *Denunciation* 4, pp. 270–1.

[107] *Denunciation* 1, p. 7. On the discrepancy between human ideas of justice and God's, see also *Ignorance*, pp. 652(3–5), 653(16ff.), 657(6–7), and Jansen, vol. 2, col. 299. For criticism see Baird, pp. 48ff.

[108] References to *Augustinus* are (unless otherwise noted) to vol. 2, by column and letter; the letters run down the middle of each page. On the topic of sect. 4 see Alflatt.

[109] *Augustinus*, 287B. 'Scholastic' in seventeenth-century writers did not always mean medieval; it was sometimes used to refer to contemporary university or college teachers.

law) excuses,[110] but ignorance, even invincible, of natural law never does.[111] Invincible ignorance of a part of natural law (total ignorance is not possible[112]) is not itself a sin,[113] but it does not excuse the sins which result from it.[114] Punishment in such cases is deserved not for not knowing, but for not doing what we do not know we ought to do. Such 'sins of ignorance',[115] and also sins of weakness, are unavoidable[116] but still imputable and punishable.[117]

Augustine gave various definitions of sin, one of which is 'anything uttered, done or desired against God's law'.[118] Sin is something not merely physical and external; it depends upon what we think we are doing. But it does not depend upon whether we think that what we think we are doing is against God's law. An act which results in a person's death is not against God's law 'Thou shalt not kill' unless we think we are killing someone, but then it may be a sin even if we do not think that killing someone is wrong. It is a sin if, as the act it was intended to be, it is in fact against God's law, even if it was not intended as a violation of God's law or as a sin.[119] To avoid sin, therefore, it is necessary[120] to know God's law and to make our decisions in obedience to it. Sin will be unavoidable if we either (a) cannot know God's law

[110] Ibid., 311B. On the distinction between natural law and divine positive law see Thomas Aquinas, *Summa*, 2-2, q.57 a.2 ad 3.

[111] *Augustinus*, 306B, 310B. For this the Jansenists could claim the authority of Gratian, 1, q.4, c.12 (vol. 1, col. 422); see *Denunciation* 1, p. 39, and *Denunciation* 4, p. 257.

[112] *Augustinus*, 310A (ch. 6), 312A.

[113] Ibid., 312B; cf. *Jansen*, pp. 279-80. Such ignorance is not a sin, but it is 'not without sin', namely the sin which causes it. See *Augustinus*, p. 279(29), *Denunciation* 1, p. 34(7-8) and a letter in *Œuvres*, vol. 3, p. 308(28).

[114] *Augustinus*, chs. 3 and 4, 291ff. Arnauld points out that a passage in which St Thomas might seem to say that invincible ignorance always excuses sin, namely *Summa*, 1-2, q.76 a.2, is really about another question, whether ignorance is itself a sin. The passage is therefore consistent with Jansen's position. See *Excuse*, p. 669(30-7).

[115] The expression 'sins of ignorance' means not sinful ignorance but sins done because of ignorance. See *Augustinus*, 298B, Arnauld, *Ignorance*, p. 664(33-4), Chéné, pp. 769-71.

[116] *Augustinus*, 292B (ch. 3), 297BC, 299A-301A.

[117] Ibid., 301BC.

[118] Augustine, *Contra faustum*, XXII.27 (*PL*, vol. 42, col. 413). Jansen does not argue explicitly from this definition, but he assumes something like it.

[119] See above, n.56.

[120] But not sufficient, as we will see in sect. 5. It is necessary also to choose out of love of God.

or (b) cannot will obedience to it.[121] A sin which is unavoidable for either of these reasons still satisfies the present definition of sin, and satisfies it fully (so the sin is formal, not material): the act is still a voluntary act against God's law, and therefore imputable and justly punishable.[122]

An act cannot be a sin unless it is intentional and therefore voluntary. But how can a sin be both voluntary and unavoidable? The assumption that an act is voluntary only if it is avoidable led to the doctrines of philosophic sin and sufficient grace[123] as attempts to meet respectively points (a) and (b) above. Proponents of these doctrines argued that there can be no voluntary (which they took to imply avoidable) sin unless the sinner (a) knows that the act is against God's law, and (b) is able (having been given any grace necessary) to choose to obey. If either knowledge or power of right choice is lacking, obedience to God's commands is impossible. It would be unjust of God to punish us for not doing the impossible. Unavoidable sin is therefore not punishable; it is merely material sin.

Arnauld answers that even after Adam's sin, and even if the necessary grace has not been given, we can always obey God's commands *if* we choose, and this conditional possibility (even if the condition is not realisable) is enough for freedom and moral responsibility.[124] To keep the commandments is within everyone's power because all they require is the

[121] 'Ignorance, therefore, and weakness are the vices which impede the will from doing good or abstaining from evil' (Augustine, *De peccatorum meritis*, II.xvii.26; quoted *Augustinus*, 294BC, and *Jansen*, p. 283). Augustine often mentions the same two causes (or passion or concupiscence as the second); see e.g. *Enchiridion*, xxii.81.

[122] In certain works written before the Pelagian controversy Augustine made—or seemed to make—avoidability essential to sin. For example, in one place he defined sin as 'the will to keep or seek what justice forbids, from which one is free to abstain', and inferred that if someone has no power to abstain we cannot consider the sin his, and that it is the height of injustice to hold anyone guilty for not doing what he could not do (*De duabus animabus*, xi.15 and xii.17 (*PL*, vol. 42, col. 105, 107)). Elsewhere he wrote, 'Sin is so voluntary an evil that it cannot be sin if it is not voluntary' (*De vera religione*, xiv.27). Later he explained that these remarks 'refer only to the sin which is not a penalty for sin ... Original sin in infants is not improperly called voluntary because it is inherited from man's first evil will' (*Retractations*, I.13, and cf. I.15 (*PL*, vol. 32, cols. 603–4, 610)). See *Augustinus*, 300AB, 302BC.

[123] Arnauld, *Denunciation* 1, pp. 7(19–27), 9(1)–10(4), *Apology*, p. 584(18–20).

[124] Compare Mill: 'this feeling, of our being able to modify our own character *if we wish*, is itself the feeling of moral freedom', even though the formation of the wish depends on external influences (*Logic*, vol. 2, p. 841). For more recent examples of similar theories, and criticism, see Campbell, pp. 122ff.

will;[125] that is (I assume he means), the commandments make allowance for external obstacles, so that a commandment requiring an external act is satisfied by genuine willingness to do it if we can. But although we can satisfy the commandments if we will, God's grace is needed to give the will.[126] Without grace sin is inevitable and obedience impossible because we cannot bring ourselves to be willing to obey, and for no other reason. Impossibility of this sort is no excuse; it is clearly just to punish those who are disobedient only because they are unwilling to obey. If this kind of impossibility were an excuse then the greater the willingness to do the wicked act the less would be the responsibility for it, which seems absurd.[127] Rather, as St Thomas says, the greater the willingness the greater the sin. The arrogant man's inability to bear insult, the miser's inability to give alms, and other vices, do not excuse. In such cases, as St Bernard says, 'the will renders it inexcusable, and the necessity incorrigible'.[128]

Our willingness to sin is one of the effects and penalties of Adam's sin, and our ignorance is another. God could not justly have created Adam originally with a defective nature,[129] lacking effective power to attain the end appropriate to an intelligent being, namely the vision of God; so in his original state Adam must have had knowledge and effective possibility of right choice sufficient to keep the commandments, avoid sin and attain his last end.[130] But although he had natural

[125] *Jansen*, p. 234(17–23), *Apology*, p. 583(22–3). Cf. Hobbes, p. 215.

[126] *Jansen*, p. 234(11–6, 24), *Apology*, p. 586(13–6, 27, 30-1). Cf. Pascal, the third and fourth of the 'Écrits sur la grâce'. The first of the Five Propositions attributed to Jansen is that God's commands are sometimes impossible. The Jansenists held that we can always keep the commandments *if we wish*, but that we cannot wish it without grace, which is not always given, not even to the just.

[127] Perhaps it seems absurd only because we do not usually consider the possibility that willingness may be necessitated.

[128] *Denunciation* 2, pp. 119, 123-4. The reference to Thomas Aquinas is to *Summa*, 2-2, q.156 a.3. For more detail on what Arnauld thought about necessity, see below, Appendix.

[129] *Necessity*, p. 220(39). According to Augustine acts resulting from defects of original nature would not be sins (*De libero arbitrio*, III.xviii.51, quoted *Augustinus*, 303); Jansen argues that then the blame would fall on God, which is unthinkable; so originally Adam's nature cannot have been defective (*Augustinus*, 857ff). Ignorance excuses if it is of a kind to which Adam was subject before the fall (*Augustinus*, 302D-303A).

[130] The claim that originally Adam must have been able to attain the vision of God was involved in controversy; see de Lubac, ch. 6. These three propositions cannot logically be held together: (1) that the vision of God was Adam's natural

power and grace sufficient to avoid sin, Adam did sin, and as a just punishment suffered an impairment of knowledge and will[131] which makes further justly punishable sins unavoidable.[132] Adam's fault is ours too, and we share the punishment. We cannot ourselves repair the impairment inflicted as punishment—only God can; but since the punishment is just he is not bound to do so, and when he does it is a grace. God gives grace to some but not to others;[133] the latter have no right to complain, since grace is not due to any;[134] to prefer

end; (2) that the vision of God cannot be attained by the unaided natural powers of any creature; and (3) that the end natural to a being must be attainable by its unaided natural powers. Proposition 2 was held generally. Some held 2 and 3, which entails rejection of 1; if God meant Adam to attain the vision of himself this was from the outset an end above his nature and any divine help toward it was gratuitous. Others, including Thomas Aquinas, Baius and Jansen, held 1 and 2 and not 3; on their premises, Adam even before the fall needed divine help to attain his natural end (see *Jansen*, pp. 167–8). Thomas Aquinas held that this help was always gratuitous. Baius and Jansen held that before the fall it was owed in justice, because if as God created him Adam needed help to attain his natural end then God could not justly withhold that help.

[131] *Denunciation* 2, p. 103(28–9). On ignorance as punishment, see *Denunciation* 1, p. 34(7–10). On weakness of will as punishment, see *Ignorance*, p. 652(18–21). Augustine: 'Man has no power to be good, either not seeing what he ought to be, or seeing it but not being strong enough to be what he sees he ought to be. Who can doubt that this is a punishment?' (*De libero arbitrio*, III.xviii.51, quoted *Augustinus*, 303). Augustine: 'It is a most just punishment for sin that each one loses what he was unwilling to use rightly when he could have done so, if he had wished, without any difficulty' (*De libero arbitrio*, III.xviii.52, quoted *Augustinus*, 304A). It seems to me that this may be true of something scarce which can be transferred to someone who can use it, but not of dispositions needed to act rightly.

[132] Augustine; 'You are much mistaken if you think there is no necessity of sinning, or if you do not understand that this necessity is the penalty of a sin committed without necessity' (*Opus imperfectum contra Julianum*, I.105 (PL, vol. 45, col. 1118), quoted *Denunciation* 1, p. 34, *Augustinus*, 300, *Jansen*, p. 288 etc.). Augustine: 'He becomes blinded, and necessarily offends more .... This darkening was already their penalty ... and by this very penalty ... they fell into worse sins still' (*De natura et gratia*, xxii.24, quoted in part (see the whole chapter) in *Augustinus*, 313). This necessity is no excuse (*Augustinus*, 301BC).

[133] Arnauld denies that after Adam's sin God gives grace to all, which some reject (*Jansen*, p. 284). See Arnauld's comments on the maxim 'God will not deny grace to those who do what is in them': 'What is in them', if it disposes them to grace, is already due to grace; it is Pelagian to say that grace can be earned as a matter of justice by the effort of natural powers not aided by grace (*Denunciation* 1, p. 8, *Necessity*, pp. 226–7, *Love*, pp. 683–4). On this maxim see Thomas Aquinas, *Summa*, 1–2, q.109 a.6, 1–2, q.112 a.3, and Oberman, *Harvest*, pp. 131–3, 44.

[134] *Necessity*, pp. 221(15–22), 272–3, *Jansen*, p. 155(14–8), *Ignorance*, p. 654. Augustine: 'The whole mass owes the penalty, and if the due penalty of damnation were given to all, undoubtedly that would not be unjust. Those freed from it by grace are called, not vessels of their own merits, but "vessels of mercy"' (*De natura et gratia*, v.5). Cf. Wendel, pp. 281–2.

one to another is not unjust except in distributing something to which all are entitled, and entitled equally, and no one is entitled to grace.[135] God is not bound in justice to repair, or give special help to overcome, impairments which he has justly inflicted as punishment for sin. So although God could not justly have created Adam originally with these defects, since the defects are man's fault God can now justly leave them unremedied. But the impairment of human powers as just punishment for sin does not impair God's rights. The fall was not God's fault; he can still justly command what he created Adam originally quite able to do, and he can still justly punish failure to obey.[136] Without grace failure is now unavoidable, so there are unavoidable sins which God may justly punish.

Consider again the doctrines intended to meet points (a) and (b) (see above). The argument that an act may be voluntary and free even if we cannot will differently, supplemented by the argument that inability to will obedience to God may be a just penalty for a sin which was effectively avoidable, explains why the doctrine of sufficient grace must be rejected—that is, why it cannot be held that God must in justice give grace to all.[137] The same reasoning also refutes

[135] *Necessity*, pp. 224-5. To me it seems unfair, or in some way wrong, when there is no scarcity and no reason for any preference, to give to one and not to another, even if neither is entitled.

[136] *Apology*, p. 613, *Denunciation* 2, p. 122(34-6), *Ignorance*, p. 657(25-6).

[137] But the Jansenist theodicy made crucial use of something like the Jesuits' doctrine of sufficient grace: what the Jesuits said to vindicate God's justice in punishing sinners the Jansenists said to vindicate God's justice in punishing Adam (and his descendants), namely that Adam was able to avoid the first sin. According to Arnauld, following Jansen, it is fundamental to Augustine's whole doctrine to distinguish between the grace of God the creator, given to Adam before he sinned, and the grace of Christ the saviour, given to some and not others after the fall (see *Jansen*, pp. 167-75, 196-201). Of the grace of God the creator the doctrine of sufficient grace is true: the Jesuits' mistake is not to realise how much difference the fall makes (compare Arnauld's remark (*Necessity*, p. 220(25-9)) that the proponents of the doctrine of sufficient grace argue like pagan philosophers ignorant of the fall). The grace of God the creator was not irresistible, it made right choice effectively possible but left sin effectively possible also, and it was given (or would have been given if the fall had not taken place) to all mankind equally (*Jansen*, pp. 154(33-7)). Like the Jesuits Arnauld offers this doctrine as part of a vindication of God's justice (see *Necessity*, pp. 220-1), and his preferences among theological theories reflect ideas of justice. Thus he prefers Jansen's theory to Calvin's because, given the sufficiency of the grace of God the creator, Adam's sin was not a predestined but an effectively free act. He prefers it to the theories of many Catholics because according to Jansen the decrees of election and reprobation did not 'precede' God's foreknowledge of Adam's sin: election is God's decision to give in Christ the grace that will infallibly

the theory of philosophic sin. Sins of ignorance are done willingly (by will of the act, not of the sin), and ignorance is a penalty for sin. God could not justly have created Adam originally without sufficient power to know the natural law, that is, the law which a creature of Adam's nature must obey to attain the end appropriate to that nature. If we cannot now avoid ignorance of natural law that is a punishment, and such ignorance therefore does not impair God's right to our obedience. So ignorance of natural law, even if it is now sometimes unavoidable, is never an excuse. Whether we call such ignorance invincible is a verbal question:[138] in view of the various senses of 'possible' (see above, and Appendix), we may say that knowledge of natural law is always possible in the sense required to justify punishment, and that ignorance of natural law is therefore never invincible in the sense in which invincible ignorance excuses; or, since knowledge may not now be effectively possible without grace which may not be given, we may say that ignorance of natural law is now sometimes in another sense invincible but not an excuse. If we follow the second usage, which is closer to common ideas, we must deny that invincible ignorance always excuses, since invincible ignorance of natural law does not. Either way ignorance of natural law, even when it is now unavoidable, does not excuse sin: when effectively avoidable it is itself a sin of negligence or self-deception, and otherwise it is a just punishment for Adam's sin.[139] Perhaps inconsistently,[140] Augustine and Arnauld concede that for sins of unavoidable

save some from the punishment justly due to all once Adam sinned, and reprobation is the decision to leave others to the punishment now due to all (see *Jansen*, pp. 151-6). On these matters see the first and second of Pascal's 'Écrits sur la grâce', especially pp. 948-54, 964-70; and cf. pp. 979-81.

[138] *Denunciations*, pp. 155-6, 238(19-21), 281-2 and *Difficulties*, pp. 375-7 (cf. Bayle, *DHC*, art. 'Rimini', rem. A, vol. 12, pp. 531-3). The ambiguity of the term enables Arnauld to discount the papal condemnation of the thesis that 'though there is an invincible ignorance of the law of nature' it does not excuse: ignorance of natural law does not excuse, but (in one sense of the term) it is not invincible. See above, n. 35.

[139] *Denunciation* 1, pp. 34-5, and *Ignorance*, pp. 657-8. Augustine: 'Ignorance is a sin in those not willing to learn, and the penalty for sin in those not able; there is therefore no legitimate excuse in one case or the other' (*Epistola* CXCIV.vi.27 (*PL*, vol. 33, col. 883), quoted *Denunciation* 1, p. 35, *Necessity*, p. 276, *Jansen*, p. 281, and *Ignorance*, p. 653).

[140] Or perhaps consistently: they may think that ignorance does not extenuate

ignorance the burning may be milder; but it will still be eternal.[141]

Ignorance and weakness of will can be remedied only by faith and strengthening grace. God has the power and the right (though no obligation) to give these gifts to anyone in any way; he could have given knowledge and strength of right choice to the Americans before the coming of the missionaries, as proponents of sufficient grace theories think he was obliged to do. That was possible in the sense that God has the power and the right; but it was not effectively possible, because in giving grace God has chosen to follow a certain order (what God does 'ordinarily', *ex lege ordinaria*), a set of self-imposed rules, some of which we can learn from scripture and from experience.[142] In accordance with these rules God does not give faith except to those who hear the gospel preached by human messengers; he does not give strength of right choice sufficient for salvation except to those who have received faith, and even to them he does not give grace to avoid sin altogether. Thus there is (ordinarily) no salvation for those who live when or where the gospel is not preached. There is no injustice in this, since faith and strengthening grace are free gifts not due in justice to anyone, and everyone could without injustice have been damned.[143]

but knowledge aggravates; see *Num.* 15:28-31. Jansen makes a similar point using a distinction between simple sin and 'prevarication' (a term not then restricted to violations of the duty of truthfulness); see *Augustinus*, 307C-308C; cf. Augustine, *Enchiridion*, xxii.81.

[141] *Denunciation* 2, pp. 128-9, *Ignorance*, p. 662, *Necessity*, pp. 270-1. In these places Arnauld quotes Augustine: the ignorance of one who does not know, though not unwilling to know, ignorant simply because he has not heard, 'does not excuse him so as not to burn in the everlasting fire, but perhaps so as to burn more mildly (*ut mitius ardeat*)' (*De gratia et libero arbitrio*, iii.5). Augustine and Arnauld quote *Lk.* 12: 47-8: the servant who did not know, and did what deserves a beating, shall be beaten lightly.

[142] *Denunciation* 2, pp. 125-8, 139(34)-140(10), 146(11-14). It is possible conditionally (it could have happened *if* God had not decided otherwise), but it is not absolutely or effectively possible—it cannot actually happen, given what God *has* decided (*Examen*, pp. 387(28)-388(33), 396(25)-397(10)). For a similar distinction in terms of God's absolute and 'ordinate' power see Oberman, *Harvest*, pp. 36-8, 473.

[143] *Examen*, pp. 393-5, *Necessity*, pp. 269-78. Arnauld quotes Augustine *De peccatorum meritis et remissione*, I.xxii.31 (those who live where they cannot hear the gospel preached), *De natura et gratia*, iv.4 (those who cannot hear because of infancy) etc., and *Rom.* 10:13-17. Those who do not hear will not be damned for not believing (see above, n. 113), but for the other sins which, not having faith and grace, they cannot avoid; *Necessity*, p. 271(10-13).

Augustine is Arnauld's main guide in all these matters, but Thomas Aquinas is also important. The references to St Thomas may be partly *ad hominem*, since the Jesuits were sworn to follow St Thomas,[144] but Arnauld's respect seems genuine. He wrote several detailed studies of St Thomas apparently to sort out his own thoughts and not for publication,[145] and his writings for publication include some extended analyses.[146] Some have read St Thomas as moving toward a liberal position on freedom of conscience but unfortunately not always drawing the conclusions which his principles imply.[147] But Arnauld's Augustinian reading may be historically correct. When St Thomas says that ignorance excuses unless knowledge is possible, he may well mean 'possible with grace' or 'possible but for original sin' (which is what Arnauld's account of possibility in the sense relevant to blame amounts to).[148] Whether anyone can be invincibly ignorant of natural law will then be not an empirical question[149] but a theological one, and St Thomas's negative answer may be exactly what he means. From that it will follow, as he says, that those who are mistaken about morality cannot avoid sin:[150] they must sin either by disobeying conscience, or by violating the moral law—for which obedience to erroneous conscience is no excuse.[151]

As a justification for punishing sins of ignorance and weakness Arnauld's theory is in my judgement unsuccessful.

[144] Cf. *Denunciation* 2, p. 124(5-8), and *Denunciation* 5, p. 347(10-11).

[145] *Disquisition, Love, Excuse.*

[146] E.g. *Dissertation*, pp. 47-67, *Difficulties*, pp. 330ff.

[147] See D'Arcy, e.g. pp. 113-21.

[148] St Thomas says that ignorance is culpable if one can and should know (*Summa*, 1-2, q.6 a.8). What if one does not realize that one can and should know? This question, with the assumption that ignorance cannot be culpable unless it is due to negligence or self-deception, leads to Terrill's theory; see above, p. 34 and cf. D'Arcy, p. 127. The assumption is not true, if 'can know' is understood to mean to 'can with grace': then ignorance of what one can and should know is culpable even if one never realized that one could and should find out.

[149] 'St Thomas was the last person to push *a priori* argument in the face of facts. He was handicapped by not having very much information about the moral values of peoples beyond the borders of Christendom' (D'Arcy, p. 138).

[150] Thomas Aquinas, *In 2 Sent.*, d.39 q.3 a.3 c and ad 5; *De veritate*, q.17 a.4 ad 3 and ad 8; cf. St Bonaventure, *In 2 Sent.*, d.39 a.1 q.3 c and ad a. This position was commonplace in the seventeenth century; see e.g. the Anglican moralists Ames, p. 13, Perkins, p. 42, Taylor, *Ductor*, vol. 9, pp. 132-7, and William Sanderson as quoted in the editor's introduction to Locke, *Two Tracts*, p. 45.

[151] *Summa*, 1-2, q.19 a.6; cf. *Denunciation* 2, p. 151(21).

Questions of justice at least as acute as those it was meant to answer arise again from several of its premisses, namely that Adam's sin is also the sin of each of his descendants,[152] that sin can rightly be punished by impairment of the knowledge and will ¡needed to act rightly,[153] and that sins resulting from this punishment can deserve more punishment. This is Christianity at its ugliest. What must we think of a father who punishes one child for another's fault[154] by leaving him ignorant of what he ought to do, and then punishes him again for not doing it, but accepts the sufferings of another innocent person (himself!) as a reason for forgiving some of his children, but not others no more guilty? God has good reasons incomprehensible to us, Arnauld says:[155] he might as well have said so at the beginning and left it at that.[156]

5. THE SIN OF NOT LOVING GOD

It is not mere coincidence that the two heresies, the theory of philosophic sin and the heresy about love of God,[157] were attacked by Arnauld and condemned by Rome together, since they are logically connected. According to Arnauld the commandment to love God as worthy of love above all things is the first commandment of natural law,[158] and as we saw in the last section he holds that even invincible ignorance of natural law is no excuse. Therefore, if we violate this commandment because we do not know God or do not think

[152] This proposition had been attacked in Augustine's time by Julian of Eclanum. For Augustine's answer see Thonnard, pp. 393ff. See also Baird, ch. 5.

[153] Contrast the view of Plato and other Greek writers that punishment is wrong unless it makes people better. This seems to be what led Origen to the conclusion that hell is not necessarily eternal. See the editors' notes to Origen, vol. 2, pp. 169, 223. See also Daniélou, pp. 276–88.

[154] And what must we think of a parent who does not do what can be done to prevent the fault in the first place? See Bayle, *DHC*, art. 'Origène', rem. E(I) and art. 'Pauliciens', rem. E, vol. 11, pp. 256, 485.

[155] *Necessity*, p. 274(7), *Ignorance*, p. 651(15–21); cf. *Augustinus*, 295A.

[156] See Bayle, *DHC*, art. 'Arminius', rem. E, vol. 2, pp. 387-9 and art. 'Pauliciens', rem. M, vol. 11, pp. 504–5.

[157] See above, n. 36. Arnauld had attacked the Jesuits on this subject before; see *Dissertation*.

[158] *Denunciation* 1, p. 33(34), *Denunciation* 2, p. 73(3–4), *Jansen*, pp. 309ff., *Infidels*, p. 383. Cf. *Mt.* 22:37, 1 *Cor.* 10:31, *Col.* 3:17. Arnauld says that this is a commandment of natural (not of divine positive) law (*Difficulties*, p. 339(8)); and that it is a commandment, not just a counsel (*Dissertation*, p. 29(18ff.)).

of him the sin is not thereby excused. It might be objected that ignorance of fact does excuse, and that God's existence is not integral to natural law but a fact external to it. Arnauld's answer is that it is not external to the law, because the first commandment of natural law refers to God. Anyone who does not know or think of God must violate this commandment because it requires that *each* action be done *consciously and explicitly* out of love of God. Forgetfulness of God is itself the sin. Thus anyone who satisfied the conditions for committing a merely philosophic sin would also in the same act commit the sin of not loving God, without excuse. Since this sin is against God, and not just against natural morality, no act can be a merely philosophic sin.

Why must each act be done out of a love of God which is conscious and explicit? According to Arnauld, following St Thomas, God is somehow the last end of every creature, including sticks and stones, but rational creatures seek God in the way appropriate to their nature, by conscious and voluntary action.[159] Some voluntary actions are not free, are therefore not subject to moral evaluation, and do not come under the commandments of the natural law.[160] What the first commandment requires of us is conscious and *free* voluntary action. There is a sense in which every free choice of every human being, even the wicked who hate God, is a seeking of God above all things, because it is a seeking of happiness which is in fact to be found only in God. But this is not enough to satisfy the commandment, because the desire for happiness is not free but necessary (even when the particular act it motivates is free), and because it is consistent with wickedness, even with explicit hatred of God.[161] Those who make themselves—their existence, pleasure, power etc.—or some other created good their last end do not act formally[162] for love of God, even though the happiness they seek can be found only in God. The good and the wicked are distinguished in part by what they identify as the object they seek.[163] To

[159] *Jansen*, p. 318(28–37); cf. Thomas Aquinas, *Summa*, 1–2, q.1 a.2.

[160] See below, Appendix, n. 4.

[161] *Love*, pp. 679–83, 686–9. On the necessary desire for happiness and the free acts it motivates, see below, Appendix.

[162] *Love*, pp. 681(6), 687(29–39), 688(12).

[163] 'Non faciunt bonos vel malos mores nisi boni vel mali amores' (Augustine, *Epistola* CLV.iv.13 (*PL*, vol. 33, col. 672); quoted *Jansen*, p. 307).

satisfy the first commandment, therefore, Arnauld holds that we must consciously and by free choice make God the end of every action.

Certain Jesuit writers, characteristically concerned to present the good life as something feasible, had suggested various less demanding interpretations of the commandment, what might be called 'constructive love' theories. They amount to this: that to obey this commandment it is enough to keep the other commandments.[164] Some Jesuits said, for example, that it is enough to have 'effective' as distinct from 'affective' love, doing what one who felt affection would do but not necessarily feeling the affection. Arnauld replies that this makes the commandment figurative, to act as if one loved God: he insists that love must be taken in its proper sense, as itself the motive of actions, an orientation of will of which feeling is a natural manifestation (though feeling may run pretty dry at times).[165] Others said that it is enough to love God 'habitually'. Arnauld replies that 'habitual' love would be consistent with total inactivity, a life spent asleep; the commandments require acts, not habits.[166] Others said that it is enough to love God 'implicitly' or 'interpretatively' or 'constructively', by doing acts which could fittingly be done out of love of God—that is, acts which violate no (other) commandment of natural law. But it is not 'implicit' love to do what could have been done for love but is not. Arnauld introduces another term, 'virtual' love. He concedes what gives these less exacting theories their plausibility, that it is not possible to be all the time conscious of God, since in carrying out some tasks—even those undertaken for love of God—our attention must become absorbed in the task; it is enough if we begin the act explicitly for love of God, which will then be its 'virtual' motive even when our attention is absorbed. A doctor, for example, is still acting for the patient's health if that was the purpose with which he began the treatment, though he cannot keep thinking of the purpose. So what this commandment requires, according to Arnauld, is that we

---

[164] *Dissertation*, p. 23(13), *Jansen*, p. 318(14–17), *Commandment*, p. 404(31). For a very demanding interpretation of the first commandment, requiring willingness to suffer eternal damnation if that should be God's will, see Burnaby, pp. 272–93.

[165] *Dissertation*, pp. 17, 20, 25–7, 37.

[166] Ibid., p. 51 (18ff.), *Jansen*, p. 319(30–3). Cf. Aristotle, *EN*, 1.8, 1099 a1–2.

begin each act out of conscious love of God, although as the act goes on the consciousness may cease.[167] (Perhaps this is too exacting. Doctors aim at the patients' health even without thinking of that purpose at the beginning of each treatment, or at first meeting each patient, or at the beginning of each day, though perhaps they have to think of it explicitly sometimes.)

Most pagans do not know God and therefore can never act explicitly for love of God.[168] They have gods, and they desire happiness, and it may be true that behind these is the true God; but to act out of love of a pagan god or for happiness is not formally to love God.[169] By natural reason some pagan philosophers did know something of the true God,[170] but knowledge is not enough: to act out of love of God a person must be made willing by grace (as we saw in the last section), and grace was not given to even the best of the pagan philosophers.[171] In giving grace God follows a certain order, and the first manifestation of grace is humility.[172] Arnauld is sure that the philosophers did not receive grace to love God above all things because they lacked humility and believed they were self-sufficient; their knowledge led to pride and made them worse.[173] Seneca examined his conscience every night and presumptuously forgave himself;[174] Cicero said that while wealth, honours, health and other goods of fortune are gifts of God, virtue and goodness are our own achievement.[175] While affecting to despise human opinion the pagan philosophers acted to their own applause.[176] Their apparent virtues were effects of

---

[167] *Dissertation*, pp. 65–7, *Jansen*, p. 319.

[168] *Denunciation* 2, p. 146(1–3), *Jansen*, pp. 318(5–6), 321(23–4), *Difficulties*, p. 332(20, 38).

[169] See texts referred to above, n. 162.

[170] Only a few, notably the Platonists: *Denunciation* 2, p. 109; cf. Augustine, *De civitate dei*, VIII.4–12.

[171] When they knew God they did not glorify him, *Rom.* 1:21. See *Jansen*, p. 322(18–20), and *Difficulties*, p. 341(31–40).

[172] *Examen*, p. 391(21), *Necessity*, p. 114.

[173] *Necessity*, pp. 89–134; *Jansen*, p. 323–9. Arnauld argues (*Examen*, p. 391(22, 39–40)) that there is no reason to think that philosophy makes anyone humble, which he apparently takes to mean that philosophers cannot be humble. Philosophers of course know better.

[174] *Necessity*, p. 108. The reference is probably to Seneca, *De ira*, III.xxxvi.3–4.

[175] *Jansen*, p. 327. The reference is to Cicero, *De natura deorum*, III.xxxvi.86–7.

[176] *Necessity*, p. 125. Arnauld quotes Augustine: 'They scorn the judgements of others, as if despising glory, ... and please themselves: but their virtue, if they have

pride and were therefore really vices.[177] To the question 'Can a philosopher who has never heard of Jesus Christ, do with the help of grace a genuinely good act?' the answer is that he could if grace were given, but since to those who have never heard of Christ it ordinarily is not, he cannot.[178]

It follows that every act of a mere philosopher or other pagan is a sin[179]—and a theological sin, since no sin, especially one against the commandment to love God, can be merely philosophic. Arnauld makes a distinction between acts good *secundum officium*, which satisfy all the other commandments of natural law, and those good also *secundum finem*, which also satisfy this first commandment. This corresponds to the familiar distinction between doing the right thing and doing it for the right reason.[180] The first commandment prescribes the right reason, namely love of God above all things. To be simply good an act must be good not only *secundum officium* but also *secundum finem*, whereas a defect in either respect is enough to make the act bad and a sin: *bonum ex integra causa, malum ex quocumque defectu*.[181] If an act comes under several commandments (and every individual act comes under the first, at least[182]) it must satisfy them all. Every act, even the most

---

any, is in another way subjected to the praise of man, for he who pleases himself is a man' (*De civitate dei*, V.20). But satisfying their own judgement is not the same as seeking their own praise.

[177] *Jansen*, p. 326, repeated in *Difficulties*, p. 342; cf. Augustine, *De civitate dei*, V.13.

[178] See *Examen*, i.e. 'Examination of this proposition: A philosopher who has not yet heard anyone speak of Jesus Christ, but knows God, can, with the help of a grace given through the mercy of Jesus Christ, do an action truly good and virtuous, before having any knowledge of Jesus Christ.'

[179] *Jansen*, pp. 303(17–8), 321(29–30), *Infidels*, p. 381(6–7), *Apology*, pp. 64–5; etc. Cf. *Augustinus*, 541ff. Luther also held that the acts of infidels are sins, and Rome condemned the proposition (Denzinger, p. 431, no. 1925). The Jansenist proposition was also condemned (ibid., p. 481, no. 2308). For Arnauld's comment on the condemnation see *Difficulties*, pp. 324, 327–46.

[180] *Infidels*, p. 381(10–11), *Denunciation* 2, p. 144(39–40). On the distinction between *secundum officium* and *secundum finem* see Augustine, *Contra Julianum*, IV.iii.21 (*PL*, vol. 44, col. 749).

[181] *Infidels*, p. 381, *Difficulties*, pp. 331, 334(40). This maxim was the reason given by those who held that a person whose conscience is in error about moral principles cannot avoid sin. See above, n. 150. St Bonaventure puts it this way: 'It is easier to destroy than to build. Goodness requires the concourse of many circumstances, evil the lack of any one' (*In 2 Sent.*, d.40 a.1 q.1 ad 4).

[182] Considered *in their species* (i.e. as a type) some acts are morally indifferent, neither required nor forbidden; but no *individual* act is morally indifferent, because

wicked, is in some way good; what makes an act bad is that
it does not have all the goodness that it ought to have,[183] and
lack of some morally necessary goodness is the kind of badness
we call sin.[184] Even the best and most apparently virtuous of
the acts of the pagan philosophers were therefore sins because
they lacked the morally necessary motive, love of God. Failure
to refer an otherwise good act to God is a venial sin[185] which
the philosophers committed in even their best acts. They were
not damned for these venial sins but for other grave sins they
were not given grace to avoid.[186]

According to Arnauld, anyone who fails to act out of love
of God above all things must make some creature (usually
himself) his end: everyone must have a last end, and if not
God then a creature; so sin against the first commandment
substitutes for our true end something unfit to be a last end.[187]
Conversely, anyone who sins seriously against any of the other
commandments sins also against the first, by turning away
from God toward some creature.[188] These points suggest
another conception of sin, as being not a violation of law so
much as a turning from one goal to another. There are hints
that the second conception underlies the first, that the laws
are directions for arriving at the goal, so that the first
commandment gives point to the others.[189]

It seems to me that Arnauld is too hard on philosophers
and pagans. It is not true that since everyone must have some
last end those who do not know the true God must make

it will be good or bad at least by being ordered or not ordered to the last end. See
Difficulties, pp. 331(25-8), 336(37)-339(5) (misprint for 337(5)); cf. Thomas Aquinas,
Summa, 1-2, q.18 a.9. A relation to the last end is *intrinsic* to an individual act
(*Difficulties*, p. 336).

[183] *Difficulties*, pp. 330(38), 334.

[184] '*Malum in genere moris* is what we call sin' (*Infidels*, p. 381; cf. *Difficulties*,
p. 331(38)). This is the most general definition. For others see next paragraph, and
above, sect. 4, and n. 122.

[185] *Dissertation*, p. 41(22-7), *Jansen*, p. 304(39), *Infidels*, p. 383(14). It is not clear
how the sin against the first and greatest commandment can be venial. However,
Arnauld distances himself from the view of St Thomas that a violation of any of the
commandments is mortal (*Dissertation*, p. 49(27-31)).

[186] See above, n. 143.

[187] *Dissertation*, p. 42(28-31), *Jansen*, pp. 306-8, 313-15, *Difficulties*, pp. 339(30)-
341(3), 343(1-7).

[188] See above, n. 59.

[189] *Denunciation* 2, p. 73(4-5). See also Thomas Aquinas, *Summa contra gentiles*,
III.116.

some creature their end. We need not definitely make any one thing our last end; we can try to keep our lives open to a range of possibilities. Arnauld acknowledges that it is not sinful to make a created good the proximate end of an action: the sin is to rest there as if in the last end.[190] But it is possible to take a step without meaning to rest there, not being sure where it will lead but believing that it is worth taking whatever the goal turns out to be; many things are worth doing on any of the likely views of the meaning of life. Why not say that acts chosen with a view to a range of possible ends are good *secundum finem*? Arnauld would probably answer that not to know what the last end is, or whether there is one, is the ignorance which is a punishment for sin and no excuse; but this is the theory criticised above at the end of section 4. As for the pride and self-sufficiency of the philosophers, the passages quoted from Cicero and Seneca do not show that every philosopher must lack humility, or even that they did. Some philosophers, such as Kant, have acknowledged that for living well supernatural help may be needed,[191] and may have prayed for it, at least hypothetically. For Arnauld to claim to know the laws of order God sets himself well enough to infer that the philosophers cannot have received any grace because they seem to him to lack humility[192] is itself presumptuous.

Arnauld's ethical theory and the theories he attacks are mirror images. The theories he attacks make contempt essential to committing sin, and will not accept that contempt can be 'constructive'—the sinner must be explicitly conscious of the relation of the act to God. His own theory makes love of God essential to avoiding sin, and will not accept that love can be 'constructive'—we must explicitly refer the act to God, at least at its beginning. Kant's ethical theory, a century later, in some ways like the Jesuits',[193] is on this point like Arnauld's

[190] *Jansen*, p. 308(11–23), *Difficulties*, p. 343(8–23, 35–7).

[191] Reason 'says that whoever, with a disposition genuinely devoted to duty, does as much as lies in his power'—see above, n. 133—'to satisfy his obligation (at least in a continual approximation to complete harmony with the law), may hope that what is not in his power will be supplied by the supreme Wisdom *in some way or other* (which can make permanent the disposition to this unceasing approximation)' (Kant, *Religion*, p. 159). This is a 'hope' which reason merely permits.

[192] See above, n. 173.

[193] Like the writers Arnauld attacked, Kant does not envisage infinite punishments, he admits the possibility of something like sufficient grace, and he says that God cannot command 'pathological' but only 'practical' love (cf. 'affective' and 'effective'

with respect for the moral law in place of love of God.[194] A middle position worth considering is this: perhaps, as Arnauld held, an act cannot be simply good if it is wrong, even if the agent does not know that it is; and perhaps, as the 'constructive love' theorists held, a right act may be (up to a point) morally good simply because it has been chosen as the kind of act it is, even without reference to a determinate further, or last, end. That is, an act may be good or bad because of the sort of act is it, apart from any thought the doer may have about the rightness or wrongness of the act or its place in any larger scheme of life. And perhaps people are good or bad because of the kinds of actions they are disposed to choose, apart from thought about the rightness or wrongness of their acts and about the meaning of life; though reflecting occasionally on these matters is among the things people ought to do.

According to Arnauld, then, sincerity is not enough. It is necessary also to be right about moral principles and to know and love the true God. It is not enough to follow conscience: if our conscience is mistaken, not only is the act wrong objectively, it may also deserve blame and punishment. Ignorance of God and his law is no excuse because it is always due to sin, our own or Adam's. Merely philosophic sin is therefore impossible: one who sins in ignorance of God and his law still offends God and, if the violation is serious, deserves eternal punishment. This moral theory is not original: Arnauld got it almost wholly from Jansen, who got it mostly from Augustine. Arnauld's polemic against philosophic sin is philosophically interesting because of the questions it raises about the relevance of the agent's intention and other thoughts to the moral value of the act, and it is historically interesting as showing what Bayle and other advocates of toleration were up against.[195] Arnauld's moral theory now seems pretty

love, above). On the first point see *Critique of Pure Reason*, pp. 638-40 (in so far as we are unworthy we 'limit our share' of happiness). On the second, see above, n. 191. On the third, see *Groundwork*, p. 67.

[194] See Kant, *Groundwork*, pp. 65-9 (where he seems to argue that an act has no moral worth unless it can have had no other motive than devotion to duty; but the most his examples prove is that only then can we *know* that the act was done for duty's sake). See also Kant, *Justice*, pp. 18-21.

[195] Bayle seems to have followed the philosophic sin controversy closely. He says that 'many people think' (1) that the doctrine of philosophic sin is a correct inference from the theory that liberty of indifference is a precondition of merit and demerit, and (2) that although it is supported by the light of reason it is inconsistent with

remote. Today most of us are merely philosophic sinners. Like Seneca we forgive ourselves each day our daily trespasses and muddle on, without fear of an eternal burning, even a mild one.

what scripture teaches about sin (*CPD*, pp. 394–5). Compare *CPD*, pp. 324, 326–7, *RQP*, p. 782. See also *DHC*, art. 'Rimini', rem. A, vol. 12, pp. 531–3, art. 'Lugo', rem. G, vol. 9, p. 537 (natural ideas clearly imply that an action is not morally good or bad unless one knows whether it is good or bad).

ESSAY II

Bayle on the Rights of Conscience

INTRODUCTION

For most of the last forty years of the sixteenth century there was civil war in France between Catholics and Calvinists, the massacre of St Bartholomew being probably the best-known incident. Eventually the Protestant Henry of Navarre was accepted as king, after becoming a Catholic. The Edict of Nantes (1598) established a religious truce. For their security the Protestants were allowed for a while to garrison certain towns, and in certain places they had permission to maintain churches and schools and to practise their religion publicly. As time went on they abandoned the opinion some Protestants had adopted during the religious wars that Christians may rightly rebel against a persecuting ruler, and took up again Calvin's (and Luther's) doctrine of non-resistance, that is, that subjects must obey the ruler except when his commands contradict God's, and even then must not rebel or resist by force.[1] Their security depended on the king's protection against Catholic zealots, and they became his most loyal subjects. During the disorders of Louis XIV's minority their loyalty was appreciated, but later the king needed them less, and once he came into conflict with the pope over the *régale* (see above, p. 14) he needed to emphasize his own Catholic orthodoxy; in any case he did sincerely hate the Protestants. From about 1660 the government campaigned more actively against Protestantism, for example by closing churches and schools permitted under the Edict of Nantes. By the end of the 1670s, when the government

---

[1] Calvin, *Institutes*, IV.xx.22ff. See also Skinner, vol. 2, pp. 16–19, 303ff. When they were persecuted later in the century some of them went back again to theories justifying rebellion, resembling the theory of Locke's second treatise. See Puaux, Dodge.

was also renewing its attack on the Jansenists, the pressure on the Protestants had become intense. In 1680 the practice began of quartering dragoons in Protestant households, which produced a flood of 'conversions'. Ministers were exiled, lay people who tried to leave the country without permission could be sentenced for life to the galleys. In 1685 the Edict of Nantes was revoked. It had been supposed to be perpetual, but the king explained that it had become unnecessary since there were no longer any Protestants in France.[2]

Pierre Bayle was born in 1647, son of a Calvinist minister. His formal schooling, delayed by his family's poverty, was at first in a Protestant school and later in the Jesuit college at Toulouse. At Toulouse he became a Catholic, and then, characteristically following the argument where it led, a Protestant again. This made him a relapsed heretic, liable to banishment.[3] He left the country, in 1670, and studied at the Calvinist college in Geneva. Four years later he returned to another part of France under an altered form of his name, and in 1675 became professor of philosophy at the Protestant college at Sedan. In 1681 the government closed the college, and (two years after Arnauld went into exile) Bayle left France for Rotterdam, where he became professor of philosophy at a college for French-speaking Protestants. He lived in Rotterdam until his death in 1706. He never became a minister, but to the end of his life belonged as a lay member to the Reformed Church. He was always poor, never married, never had onerous teaching duties, and was almost entirely devoted to reading and writing.[4]

In 1682 he published a *Letter* (in later editions *Miscellaneous Reflections*) *on the Comet*, purportedly written by a Catholic to a doctor of the Sorbonne on the question whether the comet which had appeared in 1680 was a portent of disaster. The real design of the book was perhaps to suggest to the unwary Catholic reader analogies between Catholicism and pagan superstition. It contains a great deal which is philosophically interesting, including a long argument against the claim that atheism threatens the foundations of society; Bayle argues that

[2] On the history of Calvinism in France see Chadwick, pp. 153–70, Grant, Ligou, Whiteman.

[3] Ligou, p. 219.

[4] My information on Bayle's life comes from Labrousse.

concern for honour may have the same social effects as zeal for religion. A covert purpose of this argument may have been to suggest that Catholic France might indeed be a society of practical atheists, a proposition with which the Jansenists at least would have agreed.[5] In the same year he published the *General Critique of M. Maimbourg's History of Calvinism*, in which he defended the Calvinists against a hostile account by a Catholic priest. In 1685 he published *New Letters by the Author of the General Critique*. From 1694 to 1697 he edited *News of the Republic of Letters*, a learned journal, in which he published Arnauld's controversy with Malebranche.

The French government discovered that Bayle had written the *General Critique* and, since they could not reach him, arrested his brother, a Protestant minister, who died after six months in prison. To Bayle at this time religious peace and freedom must have seemed almost a lost cause. This was the year of the revocation of the Edict of Nantes and the accession of the Catholic James II as king of England. Among the French refugees one party, led by Pierre Jurieu, until then Bayle's friend, began to advocate violent revolution against Louis XIV and the counter-persecution of Catholics. Soon William of Orange, with Jurieu's enthusiastic approval, put himself at the head of a successful rebellion against James II. These developments led Bayle into a complicated series of controversies: against Catholic persecution of Calvinists in France, in favour of toleration as a matter of principle, in favour of the doctrine of non-resistance, and in defence of himself against increasingly bitter attacks from Jurieu. *What Wholly Catholic France is Like under the Reign of Louis the Great* (1686) criticised French Catholic persecution of Protestants; the *Philosophical Commentary on the Words of Jesus Christ*, '*Compel them to come in*' (Parts 1 and 2 in 1686, Part 3 in 1687, *Supplement* 1688) argued for toleration as a matter of principle; the *Reply of a New Convert to the Letters of a Refugee* (1689) and the *Important Advice to the Refugees* (1690) (if that is a genuine work of Bayle's) were apparently intended to provoke those among the refugees who held Calvin's doctrine

---

[5] On the intentions of the *Miscellaneous Reflections* see Rex, *Bayle*, pp. 35ff. Mandeville may have been one of Bayle's students; see James, 'Mandeville and Bayle'. On Jansenist views on the possibility of a society of atheists see Sedgwick, pp. 143–5. The origin of this line of thought is perhaps Augustine's account of the Roman appetite for glory as the basis for the success of their State; see *De civitate dei*, V.13.

of non-resistance, or believed in toleration, to disown Jurieu's calls to rebellion and counter-persecution; and the *Chimerical Cabal* (1691) and various other pamphlets and books replied to Jurieu's personal attacks. All these writings were published under pseudonyms. The *Philosophical Commentary*, for example, purports to be a translation from an English work by 'John Fox', and the *Reply* and *Advice* purport to be by Catholics— they are in fact scornful attacks on Protestants, arguing that they also persecute when they can, that their doctrine of non-resistance was never sincerely held, and that their religious principles lead to republicanism.

In 1693 Bayle was dismissed from his academic post. A Rotterdam publisher came to his rescue with a pension to enable him to write the *Historical and Critical Dictionary*, his most famous work and the only book to which he attached his name. It is a biographical dictionary in which the facts of the subject's life are briefly outlined in the text of the article, which is glossed with 'remarks', relevant and irrelevant, in numerous footnotes, sometimes of enormous length, with marginal notes to the footnotes. Much of the most interesting material is in the Remarks. In the *Dictionary* Bayle continued most of the lines of thought seen in his earlier writings, but with increased emphasis on the weakness of reason, and in particular on the impossibility of any rational solution to the problem of evil. The existence of evil is a problem for any theism in which God is held to be both good and all-powerful.[6] It is a problem for Christians particularly in connection with the doctrines of original sin, predestination and grace. Why did God permit Adam to sin? Why does he leave the mass of mankind, or for that matter anyone, to be damned eternally? Indeed, why does he permit any sin at all? And why does he permit pain and so many other physical evils? Bayle refutes the various customary answers to these questions, traversing the controversies about freewill and grace among Jesuits, Jansenists, Calvinists, Arminians and others, showing that none of them can do more in the end than say that God permits sin and other evil for reasons we cannot understand. A Christian aware of the weakness of reason and the impossibility of answering these questions must simply refuse to attempt an answer.[7]

[6] See *HCD*, art. 'Manicheans', pp. 144ff.
[7] Ibid., art. 'Paulicians', pp. 166ff.

Bayle's emphasis on the weakness of reason generally and on the impossibility of answering inescapable philosophical questions about fundamental Christian doctrines have led many readers of the *Dictionary* to regard him as a sceptic and an infidel. But Bayle always rejects scepticism, and always presents himself as a Calvinist Christian. Doubt about many things, even doubt about everything, does not constitute scepticism in the classical sense of the term. In that sense a sceptic is one who practises suspense of judgement.[8] The ancient sceptics were of two schools. Academic sceptics raised difficulties against every assertion, so as to force suspense of judgement upon the Stoics, who said that a wise man should affirm nothing but what is certain. Pyrrhonian sceptics, according to Sextus Empiricus, began by seeking knowledge, but came to accept suspense of judgement as an equally satisfactory—the only available—way of achieving the real goal of the search for truth, namely peace of mind. Pyrrhonian sceptics set out to counter every argument with another equally plausible, so that no assertion would seem certain, or even more probable than its contradictory.[9] For sceptics of both kinds the purpose of inquiry was to re-establish or strengthen the disposition to suspend judgement by renewed experience of the futility of trying to reach certain (or, for the Pyrrhonians, even probable) conclusions. If the arguments heaped up on either side were criticised, that was not for the purpose of eliminating those which were unsound, but to make the project of arriving at a conclusion seem the more hopeless. Modern philosophy teachers often set out (at least, students think they do) to inculcate this ancient lesson: that since nothing is certain, and no assertion more likely to be true than its contradictory, philosophical thinking (except to learn this lesson, or perhaps as entertainment) is pointless.

Bayle was not a sceptic of this description. My impression is that he had a sharp eye for bad argument, a good memory for fact or alleged fact, a settled habit of testing every theory or

---

[8] On scepticism see Burnyeat, Penelhum, Popkin.

[9] See Sextus Empiricus, *Outlines*, I.xii.25 ff. '[N]o one of the conflicting judgments takes precedence of any other as being more probable' (ibid., I.iv.10, trans. Bury). Cf. I.xxxiii.222, 226–7. It does not seem to me that no assertion is more probable than its contradictory.

assertion on any subject he cared about by seeing what could be said on the other side, a great inventiveness in devising objections, and a compulsive urge to upset the complacency of people who think they know and do not: a latter-day Socrates, in fact.[10] When all the theories of philosophy and speculative theology, and a good part of what passed for history,[11] disintegrated under test Bayle concluded (for the time being at least) that on the matters in question certainty is not attainable. But this is not scepticism. He never says that absolutely everything is uncertain[12] and that contradictories are equally probable; he says that in religion and in other matters we must make affirmations (and not merely for practical purposes).[13] He did not substitute suspense of judgement or peace of mind for the original goal of knowledge. He did not adopt an attitude of 'carelessness', as Hume later did: he always cared a great deal to avoid errors of fact and fallacies.[14] He was—as I am myself, and as I think many students of these subjects are—a so far mostly disappointed and no longer very hopeful truth-seeker, rather than a contented practitioner of suspense of judgement. His unsparing criticism of theories and historical assertions was perhaps not motivated by much hope of arriving at sure and positive truth, but his purpose seems to have been at least to eliminate error masquerading as truth, not to show that thought is futile.

As for infidelity, Bayle's criticism of Christians and their philosophical and theological theories is not evidence of loss of

[10] 'Leibniz reports that if one asserted something, Bayle would proceed to analyze the assertion, and question it, until one was ready to give up and assert its opposite, and Bayle would then proceed to analyze *this* assertion and question it, and so on. This critical analysis, Leibniz reported, never ended as long as the opponent remained present' (Popkin, *Pyrrhonism*, pp. 27–8). He must have been hard to live with.

[11] 'I confess I hardly ever read history to find out what happened, but only to know what each nation and party says about what happened' (*CG*, 10 b23ff).

[12] Notice the 'hardly ever' in the passage quoted in the last note; a few pages later (pp. 11–12) he tries to define the possibilities of arriving at certainty in history. When he calls himself an 'historical Pyrrhonist' I think this is provocative exaggeration.

[13] See below, sect. 7.

[14] See Popkin, *Pyrrhonism*, pp. 149ff. I cannot agree with Popkin that Bayle did not really care about the problems or want to solve them (p. 153). I do not agree, either, that Bayle *aimed* at undoing 'the very effort to find rationality in the universe' (p. 26): my impression is that Bayle's general aim (if he had one) was to eliminate assertions and theories which could not withstand criticism. If very little could, that was not the critic's fault. General destruction may have been the result, but it was not the aim, and I do not think Bayle rejoiced in it.

faith. Any Christian who also cares about truth and right-
eousness will want to dissociate Christianity from fallacy, falsehood and wicked behaviour. Believers sometimes criticise their
own creed gently, not mentioning its difficulties until they can
also present the solutions, being conscious of the politics of
public discussion. The politic apologist for Christianity may
regard Bayle as irresponsible, or suspect that he is an enemy
in disguise. He never seems to care whether his criticisms of
theories meant to harmonise reason and faith may destroy his
readers' faith. But then a Calvinist may think that no real harm
can be done by the destruction of theories, since faith and
salvation are decided by God's eternal decrees and everything
is under God's providence. He criticised the behaviour of all
sorts of Christians, Protestants and Calvinists included, pretty
freely,[15] but it was never a Calvinist principle that those who
call themselves Christians or Calvinists cannot be evil-doers.
There seems to be nothing, then, in the general character of
Bayle's late writings inconsistent with the hypothesis that he
remained until his death in 1706 the Calvinist he had been all
his life, but for the short time he was a Catholic as a student of
the Jesuits at Toulouse.

* * *

Bayle's arguments on the rights of conscience grew out of a
small point in letters 20 and 21 of his *General Critique*, namely
that the true religion (whichever that is) has no more right to
persecute than the false. When this was challenged as 'an im-
pious paradox' Bayle argued for it at length in letter 9 of the
New Letters, maintaining that those who believe an error are
morally obliged to do whatever they would be obliged to do if
their belief were true, and therefore, since people have a right
to do their duty, can do it without blame. The same point is
argued again in his *Philosophical Commentary*, part II, chs. 8–10,
and again in the *Supplement*. If God commanded the orthodox
to impose orthodoxy by force, then all who think themselves
orthodox—that is, all who hold their beliefs seriously—would

---

[15] See e.g. *S*, chs. 29–31, and cf. the *Réponse du nouveau converti*, *OD*, vol. 2, pp. 562ff.
Bayle says that there is among Christians a 'perpetuity of faith in persecution' (an
allusion to the title of Arnauld's book on the Eucharist), which suggests that God has
abandoned the Christian people as he abandoned the Jews. This is strong language,
but not incompatible with Calvinism.

be obliged and morally entitled to carry out the command, and heretics would do a good act in persecuting the true Church; since God cannot have intended this he cannot have given such a command.

In this essay I will examine in section 1 the arguments on the rights of conscience given in *New Letters*, and in the other sections those given in the *Philosophical Commentary*. I do not think that in these matters Bayle changed his mind in any important way, but ideas which he only sketched out at first he later developed elaborately.[16]

1. THE RIGHTS OF TRUTH

A critic of the *General Critique* found it strange that anyone would dare to say that the truth and a lie have the same privileges: has not God given the right of entering our hearts and minds to truth alone?[17] In the *Critique* Bayle had written of the rights of Churches, but in the *New Letters*, following this critic, he writes of the rights of truth and error, as if these were persons. Later the figure can be eliminated, but for the time being let truth and error be personified. Bayle maintains that if the truth appears to us in the guise of error, and an error in the guise of truth, then the truth has no jurisdiction over us and the error succeeds to all its rights.

1.1. *Rights and duties*

Bayle's notions of right and duty can be gathered from the way he relates these terms to one another and to certain others, namely 'ought', 'responsible', 'culpable', 'blameworthy' and 'punishable'.[18] If I have a duty to do something I have no right not to do it. A right may be absolute or relative. My right is absolute if I have it in relation to every human being (Bayle never mentions rights against God and no doubt thought there are none). If I have a right in relation to you to do something

---

[16] For other treatments of Bayle's views of the rights of conscience see Rex, *Bayle*; Labrousse, *Pierre Bayle*, vol. 2, chs. 18, 19; and Jossua.

[17] The critic is quoted at 218 b43-53 (in section 1 all references in this form will be to *NL* unless otherwise indicated).

[18] See the use of these terms in 218 a32-3, 51-3, 219 b23-8, 61, 66, 220 a63-b3, b60-1, 222 b66-7, *CP* 434 a33-5.

then I am not responsible to you for that act, and you cannot
rightly blame or punish[19] me for it; conversely, if you cannot
blame or punish me for it then to do it is my right in relation
to you. Thus liability to and immunity from blame and punishment are the core of Bayle's conception of duty and right.
Of the two duty seems to be fundamental; rights arise out of
duties,[20] and consist in duties on the part of others. If I have a
duty to do something then I have a right to do it,[21] consisting
in other human beings' having a duty not to try to persuade
me voluntarily not to do it, and not to blame or punish me if I
do it. This is a crucial premiss of Bayle's case for the rights of
heretics: people have a moral right to do their duty. If, as Bayle
believes, those who believe they have a duty (even if the belief
is mistaken) really have it,[22] then it follows that they have the
corresponding rights against other people, even against those
who know that a mistake is being made. Suppose a man pre-
tends to be a woman's husband and she believes him. The true
husband may know that his rights are being usurped, and in
relation to him the impostor has no right; but in relation even
to the true husband the wife has a right to do what—because
of her mistake—is her duty. The husband has no right to dis-
suade her from doing this duty except by revealing the mistake,
and no right to blame her then or afterwards.[23]

    According to Bayle the exercise of a right may be unjust.
Sometimes a right has been acquired wrongly (for example, by
the impostor) and cannot rightly be exercised; it is not 'absolutely speaking' and in God's sight a right, but is nevertheless
'effectively' and 'relatively' a moral right because there is someone (the woman) who genuinely has some corresponding

---

[19] Or rather—since Bayle holds that earthly rulers may rightly risk injustices to
private individuals for some social benefit (220 b31-47)—those who have a moral right
do not *deserve* to be punished for exercising it, though sometimes they may rightly be
subjected to undeserved punishment. Moral and legal rights may not correspond.

[20] If there are rights which do not arise from duties Bayle never mentions them. He
seems to think that we have such rights against one another as are necessary to perform
our duties.

[21] 228 a38-40, 227 b59-60, *CP* 433 b26-32. The right is a moral liberty, not implying
any duty on the part of others to help, or even to refrain from intentional counter-action
(cf. Hart, 'Bentham', p. 176).

[22] The duty to obey conscience is basic, and other duties are secondary. The real
duty to obey conscience makes it really a duty to do what one mistakenly believes to
be a (secondary) duty. See below, p.78.

[23] See 224 b7-11, and cf. *CP* 433 a64-9.

duty.[24] Sometimes a right not wrongly acquired is unjustly exercised. For example, a king has a genuine right to levy taxes, but he may exercise it unjustly by demanding too much. Even as wrongly exercised it is, in relation to his subjects, effectively a right, because (on Bayle's political theory[25]) they have no right to call him to account; he is answerable only to God. 'Right' has two senses, the power of doing something without being (rightly) punishable for it, and the justice with which it is done: the king has a right in the first sense in relation to his subjects, though his act is not right in the second sense.[26] Since God will rightly punish those who exercise wrongly acquired rights, or exercise their own rights unjustly, the distinction is irrelevant to God; but in relation to human beings who have no jurisdiction over him, and therefore no right to punish, the king effectively has a right in the first sense to do something which is unjust.

As we will see shortly, Bayle holds that those who believe they have a duty do have it. If I mistakenly believe I have a duty to you then I do have that duty. Do you therefore have the corresponding right? Yes and no. Absolutely speaking and in God's sight you do not. But there must be a sense in which there is a right, because 'it would be self-contradictory to be obliged to do something for someone who has no right to exact it'.[27] It is a right you should not exercise. A right that cannot rightly be exercised may seem strange, and it might seem better to say that you have no right and I have no duty. But Bayle wants to say that the duty is genuine because that implies the genuineness of the right against others to which it gives rise, consisting in a duty on their part not to blame or punish me for doing it. So if my duty is genuine, but it is self-contra-dictory to have a duty to someone who has no right, Bayle

[24] 225 a39-40 (not absolutely), 218 a51-2 (effectively), 220 a4-9, 54-7 (relatively), 225 a53-63 (wrongly acquired, unjustly exercised).

[25] Bayle held the doctrine of non-resistance (see above, Introduction). See the pamphlet attributed to Bayle, *Avis aux réfugiez*, in *OD*, vol. 2, pp. 592ff. See Dodge, pp. 97-9; and Labrousse, *Pierre Bayle*, vol. 2, pp. 490-6.

[26] 218 a3-b8, 225 a53-63; cf. *CP* 434 a49-51. For the passage in Grotius to which Bayle refers, see Grotius, *De iure belli ac pacis*, vol. 2, p. 643.

[27] 225 a38-50. The doorkeeper's duty determines the rights of those wishing to enter: with respect to the doorkeeper those who lose their tickets lose their right and those who find them acquire the right (220 a4-9, cf. 52-7), because the doorkeeper *ought* to exclude the former and admit the latter (219 b23-8).

must say that you have a genuine right that you can never
rightly exercise. To avoid paradox we can say this: if I mistakenly believe I have a duty to you then I do wrong if I
voluntarily omit to do it,[28] and not if I do it, and others do
wrong if they blame or punish me for doing it, but (unless you
share the mistake) you do wrong if you call on me to do it.

1.2. *Argument from the need for notification*

Bayle claims that it is a law of God that we must accord the
rights of truth to a proposition if and only if we believe it to be
true. That this is a law he argues as follows.[29] There are an
infinity of eternal truths,[30] including moral truths (ideas of
duty), of which we know nothing; God has revealed only
some.[31] But moral truths which God has not in some way
revealed have no authority over us. [32] This shows that truth as
such, and apart from its being known to us, has no rights over
us. Truth has rights over mankind only when it is revealed to
mankind. What does this mean? Mankind in general[33] does
not exist, only individual human beings exist; and truth in
general does not exist, only particular truths exist in individual
minds.[34] It means, therefore, that a particular truth has rights

[28] Writing of the thesis of *NL* as if he were not its author, Bayle says, 'To say that
the fraud acquires all the rights of a faithful messenger relatively to the servant to
whom he presents the master's orders is an expression rather awkward ... if the author
means merely that the servant was obliged to receive the impostor, and could not do
him the least harm without perfidy towards his master, then I altogether agree' (*CP*
433 b60–434 a5). So, simply stated, the meaning is that the person imposed on does
wrong not to perform the seeming duty.

[29] 221 a29-b29.

[30] For a survey of Bayle's views on the eternal truths see Leibniz, *Theodicy*, pp. 239ff.
Bayle opposes what seems to be Descartes's opinion that God could have created an
altogether different set of moral laws.

[31] Similarly, Malebranche envisages an infinity of moral truths of which only some
are known to us; see his *Traité de morale*, pp. 19–20. (On Bayle's interest in this book
see Labrousse, *Pierre Bayle*, vol. 2, p. 261.)

[32] See *CP* 436 a61-b25, 442 b36–40; cf. 219 b1–10. This is Bayle's version of the
traditional thesis that legislation, including the moral law, does not bind unless it is
promulgated. Compare Thomas Aquinas, *Summa*, 1–2, q.90 a.4. Discovery by use of
the 'natural light' counts as revelation; see *CP* 370 a43. Compare Thomas Aquinas,
Summa, 1–2, q.90 a.4 ad 1; and Hobbes, p. 396.

[33] ' ... this man *in commune* over which we wearied ourselves when they explained
those *universals*' (221 a71-b1). Cf. Gilson, *Jean Duns Scot*, pp. 84ff.

[34] 222 a9–20.

which can be executed or exercised only over a particular person to whom that truth has been revealed.

This argument shows that to be known (or believed) is a necessary condition. But perhaps the rights of a truth depend upon two or more conditions, including (a) that it be true, and (b) that it be believed to be true. Many of his contemporaries would have regarded (a) as necessary. To prove that error in the guise of truth has the rights of truth Bayle must show that condition (b) is not only necessary but also sufficient. Consider an example.[35] A governor must obey a letter from the king, the source of its authority over him being the king's will which it expresses. But considered in itself and apart from its effect upon the governor's mind the letter has no authority. The king's will is the ultimate source, but the persuasion in the governor's mind that the letter expresses the king's will is the 'proximate foundation and immediate essence' of its authority. And if a forgery produces the same persuasion it has the same authority. If we accept that the governor must obey a convincing forgery then we must concede that the governor's duty arises from his state of mind *however* it is produced: the 'proximate foundation and immediate essence' is not only necessary but also sufficient, apart from any more remote source, to constitute the obligation. The forger has acquired the right wrongly, but the governor has a genuine duty.

Other examples support the same conclusion.[36] Suppose a man and his wife's children mistakenly believe that he is their father. While this belief lasts he cannot without injustice disinherit them, they can rightly inherit his goods, and they owe him the respect and obedience due to a father; each has all the rights and duties he or she would have if the belief were true. On the other hand, if father and child do not know their relationship and one mistreats the other, the act is no worse than the mistreatment of a stranger. Suppose a woman mistakenly thinks that a man is her husband and sleeps with him. She does not sin, indeed she would do wrong to treat him as a stranger, although the impostor has acquired a husband's rights

[35] 221 b33-67.

[36] 222 b63-223 b29, 224 a57-225 a32. The point in Bayle's terminology is that the condition is not merely a *conditio sine qua non*, but the 'whole foundation and essence' of the rights of truth, the essence being the attribute which is necessary and sufficient for the thing to be what it is (222 a52-b22). Cf. Descartes, principle 53, vol. 1, p. 240.

wrongly. On the other hand, if a woman at a masked ball makes love with her husband thinking that he is a stranger she is guilty of adultery. If we accept the moral judgements suggested in these examples then we must agree that those who mistakenly believe that they are in a certain relation really have the rights and duties of that relation, and that those who do not believe they are in a relation which really they are in do *not* have those rights and duties: that in every case it is the belief, and not the truth or falsity of the belief, which makes the moral difference.[37] To believe that a proposition is true, whether the belief is true or false, is thus the necessary and sufficient condition for owing it whatever is due to truth. If truth were a person, truth would take love for an error mistaken for truth and loved for that reason as love of herself, whereas homage given to a true proposition not believed to be true is like adultery with one's own spouse at a masked ball.[38]

Mistaken belief gives error, metaphorically, the rights of truth over those who believe it, who therefore have a genuine duty to act on their belief, and therefore (since people have the right to do their duty) the right to act on it. Perhaps this right was wrongly acquired (for example, if the belief results from self-deception), and then they will have to answer for exercising it to God on judgement day.[39] But meanwhile, and in relation to other human beings, it is a genuine right. It makes little sense to say that the error's metaphorical rights are wrongly acquired, since error, not being a person separate from the person deceived, cannot answer for the deception as the man who impersonates a woman's husband can;[40] if we become subject to the rights of an error as a result of self-deception then it is *our* right—the right to act on our erroneous belief—that is wrongly acquired. Let us eliminate the personification altogether. That a proposition (true or false) has the rights of truth over those, and only those, who believe that it is true means that those who believe it (even if their belief results from self-deception or other fault for which they will in the end answer to God) have (while they believe it) certain genuine

[37] 223 a38-40, 58-69.
[38] 225 a15-20.
[39] 226 b49-64.
[40] *CP* 434 a5-18.

moral duties[41] which other human beings cannot rightly blame or punish them for performing, or try to induce them voluntarily not to perform—though others can rightly try to change their belief or physically prevent their action.

What these duties are has not yet been determined. If we believe a proposition then presumably we must act on it, make it known to others and so on. We have different beliefs about these duties. To be consistent Bayle must say that we must do for whatever we believe to be the truth whatever we believe we must do for the truth. But he can also say, without inconsistency, that some people are wrong in what they believe, and in what they believe they ought to do for the truth, and that in some cases they can be prevented, by means which do not involve their own consent, from acting on their beliefs.

2. FOLLOWING CONSCIENCE IS AT LEAST THE LESSER EVIL

In the *Philosophical Commentary* Bayle does not talk about the rights of error personified, though he does make some use of the materials of the argument just surveyed. In this book he argues that (1) an act done against conscience is a sin; (2) of two similar sinful acts one done against conscience is the worse sin; (3) of any two acts whatever, one against conscience and the other not, even if the former is an act of a kind generally good (such as giving alms) and the other of a kind generally bad (such as beating a poor man), the act against conscience is worse, even if in both cases conscience is in error;[42] (4) not only is the act against conscience the worse sin, but the other is not a sin but a good act, at least unless the error is culpable;[43] (5) indeed, even if the error is culpable the act is good, it is the error which is to blame;[44] (6) and there may be nothing blameworthy in the dogmatic errors of a heretic.[45] From this it follows that, if persecuting heretics may be a good act on the part of the orthodox, a heretic who persecutes the orthodox may do a

[41] See *S* 500 a30-40 (that error acquires the rights of truth means that those who believe it have the obligations they would have to truth).

[42] For stages 1-3 see 422 b45-425 a64 (references in this form will from now on be to *CP* unless otherwise indicated).

[43] See *CP* pt. 2, ch. 10.

[44] See *S* ch. 3.

[45] See *CP* pt. 2, ch. 10; and *S*, especially chs. 10-19 and 22-3.

morally good act, not blameworthy in any respect and perhaps
praiseworthy.

2.1.   *Moral and natural evils*

Some of Bayle's arguments rely on a distinction and ranking of
moral and natural (or 'physical'[46]) goods and evils. Moral
goods and evils consist only in acts of free will, choices. What
makes a choice good or evil is the agent's reason for making
it—more precisely, the agent's view of the goodness or badness
of the reason: moral goods and evils are acts of free will in their
'objective' reality.[47] That is, a choice is morally good if it is
made for what the chooser believes is a morally good reason.
Physical goods and evils are everything else, including external
actions and their effects, acts and dispositions of will apart from
their objective being, beliefs[48] and other mental episodes and
dispositions.

Moral goods and evils outrank physical goods and evils;[49] at
least, the evil of acting against conscience outranks any physical
evil found in, or resulting from, human action. To act against
conscience is to do what you believe to be wrong, which satisfies
the concept of a moral evil. Although Bayle seems to hold 'the
autonomy of morals',[50] he assumes—for the reason, perhaps,
that God is the infinite good—that those who believe in God
must believe that displeasing God is wrong and that the intention to please God is the highest moral good. So to act with
the intention of obeying God is morally good. But those who
believe in God and regard their conscience as God's deputy,

[46] In scholastic terminology 'physical' did not always imply 'material'. Sometimes
the contrast is not with 'immaterial' but with 'free'—the physical is what comes about
not by free choice but by nature. Sometimes the contrast is between 'physical' and
'objective' being—see next note.

[47] 'Objective' here means 'as an object of perception or thought': 'Objective reality'
means the reality something has as such an object; see Descartes, vol. 1, p. 162. See
also Dalbiez, Wells. Mental acts and dispositions also have 'physical' or natural being
(428 a38–46), the reality they have as modifications of the thinking subject; this is
equivalent to Descartes's 'subjective' being (i.e. being in a subject as modes); cf.
Descartes, loc. cit., and see vol. 2, p. 157.

[48] On belief see below, p. 82.

[49] On the similar Stoic doctrine see Cicero, *De finibus*, III.xii.41ff. Anselm said that
the annihilation of the whole universe would be less evil than any sin; *Cur deus homo*, I.21.
More recent philosophers say that moral reasons are (perhaps not always) conclusive or
overriding.

[50] See Labrousse, *Pierre Bayle*, vol. 2, pp. 268–75.

and nevertheless act against it, are guilty of an act of hatred of God.[51] To choose to displease God is an act essentially and intrinsically evil, wrong under all circumstances (no matter what the alternative), a violation of a law from which God himself cannot dispense; obedience to conscience is thus an 'indispensable', exceptionless, absolute obligation.[52]

2.2. *Argument by comparison of evils*

Imagine two men in similar situations who both have erroneous consciences—suppose they are successively asked for help by someone in genuine distress, whom they both mistakenly believe is a fraud whom they should drive off harshly; and suppose the first obeys his conscience (for conscience's sake) and drives him off, while the second weakly or capriciously gives the help he mistakenly believes he ought to refuse. Compare the goods and evils present in these two cases: (a) the poor man's deserts; (b) the mistaken belief held by both the men he approaches; (c) their respective decisions; (d) their actions and the effects on him. With respect to (a) and (b) there is no difference. With respect to (c) the difference is in favour of one who drives the poor man off: there is the moral good of his obeying conscience,[53] there is the moral evil of the other's deciding to act against his conscience. With respect to (d) the difference goes the other way: the man who acts against his conscience does good to the poor man, the other does evil. But goods and evils under (d) are merely 'physical', whereas the evil under (c), of acting against conscience, is a great moral evil which outranks the physical evil.[54] The harsh treatment inflicted on the genuinely poor man who does not deserve it is not a moral evil, since he is not harshly treated for the reason that he is a genuinely poor man, and moral good and evil depends on intention—that is, on the reason why the act is chosen.[55] Thus

[51] 422 b45-423 a7, 424 a34-42, 425 a59. To despise what one believes (even mistakenly) to be God's will is to despise God; cf. 432 b37-40. See above, Essay I, sect. 1.

[52] 425 a47-64, 425 b19-22. Contrast the law against murder, from which dispensation is possible (433 a5-20). Cf. 374 b13.

[53] 424 a8-9, 21.

[54] Precipitation and mistake of means, if they are moral evils, are much less than the evil of disobedience to conscience (424 a71-b5). In fact they are not moral evils because there is no conscious wrongdoing; see below, sect. 4.1.

[55] 424 a67-b26.

the comparison of evils shows that the one who acts against his conscience, though it is mistaken and though he does good to one who deserves it, does the greater evil.[56] This is enough to prove that we are obliged to act in obedience to our consciences even when they are mistaken, because of the principle that if we cannot avoid evil altogether we must choose the evil which is less.

Bayle's contemporaries would generally have agreed that it is wrong to disobey one's conscience even if it is mistaken; but this does not mean that it is right to obey it, and still less that obedience must be a good act. It was generally held that one of the provisions of God's law requires obedience to one's conscience even when it is mistaken. But a distinction was generally drawn between an error of fact, which excuses if it is not due to sin, and an error of law (to which errors in faith were sometimes assimilated[57]), which does not excuse even when the error itself is not blameworthy; a woman who sleeps with someone she blamelessly mistakes for her husband does not sin, but it would be no excuse not to know that adultery is against God's law. It follows that error may make sin inevitable. If because of an error of law, or an error due to sin, I believe I ought to do (or omit) something which some provision of God's law actually forbids (or requires), then if I act on my belief I violate that provision without proper excuse. But if I do not act on it I violate the provision which requires obedience to conscience, also without excuse: I must sin either way.[58] The argument by comparison of evils does not challenge the claim

[56] Since this case, in which the person who obeys conscience mistreats someone who really deserves good treatment, is the one in which the thesis is most improbable, we can conclude universally that to avoid the greater evil we must always obey our consciences. What if it were a case of executing someone mistakenly believed to be a criminal? Would the moral evil of disobeying conscience outrank the 'merely physical' evil of that person's death? Bayle would presumably say 'Yes', which would be implausible. The argument from the beggar example perhaps tacitly relies on the idea that one can be expected to put up with a certain amount of ill-treatment.

[57] 429 b36–7. Jansen and Arnauld did not regard errors of faith as errors of law (which they took in this context to mean *natural* law), but still they denied that ignorance of faith excuses wrongdoing. They held that ignorance of truths of faith is a punishment for Adam's sin, and for that reason no excuse for resulting sins; see above, Essay I, sect. 4.

[58] Compare Thomas Aquinas, *Summa*, 1–2, q.19 a.6, and see above, p. 44. Bayle sees that the propositions that it is wrong not to obey conscience, and that it is not wrong to obey it, are not equivalent. See 427 a32–41, 430 a19–23, 433 b26–41.

that those whose consciences command what God actually forbids, or vice versa, must sin whatever they do; the argument is merely that the sin of acting against conscience is the worse sin, and that if we cannot avoid sin altogether we must avoid the worse.

3. AN ACT DONE IN OBEDIENCE TO CONSCIENCE IS A GOOD ACT

But Bayle goes on to maintain that an act done in obedience to even erroneous conscience is not a sin at all but a morally good act.[59] Provided one errs in good faith, 'an act done in consequence of a false persuasion is as good as if it had been done in consequence of a true persuasion'; 'an act opposed to a false persuasion is as bad as an act opposed to a true persuasion'.[60] By 'good' and 'bad' he does not mean simply right and wrong—that would make nonsense of the distinction between a true and a false persuasion. By 'right' he means consistent with every principle of the moral law, by 'wrong' he means forbidden by some principle of the moral law, by 'bad' he means worthy of blame and punishment, and by 'good' he means praiseworthy. His contention is that a wrong act done in the persuasion that it is right is no more blameworthy, or less praiseworthy, than it would have been if it had been right.

3.1. *Argument from how God judges us*

For the claim that an act done in accordance with conscience is a morally good act there are two arguments. The most noteworthy premiss of the first[61] is that God judges us only by the

[59] The argument presented above in sect. 1, from *NL*, already implies that an act done in obedience to erroneous conscience is not a sin; the arguments presented in this section, from *CP*, are another way to the same conclusion.

[60] 428 a3-13. 'As good as' presumably implies that some acts done in error may deserve praise and moral credit; this is not an implication Bayle draws out, but see *S* 508 b4, 17, 39, 57-8. The most that traditional scholasticism would concede is that some wrong acts done in error may be excused, not that they might deserve praise.

[61] *CP* pt. 2, ch. 9.

'objective' quality of our acts of free choice.[62] If Bayle holds
the autonomy of morals, then God is brought in presumably
because he is the infallibly just judge: what he praises or blames
really is morally good or evil.[63] It might be thought that God
judges everything according to its real nature: if a woman sleeps
with a man who is not really her husband then surely God
will judge that she has done that, and therefore that she has
committed adultery, whatever she may have thought she was
doing. But Bayle insists that in judging whether a person deserves blame and punishment God does not consider the outward act or its effects, but only the act of will;[64] and that he
distinguishes acts of will not according to the real quality of
the object chosen, but according to its 'objective' quality, the
quality the chooser believes it has, and on account of which he
or she makes the choice;[65] the real quality of the object is

[62] The proposition that moral merit and demerit depend on free choice, and the
scholastic theory of the voluntary and involuntary in human acts, seem to have been
common to most schools of thought at the time, Protestant as well as Catholic; see *S*
524 a8-10, *S* 536 b41. On the reconciliation of the doctrine of predestination with
philosophical morality see 439 a37-b9. But it was contentious to say that moral merit
and demerit depend on the 'objective quality' of voluntary acts, i.e. on the moral
quality of the act as the agent sees it; see above, Essay I, n. 56.

[63] 219 a26-7, and see above, n. 50.

[64] 423 b69-424 a6, 424 b8-51, 428 b21-36, 429 a45-50, 432 b7-14. Abelard says
something similar: 'God considers only the mind in rewarding good or evil, not the
results of the deeds. . . . Works . . . are all indifferent in themselves' (p. 45; cf. pp. 13,
15, 25, 27, 29, 47, 49, 53). St Augustine says: 'Even if a man finds no opportunity to
lie with the wife of another, but . . . would if he got the chance, he is no less guilty
than if he were caught in the act' (*De libero arbitrio*, I.iii.8. According to Thomas
Aquinas the external act is not morally indifferent ('the interior act of will and the
external act, as considered morally, are one act'), but if completion of the act is
prevented by some chance, that makes no difference to the reward or punishment due;
see *Summa*, 1-2, q.20 a.3 and a.4. In effect, Bayle takes the view that completion as
much as non-completion is a matter of chance, since it always depends on other factors
besides the agent's choice, so that the external act never makes any difference to the
praise or blame due; and he takes that to mean that external acts have no moral value.
For fourteenth-century discussion of this question see Duns Scotus, *God and Creatures*,
pp. 399ff., and Adams and Wood.

[65] 428 a38-46, 428 b13-21, *S* 537 a56-61. The reference to Thomas Aquinas at 537
b1 is incorrect; presumably it should be to *Summa*, 1-2, q.19 a.2. Bayle misrepresents
St Thomas's position. See *Summa*, 1-2, q.18 a.6, where he distinguishes the object from
the end the agent has in mind. By 'the object' St Thomas means either the consequence
of the external action or the things which the action affects—'the subjects to which it
tends' in Bayle's phrase—which may not be what the agent has in mind, and therefore
not something 'objective' in Bayle's sense. In 1-2, q.18 a.4 St Thomas says that for an
act to be morally good it must be good both in its end and in its object—so it is not
enough to be good 'objectively'.

accidental, and therefore morally irrelevant.[66] These are points already noticed.[67] A new point is this, that in judging moral desert God distinguishes acts of choice by the dispositions they manifest;[68] for example, God judges one who acts out of love for an error mistaken for truth as if he acts out of love of truth, because the disposition is the same.[69] It might be thought that some sort of utilitarianism lies behind this, that Bayle thinks the act should be judged by the disposition it manifests because in the long run judging by disposition will have good effects, by encouraging dispositions which generally have good effects. But although he sometimes refers to the acts the disposition would prompt if there were no error,[70] he is talking about God's judgement on the last day when the long run is over. The point of referring to the disposition and the hypothetical acts it would prompt under other circumstances is to make clear the intrinsic and actual moral value of this act.[71] Whatever the consequences of the act or of the disposition, if the act is done because it is believed to be right then it is a morally good act.

[66] 428 a48–51, 428 b2–3, 429 b4–11, *S* 526 b67–70, *S* 529 b33–5, 54–7.

[67] See above, sect. 2.1.

[68] For examples of judgement by reference to dispositions see *NL* 220 b11, 424 a16–25, 37–42, 56–61, 428 a51–3, 468 b17–24. Sometimes Bayle puts it in terms of the dispositions God 'sees' in the soul: 425 b63–5, 426 a25–9, 428 a56, 432 b31–44, 61–8. According to Hume when we praise or blame acts 'the ultimate object [of evaluation] ... is the motive that produced them', the action being relevant merely as a sign of the disposition (see Raphael, sect. 512 and 628). Bayle may also have thought this, but I think he thought rather that the object of praise or blame is the act of the will, though (for some reason) he thought that the quality of a choice is most easily conveyed by reference to the disposition to make such choices.

[69] *S* 529 b3–9, *S* 537 a1–61 (a miser who loves fake gold pieces loves gold; a lover of ancient medals, or of beauty, who has poor judgement really loves these objects). It seems strange to say that someone loves X if he loves Y because he thinks it is X—in fact he loves Y. The disposition manifested in the choice is the same, and that, in Bayle's view, is apparently what reveals the moral quality of the choice.

[70] 428 b10–12, *S* 529 b17–18, 42–4, 70-a5, *S* 533 a31–36 (leave the man altogether the same, and substitute the truth in place of what he now loves, which is false, and he will love this object as he loved the other). See above, p. 66.

[71] Utilitarian considerations are relevant to human judgement, but God judges by real intrinsic value. Human judges cannot search the heart and are concerned chiefly to repress harmful consequences: 432 b5–15, *S* 517 b21–9, *NL* 220 b31–47. Cf. Abelard, pp. 39–45. See above, n. 19.

3.2. *Argument from the generality of laws*

The most noteworthy premiss of the second argument is that God rules and judges us ordinarily through general laws.[72] If a ruler addresses to all his subjects a law in general terms requiring As to treat Bs in mode C, then each subject is obliged and *authorised* to decide whether he or she belongs to category A, and if so then who belongs to category B and which acts would fit description C.[73] A ruler ought to take account of the capacities of his subjects;[74] if he knows that they are fallible but does not provide enough specific guidance to save them from mistakes, then he must be understood to authorise them to act on the law as they fallibly interpret it.[75] To act on one's interpretation of a law which one is obliged and authorised to interpret is to obey it—even if one's interpretation is mistaken. This is the vital point. Those who are obliged and authorised to act on their own fallible interpretation, if they act on a mistaken interpretation, are not merely excused of disobedience: they actually obey.[76] We might be inclined to make a distinction, and say that they obey their superior's implied higher-order command to act on this law as they interpret it, but do not actually obey this law itself if their interpretation is wrong. But Bayle makes no such distinction: those who act on a mistaken interpretation of a law they are obliged and authorised to interpret actually obey that law. If he thinks this because they have the same disposition of choice then this

[72] For the second argument see *CP* pt. 2, ch. 10. For Bayle's views on the generality of laws see Riley, who shows that Bayle at first entertained, and later rejected, Malebranche's novel idea that it would be unworthy of God's wisdom for him to make exceptions to physical laws. There was no novelty, however, in the idea that moral laws are general; see Thomas Aquinas, *Summa*, 1-2, q.94 a.2. To some moral laws God might make particular exceptions (as when he ordered Abraham to sacrifice his son), but others were supposed to be absolutely exceptionless; see above, n. 52. It was also supposed that in his treatment of mankind God follows certain general policies, with occasional exceptions; see above, p. 43.

[73] 434 b6, 11, 56, 61-5, 435 b59-63, *S* 509 b10-13.

[74] 437 a24-7, 69-72, 436 b42-71.

[75] 435 b20-436 a27 (a king who commands his judges to punish the guilty and acquit the innocent obliges and therefore authorises them to behave thus to those who *seem* guilty or innocent, and the judges are not to blame if, after proper inquiry, they acquit some who are really guilty and punish some who are really innocent), *S* 516 a52-517 a31 (the judges are not to blame, just as physicians are not to blame for killing some of their patients), *S* 509 b42-510 b6.

[76] *S* 509 a29, *S* 509 b61-2, *S* 510 b55-6, *S* 511 a37, *S* 513 a52-65, *S* 513 b36, 46.

argument is a variant of the argument from how God judges us.

Suppose, then, that God has commanded those who possess the truth to compel everyone else to accept it. He has not given enough specific guidance to prevent mistakes in carrying out the command. It is addressed to all who hear the gospel,[77] and does not specify which of the many disputed doctrines is the truth.[78] God knows that we are fallible, that what seems true to us even after thorough study is often not true, that real truths have no mark that we can perceive to distinguish them from merely apparent truths.[79] If he has given this command he has obliged and authorised us all to compel acceptance of whatever seems to each of us to be true.[80] The heretics, then, whichever they are, when they persecute the true Church because it seems to them to be in error, actually obey the alleged command and do a good act.

3.3. *The basic commandment*

Bayle does not believe that such a command has been given, but still he seems to believe that those who think it has and do what they think has been commanded do a good act.[81] He seems to have in mind something like this. The moral law is a hierarchy of practical principles with just one basic commandment, 'Seek the truth and act on it',[82] or even—since we are not obliged to seek unless we think it true that we ought

---

[77] 392 b1-31, 434 b5-435 a65.

[78] 434 b40-6.

[79] 437 a2-13, 437 b54-438 b43. Grace does not provide any criterion (439 a9-32, and *S* ch. 23). God can give inspirations together with the certain knowledge of being inspired by God, as he inspired the prophets (454 a7-20, *S* 545 a27-35). But ordinarily grace is 'imperceptible', 'unknown', 'invisible'. See *S* 545 a18-22, *S* 545 b14-19.

[80] 434 b3-17, 435 b6-19.

[81] 433 b38-41, *S* 540 a1-4. Their act is good if done in good faith. But Bayle thinks that the belief that one must persecute is unlikely to be held in good faith, especially by those who act on it and find themselves doing things which they must know are wrong (540 a7-33).

[82] 'God has imposed on us a duty proportioned to our power, namely to seek the truth, and to take our stand on what seems true after sincere inquiry, to love this apparent truth, and to rule ourselves by its precepts however difficult they may be' (437 b38-45). See also 436 b30-5, 437 a18-24, 438 b48-51, 62-66, *S* 503 a46-52. Similarly Malebranche says that 'love of order' (i.e. of the system of truths of practical reason) is the fundamental, in fact the only, virtue; see Malebranche, pp. 19, 24, 28.

to seek[83]—simply 'Act on the truth'. On this theory other, secondary, duties will be imposed by the various particular practical truths as we come to know them.[84] For example, if it is true that we ought to do no murder, then doing no murder will be required by the single basic commandment as soon as we find out that 'we ought to do no murder' is a practical truth—that is, as soon as we find out that murder is wrong. The argument that a commandment addressed in general terms to fallible subjects must authorise them to act on their possibly mistaken interpretations applies to this basic commandment, interpretation in this case being deciding what is true. We obey the basic commandment, therefore, and do a morally good act, if we act on whatever *seems* true about what we ought to do— that is, if we do whatever seems right, even if really it is not. Therefore, although it is not true that God has commanded us to impose the truth by force, those who think it is true, and for that reason impose by force what they think is the truth, do a morally good act.

If by 'conscience' we mean the self as deciding what it is right to do in a particular case,[85] and if it is enough to do what seems right, then it is enough in each case to follow conscience. 'Follow conscience' is simply the basic commandment in other words. As Bayle says, the interior sentiment of conscience, its

[83] 442 a57-b23. This is less exacting than what Thomas Aquinas says in *Summa*, 1-2, q.6 a.8, namely that ignorance is voluntary if there is something we ought to know and could find out (whether we know that this is so or not); see above, Essay I, n. 148.

[84] See above, sect. 1.2. On this account, the moral law consists, strictly speaking, of one basic imperative and a number of practical truths which are not themselves imperatives. But in Bayle's time this distinction would not have been regarded as important.

[85] See Hunter for a forceful Humean attack on Conscience as an infallible agency distinct from the person. (This is not Bayle's notion of conscience, nor as far as I know that of any of his contemporaries or predecessors—no one thought of it as infallible, or as distinct from the self.) Other recent writers say that conscience does not make judgements but merely enforces them. '[C]onscience is not a special unerring faculty for making ethical judgments .... One's conscience is a sanction against doing what one believes to be wrong' (McGuire, p. 259). 'Conscience ... does not tell the agent what is right or wrong ... either in individual concrete instances or as a matter of principle. ... The role of conscience is purely and simply to "enforce" our moral knowledge or belief' (Fuss, pp. 116-18). In my view conscience not only enforces but also judges. My conscience is myself, considered as judging what is right to do in a particular instance and/or enforcing the decision. 'I told myself' does not imply a speaker distinct from myself, and neither does 'My conscience told me'. That one can have a dialogue with oneself is perhaps puzzling, but it is a fact.

sense of conviction, the 'taste' of truth which it finds in some proposition about what ought to be done, is the distinguishing character or criterion of morally good action.[86] Conscience is not a touchstone of what really is right, of the absolute truth of propositions about what we morally ought to do. Except for mathematical and metaphysical evidence there is no criterion of absolute truth,[87] in particular none of true moral judgements of particular actions.[88] If God required that we act only on absolute truth certainly known as such, we would be reduced to more-than-Pyrrhonian suspense even of practical judgement.[89] Conscience is the touchstone of 'relative' truth, of truth 'for me',[90] the touchstone for discerning what at the moment of decision I am obliged and authorised to do, given that the commandments are in general terms which I must interpret and apply. 'God demands only that we search for truth sincerely and diligently, and that we discern it by the sentiment of conscience, in such a way that if the combination of circumstances prevents us from finding absolute truth, and makes us find the taste of truth in an object which is false, this putative and relative truth should hold for us the place of real truth.'[91]

This is not relativism or subjectivism or scepticism, but merely a combination of his doctrine of the basic commandment with fallibilism.[92] The basic commandment is not

[86] 437 b45-8, 440 b44-7, 441 a39-43, 441 b18-66. Cf. Jurieu, as reported in Popkin, *Pyrrhonism*, p. 167.

[87] On mathematical and metaphysical certainty see 437 a6, 437 b58-60.

[88] There are self-evident *general* moral propositions; although Bayle does not actually say so, he seems to hold that they are as evident and certain as the propositions of mathematics. See 368 b47-55, 369 a9-13, 370 a35-43, 370 a59-b1. But a judgement of conscience is not a universal proposition but a judgement of the rightness or wrongness of some particular act, and for such judgements there is no criterion.

[89] On suspense of practical judgement see *NL* 226 b9-16, *NL* 228 a15-51, 427 a47-b21, 436 a28-41, 440 b63-441 a21.

[90] For the terms 'true for me' and 'relative truth' see *NL* 219 a2-32. According to Bayle these are scholastic expressions which mean simply what seems to me to be true (*NL* 219 a32-8).

[91] 441 a65-b3; cf. 438 b53-4. Bayle suggests an analogy between his doctrine of conscience and Descartes's doctrine of sensation: just as sensation is given not as a means to absolute truth but only to preserve the composite of body and soul from death, so conscience is given not as a means to absolute truth but to preserve the soul from damnation; see Descartes, vol. 1, pp. 193-4, and cf. 440 b12-40, 441 a46-57.

[92] By 'fallibilism' I mean that any proposition which seems true may actually be false, by 'scepticism' that one should always suspend judgement, by 'relativism' that two people (for example, from different cultures) may make assertions which negate one another yet may both be right. Fallibilism does not imply scepticism except on the assumption that we must suspend judgement except where there is no possibility

'Do whatever you *believe* is right', as if it does not matter what
you believe as long as you act on it, but 'Do whatever you
believe is *right*'. Between these two formulae there can be no
practical difference until we realise that our beliefs may not be
correct, and even then there can be no practical difference at
any given moment: the difference is in behaviour over time. If
we realise that some of our beliefs may be false, and that God
wants us to act on what is true, then we will try to replace
beliefs which merely seem true with beliefs which are true,
though we will never be sure we have succeeded. But at the
moment of decision we must act on what at that moment seems
true. Bayle takes a lenient view of people who refuse to inquire;
if they do not believe that it is true that they have a duty to
inquire, then in not inquiring they do not disobey the commandment to act on the truth.[93] We must act on what seems
true after whatever inquiry (if any) it seems true that we ought
to make; but in truth we ought to inquire.[94]

The thesis that a person who obeys an erroneous conscience
may do a morally good act therefore does not mean that it
is simply right to do whatever you think is right. You have
(conditionally—given your belief) a duty to do whatever you
think you have a duty to do, but this does not mean that your
duties (simply) are whatever you think they are. The duty to
obey conscience is really a duty, and the basic duty. If you
mistakenly think you have some secondary duty which otherwise you would not have, then to do what you mistakenly think
is your duty is—by virtue of the duty to obey conscience, and
given your mistake, but not otherwise—really a duty, and you
really have the right to do it: but the mistake is still a mistake.

of error, which is not true. On fallibilism see Chisholm, 'Fallibilism'. For Bayle's
fallibilism see above, n. 79. See also 377 a34-b16 (we all know by experience that we
are prone to error, and see—or think we see—the falsity of much we used to think
true; this gives rise to a general mistrust of our present opinions, which—even before
we have any particular reason for doubting—ought to make us ready to listen, for
example, to missionaries from Australia (on the strange beliefs of the Australians see
DHC, art. 'Sadeur')); and 414 b39-65.

[93] 'It is sometimes permitted to have zeal for opinions one has not examined' (*NL*
226 b35-44 (not ironic, I think)). See below, sect. 4.2, on opinionatedness.

[94] 443 a9-15 (although God is content that we should search and then act on what
seems true, he wants us to correct our beliefs, and to correct one another, when
possible).

4. CULPABLE ERROR

Of the points listed at the beginning of section 2 we have covered 1–4. Usually Bayle says that an act done in error is morally as good as if the error had been truth 'if the error is inculpable'.[95] But this 'if' means '*at least* if', since in fact he holds (5) that the act is good even if the error is culpable.

The argument for this is by analogy. If a usurper seizes power wrongly, but after that rules well in accordance with the laws God gives rulers, then on judgement day he will be blamed for the usurpation but not in addition for acts of government which would have satisfied the law of God perfectly if he had been the lawful ruler. Similarly, those who culpably fall into error (for example through negligence or self-deception) will be blamed for the error but not for acts which would have been right if the error had been the truth.[96] This seems plausible. If we reject it and say that culpable error does not excuse, and simply blame those who ought to know better as if they do know better, then blame will depend on luck. If a motorist too drunk to know what he is doing happens to kill someone he will be to blame for homicide, but if by good luck he arrives home without an accident he escapes that blame. On Bayle's theory, however, someone who drinks, knowing he may drive under the influence of alcohol and that this may lead to an accident, is very much to blame even if there is no accident, and no more to blame if there is.[97] The moral irrelevance of luck or chance follows from the conception of a moral good. Moral goods and evils are acts of free choice whereas physical goods and evils include whatever is determined by chance— that is, whatever is accidental in relation to the agent's will, whatever depends on any other cause.[98]

[95] Or 'involuntary', 'invincible', 'sincere' or 'in good faith', expressions Bayle treats as equivalent. For examples of his use of these terms see 427 b30, 430 a69-b2, 435 b13-15, 30-31, 437 b42-3, 438 b63.

[96] *S* 508 a56-b15.

[97] Physical results are morally irrelevant; see above, n. 64. Anything that depends on luck is morally irrelevant: *S* 529 b41-57, *S* 543 a56-b5 (heaven is not won at cross and pile—a game of chance), *NL* 226 a51-5. (Contrast Williams, *Moral Luck*, pp. 20ff. Bayle would deny Williams's claim that a decision made by an unjustifiable process of deliberation can be justified by a successful outcome. On 'moral luck' see also Nagel, N. Richards, Parker, and Jensen.)

[98] Compare Aristotle's notion of a chance event as one of a kind that could have been intentional, but was not, being (under the description suggesting intention) produced by some cause *per accidens* (*Phys.*, II.5, 197 a5-8). On the conception of a

4.1. *The moral irrelevance of being right*

Bayle soon passes to point 6, that the dogmatic errors of a
heretic may be inculpable: if this is true then point 5 need not
be insisted on, since it is not essential to the argument for an
end to the persecution of supposedly heretical Christians.[99] The
thought behind 5 is also behind much of what he says about 6:
someone who thinks under the influence of bad motives is to
blame even if by good luck he arrives at the truth, and no more
to blame if he does not—the actual truth or falsity of the
resulting beliefs is morally irrelevant. The morality of thinking
depends on exactly the same principles as determine the morality of acts or omissions of any sort.[100] Let us go into these
principles further.[101] Like other activities, thinking is morally
good or bad only in so far as it involves free choices, which get
their moral value from the reason (motive, intention) for which
the choice is made. The motive which should direct our thinking is the firm intention to use all our strength to know (so that
we may do) God's will;[102] that is, the motive of thinking, as
of all other activities, should be zeal to carry out the basic
commandment. Bad motives include love of ease in preference
to truth, a spirit of contradiction, jealousy of rivals, vanity
attaching us to opinions we have defended publicly.[103] For an
act to be blameworthy, however, it is not enough that the
motives be bad; we must realise their badness at the time—or
at least fail to examine their moral quality because of the
influence of motives we do realise are bad. (For example, I
might refuse to consider the possibility that my thinking is being
influenced by jealousy of a rival, because I wish to continue to
think well of myself—and I might realise that this is my motive,
and that it is bad.) Morality depends on the *objective* quality of
moral good see above, sect. 2.1.

[99] Occasionally Bayle says that acts done in accordance with conscience may be
sinful; see *S* 498 a22–32. His principles really imply that such an act cannot be a sin,
even if there is culpable error. I suspect that he did not himself consistently see this
implication, but his main line of argument does not depend on it—for that it is enough
that heretics should think themselves obliged to persecute.

[100] Bayle does not say this explicitly, but it seems reasonable to attribute it to him
in view of *S* 524 a4–7 and *S* 536 a71–b3, and the general uniformity of his treatment of
the morality of mental acts with that of acts of other kinds (see e.g. 442 a31–44).

[101] See above, sect. 3.1.

[102] 443 b20–1.

[103] *S* 531 a48–532 a10, *S* 535 b51–536 a22.

the motive—'objective' in Descartes's sense: that is, morality depends on the motive *as the agent sees it*. This is because an act is blameworthy only if it is voluntarily bad—that is, chosen in the belief that the choice is bad. It would be unjust to require repression of motives we do not know we have, or do not know are bad.[104] So we deserve blame not in so far as the motives by which our conduct is actually influenced are actually bad, but only in so far as we know (or believe) at the time that our action is influenced by motives we believe to be bad, that is, in so far as our mental activity is against conscience. Culpability in thinking, as in other activity, thus requires bad motives which cause the act with knowledge of the cause, and with knowledge of its badness—that is, so that we are at the same time conscious of the disorder of the motive.[105] This is simply an application of the principle Arnauld regarded as the basis of the doctrine of philosophic sin (see above, Essay I, sect. 2).

Ignorance or error is excused when it is due to circumstances outside the person's control, or to other inculpable ignorance or error, or to the influence of some other inculpable disposition which makes ignorance or error unavoidable by any free choice. For example, if a motive results from some habitual disposition it is not culpable unless the disposition is due to acts suspected or known when they were done to be bad.[106] Similarly, failure to find out something we could easily find out is not culpable negligence unless we know there may be something to be found out and wilfully refuse to inquire;[107] ignorance of the need to inquire excuses the error. Those who deceive themselves culpably, therefore, must have at least an inkling that the motives which influence them are bad, and fail—because of some motive they realise is not good—to examine their motives more closely.[108] Self-deception or negligence is not culpable, then, even if it results from envy or idleness or other actually wrong motive, except in so far as it results directly or indirectly

---

[104] *S* 533 b46–534 a37.

[105] *S* 532 b29–32, *S* 531 b20–1, 442 a31–3, 536 b44–9.

[106] 442 b51–3. Others held that we are responsible for acts which we cannot help doing, given our present dispositions, if those dispositions were formed by acts we could have chosen not to do, even if it did not occur to us at the time that the acts were bad or that we were forming a disposition. See Aristotle, *EN*, III.5.

[107] See above, n. 83.

[108] *S* 534 a27–37.

from conscious choices made in the knowledge that they were
bad.[109]

Natural dispositions do not merit praise or blame. For example, the love of what seems true is a disposition without
moral value since it is an impulse of nature and not a matter of
free choice.[110] We cannot help assenting to all propositions,
and only those, which seem true, and error can gain acceptance
only under the guise of truth: no one, no matter how wicked,
can wilfully believe what seems false.[111] We therefore deserve
no moral credit for believing what seems to us to be true, and
no blame for disbelieving what seems false. Also by nature, and
apart from the effects of original sin, every child is susceptible
to education; a young child cannot help receiving as true what
it is taught by its parents and other elders.[112] Also by nature—
not by universal human nature, but by each person's particular
constitution (as modified by education and acquired beliefs)—
some people are more or less susceptible than others to this or
that kind or item of evidence. A reason which is enough to
enlighten one person may not be enough to enlighten another
with an equal love of truth, and this is a difference of no moral
significance.[113] Finally, it is a merely natural good or evil for
the beliefs we arrive at to be actually true or false.[114] So to have

[109] Bayle holds that belief is voluntary not directly but indirectly, inasmuch as
various voluntary acts and omissions may result in belief; see 385 b35–386 b24, 418
b2–3, *S* 520 a42-b18. From the argument for point 5 above it would then follow that
error itself is *never* culpable, but only certain acts and omissions of self-deception or
negligence, which deserve blame even if the resulting belief is true: the error stands to
those acts and omissions as acts done in error stand to the error. See above, Essay I, n.
101. But we are not to blame even for such acts and omissions if they are the unavoidable results of certain dispositions (laziness, envy, etc.), but only for prior acts or
omissions from which those dispositions result—and not even for those, if they are in
turn the consequence of prior dispositions. We deserve blame or credit only for original,
undetermined acts of free choice done with awareness of their moral quality. Bayle
does not draw all of these conclusions, but they seem to follow from his premises.

[110] *S* 528 a68–71. Arnauld also thought that naturally necessary acts cannot be
morally good or bad; see below, Appendix, n. 4.

[111] *S* 527 a29–36, b32–45.

[112] *S* 526 b1–5, 29–35, *S* 526 b63–527 a1, *S* 528 a17–23, b21–24. Bayle seems to
think that the mere personal influence of parents and others is an original source of
beliefs. Contrast Hume's opinion that trust in testimony is the result of experience; see
his 'Of miracles'.

[113] 396 b26–35, 397 a34–44, 442 b42–6, 443 b17–216 ('It is not for being more
intelligent … but for the stronger intention of using all one's forces to know and do
what God wills'), *S* 532 a13–16, 23–5.

[114] *S* 531 a41–51, 69-b3, *S* 532 b4–7, 43–6, *S* 533 a56-b32.

been brought up in a true belief, or to have been susceptible to true teaching, or to believe what is actually true, or what seems true, are all natural, not moral perfections, and their opposites are non-moral evils.

How much scope does this leave for moral good or evil in the conduct of thought? Bayle does not ask himself this question, but I suppose he would say that there can be moral good and evil in thinking only because there are degrees of zeal in seeking truth, degrees which are subject in some way to free choice. By nature everyone desires to know the truth, but if the intensity or effectiveness of this desire depends on free choice then people can deserve praise for the degree of zeal they show for discovering the truth (or holding to it if they think they have it), or blame for neglecting it for other ends.[115]

4.2. *The errors of heretics*

Bayle argues at length that the opinions of the various sects of Christians of his time could result from good or at least innocent motives. A heretic may even be led further into what is actually error by zeal for truth, for example if education leads him to think that truth is to be found in some book or institution where in fact it is not; he is like a zealous messenger misdirected and riding further away from his goal, hurried away precisely by his zeal to arrive at the goal.[116] On the other hand, people may become or remain orthodox because of bad motives, and then they deserve blame just as much as they would if their beliefs were actually false, since being right is morally irrelevant. Given equal zeal for truth, there is no moral superiority in being orthodox.[117]

[115] Perhaps he should say: for the previous choices which fostered or weakened such zeal. See above, n. 109.

[116] 527 a54-b25.

[117] 527 b53-7 (there is no less sin in propagating orthodoxy believing it heretical than vice versa), 532 b58-533 a16 (remaining in true religion from bad motives as bad as remaining in false religion from those motives). Compare Locke: 'The great division among Christians is about opinions. Every sect has its set of them, and that is called orthodoxy; and he that professes his assent to them, though with an implicit faith and without examining, is orthodox and in the way to salvation; but, if he examines, and thereupon questions any one of them, he is presently suspected of heresy, and, if he oppose them or hold the contrary, he is presently condemned as in a damnable error and in the sure way to perdition. Of this one may say that there is nor can be nothing more wrong. For he that examines, and upon a fair examination

Many of Bayle's contemporaries would have held that the errors of heretics are culpable, or at least do not excuse resulting acts, because either (1) they are errors of law, or they are always due to sin, either (2) to original sin or (3) to the personal sins of the heretic, or for several of these reasons. To the first reason Bayle replies that it assumes that errors of law cannot be invincible, i.e. involuntary. It will not do to say that one kind of error excuses and the other does not simply because they are errors about different sorts of things. There must be some relation to the fundamental moral idea of free choice. So if an error of law can be involuntary it will be innocent and will excuse just as much as any error of fact and for the same formal reason, namely that it is not the result of free choice.[118] In any case a question of moral and religious law is reducible to a question of fact, namely whether God has revealed a certain proposition.[119] Dogmatic truths do not have the clarity and evidence of mathematical and metaphysical truths.[120] Many dogmatic propositions are related to matters which depend upon God's free choice, so they are contingent truths; there may be good arguments for the various contending dogmas, since they may all represent things God could quite reasonably have done, though as a matter of contingent fact he chose to act one way and not another; and he may not have chosen what seems more probable.[121] The questions which divide Christians are therefore difficult, just as difficult as the questions of fact decided by courts of law, in which, it is generally agreed, error may be involuntary and inculpable.[122]

The second reason given why a heretic's error cannot excuse was that it is always due to sin,[123] to original sin at least. The followers of St Augustine held that error or ignorance may be a penalty justly inflicted on the human race for original sin; that although such error is not itself a sin deserving punishment

embraces an error for the truth, has done his duty more than he who embraces the profession of the truth (for the truths themselves he does not embrace) without having examined whether it be true or no' (Bourne, vol. 1, p. 306).

[118] 430 a24-b37.

[119] 430 a10-18, *S* 511 b54-67 and n., *S* 517 a41-b3.

[120] 437 a2-6, b57-60, 438 a54-b4.

[121] *S* 546 b10-22, *S* 547 b57-548 a62. See also *DHC*, art. 'Synergists', rem. C, vol. 13, pp. 315-17.

[122] *S* chs. 10-12 illustrate the difficulties with a survey of the disputes among the various parties of Catholics and Protestants. See *S* 542 a64-543 a31.

[123] *S* 514 b17-20 (almost all Christians suppose that our ignorance is due to sin).

it does not excuse sins which result from it, since Adam's sin does not reduce God's rights; and that God is therefore entitled to treat us as if we knew what we would have known but for original sin.[124] Bayle answers that it would be unreasonable on God's part not to take account of the effects of original sin since they take place because of laws which he freely chose.[125] And dogmatic errors are not all due to original sin; mostly they are due to human nature as it was originally created, before Adam sinned. Although our souls are infected by original sin it is not true that in everything they act *as* infected by sin; some of our original nature remains, and is the source of some of what we do and of some of our errors.[126] The union of soul and body, and the consequent confusion and weakness of our reasoning power, especially in childhood, are part of our nature as originally created.[127] Receptivity to what our parents teach is natural, and not due to original sin or to any other sin—or if it is, then the true belief of the orthodox (whichever they are) is also due to sin, since the beliefs of most members of all sects are probably due to education.[128]

The third reason was that a heretic must in every case be led into or kept in error by some personal vice or sin—negligence, pride, temerity or the like. In reply Bayle observes that the Christian sects all agree on the doctrines which come most into conflict with vice—doctrines forbidding revenge, commanding us to love our enemies, live soberly, chastely, humbly and so on. The disagreements are on matters which do not make the yoke of morality heavier or lighter. In fact people seem to be attracted to a religion if it is demanding.[129] Some doctrinal disputes arise because of the difficulty of reconciling certain of God's attributes with one another (for example, his lordship with his equity); different solutions may all be proposed with good motives.[130] As for pride, no one says 'God says so, but I

---

[124] 437 a41-50. See above, Essay I, sect. 4.

[125] 437 b1-13. The answer seems to beg the question: it was God's right to make the choice.

[126] *S* 526 b28-63, *S* 528 a10-16. See above, Essay I, n. 129.

[127] 437 a53-72, *S* 534 a41-66, *S* 514 b20-515 a6.

[128] *S* 526 a28-b39. Religious belief is mostly due to 'the imperious force of education': *S* 525 a17-32, *S* 522 a37-40, *S* 526 a11-17, *S* 543 a20, 440 a33-60 (if we had been born in China we would have followed the Chinese religion, if the Chinese had been born in England they would have been Christians).

[129] 439 b29-36, *S* 534 b69-535 b2.

[130] *S* 548 a63-b22; *DHC*, art. 'Synergists', rem. B, vol. 13, p. 313.

know better than God'. It cannot be fairly said that members
of any sect have too much pride to submit their lights to God;
the dispute is not whether what God has revealed is true, but
only whether he has revealed this or that.[131] As for self-interest,
it is not always the reason why people adopt religious opinions.
The French Protestants, Polish Socinians and Jews in every
Christian land have persisted in beliefs it would have been in
their interest to abandon.[132]

As for prepossession or prejudice, it is true that many people
look most favourably on their own side's arguments and think
about them most and know them best, and do not give enough
consideration to the other side. But this is true of all sects, not
only of those who are in fact in the wrong. And it is not true
that error is always due to such prejudiced behaviour. Even
impartial judges, such as Chinese philosophers might be, would
find it difficult to decide the points which divide Christian
sects.[133] It is said that no one can remain in error who makes
unprejudiced use of the means of information which are at
hand. But there is a complicated dispute about what the proper
means of information are.[134] In any case it is absurd to suggest
that *all* who have remained in error have (for example) read
the bible without prayer and docility, not desiring to find out
the truth but seeking confirmation of their prejudices, carefully
repressing all truer thoughts which the book suggests.[135]

As for opinionatedness, to refuse to change one's religion
even though one has been silenced in argument need not be
due to that fault. Someone who is quick-witted, articulate and
well prepared may silence someone who is really right but lacks
self-confidence or presence of mind.[136] Those who realise this
are entitled to hold to their position even though they can give
no reasons. Repressing doubts that arise in the mind, or refusing
to listen or to investigate, may not show lack of love for truth;

---

[131] 440 a1–32 (not even the devil can doubt what he believes God has affirmed).

[132] *S* ch. 14.

[133] *S* ch. 11. On preoccupation see *DHC*, art. 'Pellisson', rem. D, E, vol. 11, pp. 528–30. On unfair controversy see art. 'Chrysippe', rem. G, vol. 5, pp. 167–9. At the time there was great interest in Chinese philosophers; see Rowbotham, pp. 249ff.

[134] 438 a32–b26, *S* 521 a4–b10, 499 a15–26. See *DHC*, art. 'Nicolle', rem. C, vol. 11, pp. 141–6; *NL* 334 a33–b5. This dispute encourages Pyrrhonism and religious indifference: *NL* 334 b9–15; *S* 499 a25–6; art. 'Nicolle', p. 145.

[135] *S* 524 a30–525 a51.

[136] 396 a38–b21.

it may be due to a conviction that one already has the truth, together with fear of deception by crafty antagonists. This fear is often the result of education, and susceptibility to education is a physical (not moral) defect at most, while the desire to hold fast to what seems to be the truth (which is often what makes the mis-educated refuse to examine) is a 'physical' perfection at least, and perhaps a moral perfection.[137]

It may be said that those who fall into error are guilty of temerity, in imprudently affirming what (since it is false) can-not be evident.[138] Descartes's notion of temerity is very ex-acting; he says that since assent is an act of will error is always voluntary and avoidable. But then, since some errors of fact must surely still excuse, there must be some errors which are voluntary but not culpable, and religious error may be in this category.[139] Descartes's maxim of assenting only to what is clear and distinct does not apply to religious questions; we must affirm and live by whatever religion conscience finds has the 'taste' of truth.[140] In deciding religious questions we cannot wait for conclusive evidence.[141] In the questions debated

[137] *S* 525 b53-66, *S* 528 b56-529 a68, *S* 532 a32-61, *NL* 249 b2-43. Parents and ministers do not encourage critical examination; see *S* 530 a6-b2, *S* 532 a62-7, *S* 547 a41-b8.

[138] On temerity see 378 b62-379 a2, *S* 544 a39-60, *S* 545 a1-4, *S* 545 b67-546 a36. According to 'philosophical minds' the proper use of reason requires suspense of judgement until indubitable evidence forces assent: *DHC*, art. 'Nicolle', p. 145. Bayle does not agree with this (although he thinks there should be a proper inquiry—it is not good enough to be right by chance; see 435 b24-31, 544 a52-65). And he may not agree with the proposition that what is false cannot seem, or even be, evident; see Popkin, 'Bayle's Place'.

[139] *S* 530 b58-531 a40, *S* 534 b1-53.

[140] 438 a45-55, *S* 533 b33-44, *S* 544 a69-b12; cf. *S* 542 b19-37. See above, sect. 3.3. See also *NL* Letter 12 (especially 244 a41-b19, 245 a62-b17, 245 b30-44), directed against Arnauld (see his *Œuvres*, vol. 14, pp. 711-23) In this letter Bayle argues that we may have to judge people's motives without certainty, and generalises to the conclusion that Descartes's rules are not applicable outside speculative philosophy. Descartes and the ancient sceptics would have agreed that in practical matters one must act on propositions which are uncertain.

[141] A distinction had often been drawn between certainty of evidence and certainty of adherence (see Thomas Aquinas, *De veritate*, q.14 a.1; Ockham, in Baudry, pp. 43-4; Hooker, 'Sermon', prefixed to *Ecclesiastical Polity*, vol. 1, pp. 2-3; Chillingworth, pp. 27-9, 86). Traditionally it was held that those who have faith have 'certainty of adherence', that is, that they cling firmly by act of will to truths for which they may not have evidence. (Not everyone held that faith requires certainty of any kind: 'God desires that ... the strength of our faith be equal or proportionable to the credibility of the motives to it' (Chillingworth, p. 27).) Since the truths of faith include some speculative propositions, it was traditionally held that Christians must be certain (with certainty of adherence) of some speculative truths. Recently Arnauld's associate,

among the Christian sects none of the arguments goes beyond probability and the probabilities are not overwhelmingly in favour of any sect.[142] The fact that assent is voluntary is not enough to show that error in such questions is culpable. Some say that those who are given God's grace will be guided to the right decision, and that only those who follow such guidance escape the guilt of temerity. But we cannot know when grace is leading us, since it is imperceptible, and truths to which it leads us have no mark to distinguish them from beliefs which we wrongly think are due to grace; the influence of grace therefore provides no criterion of non-temerarious decision. We cannot be rationally assured of having the truth except by argument, and grace does not provide arguments—it does not teach Greek or Hebrew, logic or historical fact.[143]

Thus Bayle replies in detail to the objections which might stand in the way of his thesis that there is no correlation between orthodoxy and moral merit, or between heresy and demerit. He does not try to prove that no one's errors are ever blameworthy, merely that there can be no presumption that those who belong to one or other of the Christian sects of his time are to blame for their errors. Some controversies may be simpler, and there may be some opinions which no one can hold without wickedness. Whether the beliefs of one side are more likely to result from some moral fault is a question that needs to be decided (if it needs to be decided) separately for every conflict.

Nicole, in controversy with the Calvinists, had said that choice of religion requires certainty *of evidence* (see above, n. 138). Bayle reasserts the earlier position (cf. Jurieu, in Popkin, *Pyrrhonism*, pp. 166-8). He accepts that faith includes speculative elements and that it is a kind of certainty (*DHC*, art. 'Pyrrho', rem. B, first para., vol. 12, p. 101), but not that it requires indubitable evidence. On this see *NL* 334 b30-55 and *DHC*, art. 'Nicolle', rem. C, pp. 145-6. According to Bayle the dispute over the rule of faith (see above, n. 134) leads to religious scepticism *only* on the assumption that the right use of reason requires that a religious commitment be based on certainty of evidence. He presents the dispute over the rule of faith as an antinomy that can be resolved only by adopting his view that in moral and religious matters conscience (which does not wait for evident certainty) is a sufficient guide; see 438 a47-52 and b44-51, and *S* 499 a28 ('it is necessary to come over to my system').

[142] *S* ch. 24.

[143] See above, n. 79. On the other hand, having true beliefs is no assurance of grace, since it is possible to achieve probable knowledge of religious truths without grace ('historical faith'). See *S* 543 b27-544 a28.

5. THE RIGHT TO PERSECUTE

Originally, in the *General Critique*, Bayle argued that if the true Church has the right or duty to persecute then heretics have it too. The argument of the *Philosophical Commentary*, as we have seen, moves toward the conclusion that—whether or not the true Church has or claims the right to persecute—those who *believe* they have it do have it,[144] and have it even if their belief that they do is a culpable error. But he also gives several arguments to show that indeed it is an error, that in truth no one has it.

5.1. *The reciprocity argument*

The first of these I call the reciprocity argument.[145] Suppose that the saying, 'Compel them to come in',[146] or some other of Jesus's sayings, was meant as a command to persecute. Then the various Christian sects will feel obliged to persecute non-Christians and one another reciprocally, which will lead to civil wars, rebellions,[147] the exclusion or even extermination of Christians by conscientious infidel rulers,[148] and other evils. Persecution essentially[149] requires acts which would be wrong except that they are supposed to have been commanded to be done in the cause of truth,[150] and Bayle argues that once any exception is made to the ordinary laws of morality the moral boundaries are obliterated altogether.[151] The evils of reciprocal

[144] See above, p. 78.

[145] The main passages relating to this argument are: *CG* 87 b28-88 a11, *CG* 94 a22-b2, 375 b66-376 a72, *CP* pt. 1, ch. 10, 425 a65-427 a41, 434 a59-435 b19, *CP* pt. 2, ch. 11, 461 b8-36, *S* chs. 1, 2, 20.

[146] Bossuet, bishop of Meaux, preached a sermon on this text 'according to the principles of St Augustine' in the presence of the king shortly after the revocation of the edict of Nantes. The sermon, not now extant, is said to have made a great impression. See Truchet, vol. 2, p. 46. Perhaps this incident gave Bayle his theme. On the influence of 'the principles of St Augustine' see Orcibal, *Louis XIV*, pp. 114-15; the pamphlet *La Conformité* mentioned there is the source of the passages from Augustine which Bayle discusses in *CP* pt. 3. For passages from Augustine on compulsion see Lecler, vol. 1, pp. 57-9. But some of the most striking of these passages are not among those quoted by Bayle in *CP* pt. 3, or among those quoted by Arnauld in his *Apologie pour les Catholiques, Œuvres*, vol. 14, pp. 717ff.

[147] 376 a23-55, 376 b1-52, 378 a45-b23.

[148] 378 b24-380 b25, *S* 539 a53-b9; *DHC*, art. 'Japon', rem. E, vol. 8, pp. 328-9.

[149] 382 b12-69, 389 b50-64, 390 a67-391 a1.

[150] 375 a57-b21.

[151] 361 a43-65, 375 b22-376 b63, 378 a67-b4, 382 b70-383 a46, 402 a51-b26, 454 a39-b32, 456 b14-458 a59, *S* chs. 26-8.

persecution are thus very great. Jesus (if he is God) must have
foreseen all these evils and would (if he had given such a command) be chiefly responsible for them.[152] Since God's responsibility for such evils is unthinkable, the supposition that
Jesus commanded persecution must be false.

It may be said that only the *true* Church has been commanded to persecute, and that therefore it alone has the right
to do so.[153] But being alone entitled to persecute will not do
the true Church any good. Since every sect regards itself as a
true Church they will all take the command as addressed to
themselves[154] and will in fact persecute, whether they have a
right to or not,[155] and the true Church (and everyone else) will
be deprived of the protection against persecution which the
laws of morality might otherwise have given. Its only defence
will be to claim that it is the true Church and call on its
persecutors to look into its claim, postponing what they regard
as their duty until they have examined all the controversies—
which they will reasonably refuse to do. That the true Church
(whichever that is) is left with such a weak defence is one of
the evils resulting from the alleged command to persecute.[156]
Not only *will* all sects persecute, but (according to the reasoning
presented in the earlier sections of this essay) persecution will
be their duty and therefore their right, both in the sense that
no human being can rightly blame or punish them for it or try

[152] 376 a5–15, 380 b15–25, *S* 512 a24–9, *S* 513 a35–6. Why is Jesus not to blame
for saying something that could be mistaken for a command to persecute, since if he
was God he must have foreseen the mistake? Bayle would presumably answer that God
has in fact clearly forbidden persecution, and the mistake is due to the self-deception of
persecutors, for which God is no more to blame than for the other sins of mankind; see
above, n. 81.

[153] 'We can coerce you because we are in the right, but you cannot coerce us
because you are in the wrong': Bayle calls this the 'perpetual motion machine' because
every time it is knocked down it rises again. See *S* 506 a46–50, *S* 507 b20–9, 359 b32–
35, 389 b13–20, 392 a19–23, 421 b40–57, *S* 539 a19–36. For illustrations see the
passages quoted from Augustine and Bayle's comments in pt. 3, chs. 12, 20, 32, 33.
This 'perpetual motion machine' cannot be dismissed as absurd; it always arises again
because there is something in it. See below, Essay III, sect. 1.

[154] *CG* 87 b63–88 a6, *CG* 94 a33–58, 391 b36–40, 51–8.

[155] 444 a1–b8, 375 b66–376 a8, 462 a41–8, *S* 508 a16–25.

[156] 391 b47–392 a10, 461 b13–28 (Bayle turns against Bossuet his words about the
helplessness of the Church), *S* 506 a20–b19 (it is contrary to all appearances that God
should have left his Church so helpless), *S* 507 b52–66, *S* 538 a11–49 (what would
become of God's wisdom, goodness and justice if he had put the same weapons into the
hands of the Church and its persecutors? See also *S* 507 b35–42). Compare Thucydides
V.xvii.90, III.x.84.

to induce them voluntarily not to do it,[157] and in the sense that even in God's sight they do nothing blameworthy or punishable—they will not be condemned for it even on judgement day.[158]

Since persecution may happen even without a command a prohibition is needed. Persecution should be outlawed by treaty between sects,[159] or it should be regarded as contrary to the law of nations.[160] Since persecution always violates some ordinary rule of morality, it is in fact prohibited by the law of nature—God's law, which the Gospel law confirms.[161] Since God must have foreseen and provided against the evils of reciprocal persecution[162] he must have intended the rules of morality as 'common principles', binding on all sects alike,[163] including the true Church, and never to be suspended without an explicit command.[164]

With this reciprocity argument there are some difficulties. First, it is meant to show that there is no moral right to persecute, yet Bayle must admit that those who believe they have the duty to persecute have a genuine moral right to do so. This is implied by the arguments presented in the earlier parts of

[157] 391 b59-67 (true Christians could not justly blame their persecutors, or expect them to stop). See above, sect. 1.1.

[158] Pt. 2, ch. 10, 443 b36-58, *S* chs. 3-20. In *S* chs. 5-7 (and cf. chs. 9, 22) Bayle examines the responsibility of each functionary, supposing the ruler entrusts the coercion of heretics to officials, as he can rightly do. Bayle argues that provided all act with due care and in good faith neither the ruler nor his judges nor their theological advisers are to blame if the wrong people are coerced. He concludes (*S* 513 a19-34) that if all these functions are carried out by one person that person is not to blame. Only God, if he had commanded persecution, would be responsible for persecution of the truth. (See above, n. 152). Heretic persecutors acting in good faith are blameless, and may even deserve praise (see above, n. 60).

[159] 361 b13-38.

[160] *CG* 88 a8-11 (a sort of Law of Nations should be established among religions, to which the true religion should be subject as much as others), 444 b9-15 (if the true Church had a right to persecute it ought to lie forever dormant).

[161] *CG* 93 b66-94 a3, 376 a57-60, *S* 506 b20-58. In *CP* pt. 1, chs. 1-3, Bayle argues that the interpretation of scripture must be guided by natural law, and that persecution is contrary to natural law and to the spirit of the Gospel.

[162] 435 a33-9, 391 a64-b7.

[163] *NL* 227 a66, 391 b4, 64, 392 a30-7, 397 a70-b7, 421 b14-16, 422 a22-3, 467 a23-4, *S* 507 a29-50. The principles are common in the sense that they are to be accepted by all parties and applied in the same sense, so as to give the same practical conclusions. Appeal to principles which are not common is a *petitio principii*.

[164] Bayle thinks that by explicit command God may on occasion suspend moral rules, except the rule (equivalent to the basic commandment) that one must do what one believes is one's duty; see above, n. 52.

this essay, and Bayle acknowledges the implication in the course of developing the reciprocity argument.[165] In answer to this difficulty he says that the reciprocity argument is a *reductio ad absurdum*,[166] showing that if (P) God had commanded persecution it would follow (Q) that in persecuting the true Church heretics do a morally good act. But this is not the structure of the reciprocity argument, the premisses used in the derivation of Q do not include P, and Q is not, in Bayle's opinion, absurd but true. The absurdity is that God would be responsible for certain evils, and that would follow whether or not the acts of heretic persecutors are sins. That heretics would do a good act in persecuting the truth follows not from the hypothesis that God has commanded persecution, but from the fact that they *believe* he has, together with the principles of Bayle's own ethical theory. The true answer to the difficulty is that in Bayle's ethics an act may be morally good, and a person may have a genuine moral right to do it, and yet it may be in truth a wrong act: and a morally virtuous person will want to do, and will want to lead others to do, what is actually right. So, as Bayle says, even if those who persecute do so sincerely and err involuntarily we ought to correct their error, which is the purpose of the reciprocity argument and of his book.[167] The argument is meant to lead persecutors who may not have been to blame for persecuting to see that persecution is wrong, and they will then deserve blame if they persecute knowing that it is wrong. (The point of course is not to make them blameworthy, but to make them stop: if they are sincere they will stop when they realize that persecution is wrong.) While they think that persecution is right no one can rightly try to persuade them not to persecute[168] except by entering into the ocean of theological controversy to show them that their Church is not the true Church. The reciprocity argument avoids those controversies and instead corrects the error about persecution.

A second difficulty is with the 'common principles' which the argument is supposed to confirm. In arguing that any exception to ordinary moral rules obliterates moral boundaries altogether, Bayle commits a fallacy. He accepts the rightness

[165] 430 b42–8, 60–7; and see above.
[166] *S* 539 b43–65, *S* 540 a7–33.
[167] 430 b69–431 a2, *S* 540 a34–52; and see above, n. 94.
[168] See above, sect. I.I.

of capital punishment and of other acts done by the ruler and his authorised agents for the purpose of repressing crime, acts that would be wrong if done by others or for other purposes; in that sense they are exceptions to the ordinary rules of morality. But to repress crime the ruler may not do just anything: his action is still subject to some moral restrictions. The fallacy is to take the proposition, 'That *certain things* which might be unjust if not done in favour of the true religion (or for some other legitimate purpose) become just if done in its favour', as equivalent to the proposition, 'That *whatever* is done for a legitimate purpose is just'.[169] This leads to an exaggeration of the evils following from the supposed command to persecute. It also forces an 'all or nothing' choice: either the moral boundaries are obliterated altogether, or *nothing* is to be done by rulers which would not be just if done by anyone for any purpose. As far as the reciprocity argument goes various intermediate positions are possible. Consider, for example, the rule *cuius regio eius religio*: this rule would not lead to reciprocal persecution, since it forbids rulers to attempt to impose a religion in another ruler's territory, and authorises none but rulers to enforce any religion. It might be objected that it is pointless to impose different religions in different places, but there may be some secular or even religious point in religious uniformity even if the favoured religion is not enforced as the only one that is true. The *cuius regio* rule leaves open the question what means may be used, but this is true also of the principle that the ruler may repress crime by means not available to everyone for every purpose.[170] The moral code may forbid some actions as wrong intrinsically and never to be done by anyone for any purpose, and these will of course not be available to rulers for repressing crime, or for imposing religion.

5.2. *The argument against forcing consciences*

Bayle has another argument which might be used to reinforce the reciprocity argument by forbidding coercion in religious matters by rulers. The argument runs as follows. Anyone not

[169] See above, n. 151.

[170] Bayle says that since the 'compel them' command is general, if it derogates from any moral rule it derogates from them all; 402 b14-17. But it is 'general' in the sense of indefinite or vague, not specifying the means to be used. It does not specify whether and how other rules of morality are affected.

an atheist must regard conscience as the voice of God; to act against one's conscience, therefore, implies hatred of or contempt for God, and to act thus is evil intrinsically, not justifiable under any circumstances. Neither of the two possible sources of the ruler's authority, God and the people, can be supposed to have authorised the ruler to try to make people do an intrinsically evil act: not God, because that would mean that God might confer a power of trying to make someone act in contempt of himself; not the people, because the parties to the social contract cannot be supposed to have given anyone power to make them do anything that implies contempt of God. The ruler therefore can have no right to try to force anyone to act against conscience.[171]

The difficulty with this argument is that conscience cannot literally be forced, it can only be tempted. The body can be forced; but without consent, which on Bayle's account is an interior act of will, there is no action attributable to the person forced; and the will cannot be forced to consent.[172] Force or threat of force to the body may constitute temptation, but it might be argued that those who consent are themselves responsible for what they consent to against conscience. Bayle denounces the tempter as a sharer in the guilt of the hypocrisy and acts against conscience which temptations cause.[173] But some distinctions need to be drawn. Temptation may be directly intended or incidental; it may be strong, or so weak that a reasonably conscientious person would successfully resist it; it may be temptation to do what both parties regard as wrong, or temptation (if that is the right word) to do what the tempter regards as right. A person who directly intends to subject another to strong temptation to do what both regard as wrong clearly does something wrong. But it is impossible to make laws, or even simply to live, without incidentally exposing others to at least weak temptation to do what they may regard as

---

[171] 384 b6–385 a18. If a community does provide for the enforcement of religion it is on the rash assumption that they will never change their minds. Such provisions are *ultra vires*: 384 b45–66.

[172] 496 a12–41. That the will cannot literally be forced was a Stoic commonplace. See Augustine, *De civitate dei*, V.10, and cf. I.18, on rape. See below, Appendix.

[173] 382 b39–48 (that of tempter is one of the Devil's most odious qualities), 362 b63–7, 406 a25–62, 406 b6–9, 55–63, 409 a61–b15 (to offer heretics a pardon is worse than remorseless killing, because it tempts to religious hypocrisy (the worst sin—cf. 379 b9–11)), 425 b67–71.

wrong.[174] I believe there is a duty not to tempt people even incidentally, even to actions which they are mistaken in regarding as wrong; but this is merely a *prima facie* duty.[175] Bayle ought to agree, since he holds (as we will see) that the ruler may enforce certain kinds of laws even against those who believe they have a duty to violate them. So it would seem that, in at least some cases, if the ruler regards the commanded act as right he may rightly exact it even from those who regard it as wrong, if he has a weighty enough reason. What Bayle needs to show is that the reasons in favour of religious uniformity can never be weighty enough.

6. THE RULER MUST PREVENT PERSECUTION

In Bayle's time there were various theories about the functions of the secular ruler. Some held simply that the ruler should do as much good, of whatever sort, as he can by any available morally permissible means.[176] Others imposed restrictions on ends or means or both. According to some the ruler's proper means is force: only the ruler (or his agents) may use force, and whatever he does (at least as ruler) is done by that means.[177] According to some the only legitimate end of the ruler's acts as ruler is to enforce God's law; or (since only God can 'search hearts' and judge inner acts) to enforce outward conformity

---

[174] During the eighteenth century English dissenters and Whigs stretched the terms 'persecution' and 'punishment' and 'liberty of conscience' until even quite incidental temptation, anything that would make membership of one sect more or less advantageous than membership of another, could be represented as a violation of liberty of conscience. The interpretation of the First Amendment to the U.S. Constitution has been influenced by similar ideas.

[175] This is the view of Sidgwick, p. 208, and Kant, *Virtue*, pp. 52–3.

[176] 'Whatsoever a company of people gathered together may judge tending to the public good ... that they have liberty to do, so long as it is not sinful, and they may put this into the ministerial power, to attend to it ... [including] what may be done in a lawful way for the preserving of their religion as well as for the feeding of their bodies' (Philip Nye, quoted in Woodhouse, pp. 159–60). Compare the antagonist whom Locke quotes in his *Second Letter*, p. 11.

[177] Locke, for example, held that only the magistrate and his agents may use force, and that whatever the magistrate does as magistrate is done by coercive means. See *Toleration*, pp. 11–12, 16, 17, 23. This view was common among Dutch Protestants in the seventeenth century; see Nobbs, pp. 256–7.

with it;[178] or to enforce the 'second table' of the ten commandments, that is, those provisions of God's law which regulate human intercourse in this world. Others held that the ruler's function is to enforce 'political laws' designed to secure peace (and perhaps prosperity) in this world, laws which by coincidence may overlap with God's law, but not to enforce them as being divinely ordained.[179] Some of these options may be combined; thus Locke and others held that the magistrate is restricted to the use of coercive means for 'political' ends.

6.1. *The simple argument*

Mostly, Bayle's theory is like Locke's: the ruler has no concern with conscience or religion or morality as such, but is to use coercive means to enforce 'political laws' designed to protect the this-worldly peace and security of society and its members, without concern for conscience.[180] Thus he says that in punishing the murderer whose conscience tells him to kill, the ruler is not obliged to have any regard to conscience; if someone believes he ought to commit murder then morally he is obliged to do so, but the ruler can punish him without taking any account of his moral obligation.[181] Similarly the ruler can

[178] 'The civil authority is the keeper of the whole law where outward discipline is concerned. Just as it prohibits and punishes by force murder, theft, and similar offences against the second table of the Ten Commandments, so it must, all the more, prohibit and punish outward offences against the first table, that is, the worship of idols, blasphemous doctrine, perjury, and open profanation of divinely instituted ceremonies' (Melanchthon, quoted in Lecler, vol. 1, p. 246; and see pp. 156-7, 245-8). Compare Calvin, pp. 847, 1495.

[179] Locke: 'The law maker hath nothing to do with moral virtues and vices, nor ought to enjoin the duties of the second table any otherwise than barely as they are subservient to the good and preservation of mankind under government. For, could public societies well subsist, or men enjoy peace or safety, without the enforcing of those duties ... the law-maker ought ... leave the practice of these entirely to the discretion and consciences of his people' (Bourne, vol. 1, pp. 181-2; cf. *Toleration*, pp. 36-7, 41-3, 10-13). Cf. Walaeus in Nobbs, p. 12. This view goes back to Marsilius of Padua.

[180] 408 b41-53 (punishable as felony and sedition, not as a sin against moral and metaphysical obligation; Gospel precepts are not political laws except those without which human society could not subsist), 412 a13-43, 416 b61-417 a3, 418 a18-24, *S* 559 b66-560 a7.

[181] 408 b54-63 (the sovereign does not lose the power to punish murder even if it is done in obedience to conscience), 431 a8-17 (the ruler need consider conscience only when public peace is not at stake), 433 b12-18, *NL* 220 b31-38 (the aim of human justice is the welfare of society, and it does not always examine whether those punished deserve it). Compare Locke: 'such a private person is to abstain from the actions that

coerce without hesitation any religious innovator whose doctrines are destructive of human society.[182] On this theory the
argument to show that the ruler must repress persecution
is simple: persecution is destructive of peace and security, a
violation of the laws which the ruler must enforce without regard to what people believe in conscience they ought to do.[183]
Political laws thus include the moral rules which the reciprocity
argument reaffirms and shows to be 'common' principles ruling
out persecution even by the true Church. In enforcing political
laws the ruler therefore represses persecution. That the true
Church has no special right to persecute, and in general no
rights that error does not have, means that the magistrate must
prevent persecution even by the Church he regards as true.

However Bayle says various things that are inconsistent with
this simple theory. For example, he says that the ruler can act
as 'nursing father' to what he regards as the true religion—
sponsor reformation, act against scandals in clerical life, endow
orthodox colleges, supply money and prestige[184]—as long as
he does not impose religious unity by force. In justifying the
enforcement of political but not religious laws Bayle argues
that people's consciences generally support the former but not
necessarily the latter,[185] a consideration that would have been
irrelevant if conscience were for the ruler simply of no account.
He says also that the ruler may punish people for acting against
their consciences, even if their conscience is in error, and even
if they act in religious matters and without violation of political
law, provided he can be sure they do act against conscience.[186]

he judges unlawful; and he is to undergo the punishment, which is not unlawful for
him to bear [whether it is deserved or not]; the private judgement of any person
concerning a law enacted in political matters, for the public good, does not take away
the obligation of that law, nor deserve a dispensation' (*Toleration*, p. 43). See also
Bourne, vol. 1, pp. 178–9.

[182] 412 a19–28 (a sect which breaks the bonds of society ought to be driven away),
431 b43–52 (in such cases the sovereign does not consider the claims of conscience),
416 a43–6.

[183] 378 b24–47, 379 b42–6.

[184] 416 a67-b34, 417 b4-11, *S* 560 b23–54. Cf. Acronius and Walaeus in Nobbs,
p. 20.

[185] 468 a43–64 (this is the great and capital reason which puts a difference between
civil and religious matters, with respect to the sovereign's jurisdiction), 417 a4-18, 432
a26–36. Bayle seems to admit that there is some force in the objection that the judges
should not punish those who 'only do their duty' by obeying their consciences; cf. 432
a20–3.

[186] 428 b37–66, 429 b25–9, 472 b61-493 a5 ('493' is a misprint), 379 a55–60, b7–

His various remarks could mostly be harmonised if we attribute to him (as something he held in the back of his mind, not clearly) a more complex theory along the following lines: (1) The ruler is to do as much good of whatever sort as he can by any morally legitimate means. (2) The ruler cannot generally judge people's motives with much assurance.[187] (3) People's consciences generally sanction the rules needed to secure this-worldly peace, but (4) otherwise disagree, especially about religion. (5) Moral goods and evils greatly exceed other goods and evils, but (6) not so as to rule out sometimes doing or risking some moral evil for the probability of avoiding much non-moral evil.[188] (7) The greatest (or only) moral evil is to decide to act against one's conscience. From these premisses follow: (8) the ruler should do what can be done without tempting consciences to foster what he regards as the true religion; and (9) he should punish acts of impiety done against conscience, in the few cases (if there are any) in which he can be sure they are such, but (10) otherwise he should inflict punishment only to enforce political laws. Since (10) rests on (2) and (3), which are propositions of contingent fact, it is merely a rule of thumb; the 'simple theory' is (10) treated as an independent principle. Notice that on this more complex theory the overlap of political laws with part of God's law need not be mere coincidence, and there is no reason why the ruler should not be said to be enforcing God's law as such in so far as it secures peace in this world (the 'second table' of the decalogue). Serving God is one of the sorts of good things the ruler may rightly do.

6.2. *The right of the conscientious persecutor*

On this more elaborate theory the argument that the ruler must prevent persecution cannot be simple, since there are people who believe they are obliged to persecute, and on this theory their consciences cannot be simply disregarded. If they

12, 409 a10–19.

[187] God alone is the searcher of hearts: 395 b46–7, *S* 514 a54–65, *S* 517 b9–33 (this is why ignorance of law does not excuse at human tribunals, but does at God's). This reason was commonly given for restricting the ruler to outward matters. See Luther, *Secular Authority*, p. 253; Hobbes, pp. 501, 576; Grotius, II.iv.3, vol. 2, p. 221; Nobbs, pp. 78–9. See above, n. 71.

[188] See above, n. 19. This assumes that moral evil does not, after all, always outrank physical evil; see above, n. 49.

could be physically restrained there would be no violation of their consciences, but in practice they must often be restrained by threat. In repressing persecution the ruler may therefore be tempting the consciences of many who believe they have a religious duty to persecute.[189] Bayle does not seem to see any problem. He does not give any argument from the premisses of the more elaborate theory to the conclusion that the ruler must prevent persecution—in arguing that point he writes as if he held simply that the ruler must preserve peace without concern for conscience. If he had taken account of effects on conscience he might have argued that persecution tempts more consciences than the repression of persecution does (which will not always be true). Or he might have argued that incidental temptation is not as bad as direct and intentional temptation, and that tempting persecutors is only a side-effect of the ruler's attempt to preserve peace and protect conscience from direct violation, whereas the persecutor's intention is precisely to induce people to change religion against their consciences. It would follow that the ruler ought to take precautions—even if that may, as a side-effect, tempt some persecutors voluntarily not to do what they think they ought to do—so that no one can subject others to direct temptation to act against their consciences. But this is an argument Bayle does not use.

6.3. *Precautions*

He does say, however, that the ruler should control persecution as far as possible by means which do not tempt the consciences of those who think they ought to persecute.[190] This is in effect his reply to the common question whether we must tolerate the intolerant: we cannot persecute them, but we must prevent them from persecuting others, and we can take precautions against them.[191] He agreed with many of his Protestant con temporaries that toleration should not extend to atheists or

---

[189] 426 b15-59, 430 b60-7.

[190] See above, sect. 5.2.

[191] 411 b54-5, 412 b5-6, 413 b2-13, *S* 560 a50-2. Bayle calls this policy 'non-toleration'. This does not mean persecution. It is what Paley later called 'partial toleration', which he explained as unmolested profession and exercise of religion but with exclusion from positions of trust in the State; see Henriques, pp. 69-70.

Catholics, as sects dangerous to society.[192] The argument against forcing consciences does not apply to atheists because they do not regard conscience as the voice of God,[193] and they are believed[194] to attack the foundations of peace in this world, which the ruler must defend. As for Catholics, since they do regard conscience as the voice of God their consciences are not to be forced or tempted. But they will persecute others if they can,[195] so precautions must be taken against them.[196] The ruler must repress persecution and need not wait until acts of persecution are actually taking place. He must make sure that Catholics will never get the power to persecute, acting against them not as holding a false religion but as endangering public security.[197] He may prevent seditious preaching, exclude Catholics from public office, and even—if milder measures are not enough—send them into exile (allowing them to take their possessions).[198] But this non-toleration must not become persecution: there must be no attacks on their persons or properties, they must be allowed to practise their religion at least in private and to bring up their children as Catholics, and they must not be forced to attend religious exercises against their consciences.[199] Precautions must as far as possible be managed so as not to tempt their consciences; for example, disqualification from office must apply for life even to those who convert, and to their older children.[200] If we do not take incidental temptation so seriously this may sound like disguised persecution, but Bayle's intention is to protect integrity of conscience.

[192] Locke, *Toleration*, pp. 45–7; Bayle, *DHC*, art. 'Milton', rem. O, vol. 10, pp. 459–60.

[193] 431 a34–42. Some held that atheists have no conscience. Bayle does not seem to mean this (422 b56 acknowledges that atheists may have consciences), but rather that an atheist cannot claim that his conscience represents any authority greater than that of human laws; cf. 431 a46–7.

[194] 431 a24–30. Bayle is not being altogether frank: he did not himself believe that atheism undermines the foundations of society. See *PD*, pp. 75–122, and *CPD*, pp. 351–71.

[195] 358 a52–61.

[196] 361 a14–43, 412 b53–413 a2.

[197] 361 a10–16 (the false religion of the papists, considered simply as false, is not a just reason for laws against them), 412 a47–9, 412 b43–8.

[198] 361 a66–b12, 385 a25–37, *S* 560 a21–7. A Catholic ruler may take similar precautions against Protestants; cf. *Avis*, *OD*, vol. 2, pp. 612ff.

[199] 359 a9–13 (no reprisals), 412 b14–26, 414 a47–58 (public display not essential to religious liberty).

[200] 361 a3–8, 412 b26–37.

7. SCEPTICISM AND TOLERATION

In his excellent book on Bayle, Walter Rex suggests that in the end Bayle's scepticism destroys his case for toleration. He says that to oppose acts of persecution Bayle at first appealed to the 'natural light' as showing with 'absolute certainty that such acts were contrary to God's moral law'. But in the end 'the criterium of natural light has virtually disappeared and the fallible but absolute judgment of conscience has been put in its place'. Against the persecutor's claim that his conscience obliges him to persecute, 'Bayle is reduced to the mere assertion that persecution *is* a crime, with very little logic to substantiate it'. Although he keeps saying that we must examine our beliefs, 'Bayle's statement that there is no way to be certain of having found the truth would appear ... to undermine completely the doctrine of the necessity of examination'; 'There seems to be nothing left but ruins. One wonders if even the idea of tolerance remains'.[201]

I do not share this unfavourable assessment. To begin with the last point: the impossibility of being certain does not mean that examination is unnecessary. We may be wrong about some things, and examination may reveal some of our mistakes (though possibly we sometimes change our minds when we should not).[202] And the impossibility of arriving at certainty does not make examination futile. It is reasonable to examine as long as it seems possible that examination may significantly improve our chances of believing what is actually true, even if we will never be sure it is true. Perhaps the natural light is dim but still a light. Bayle's fallibilism therefore does not imply the rejection of examination.

And fallibilism is not scepticism.[203] The ancient sceptics practised suspense of judgement, affirming nothing, since nothing is certain (or even, as it seemed to the Pyrrhonists, more probable than its contrary).[204] Bayle always rejected scepticism, not only in religion but generally, and I think we should take him at his word.[205] In religion it seemed to him essential to reject

[201] Rex, *Bayle*, pp. 181–5.

[202] See 377 a38–40 (everyone on growing older sees, 'or believes he sees', the falsity of many things he had believed).

[203] See above, Introduction.

[204] See Cicero, *Academica*, II.xx.66–7.

[205] See *EMT*, 42 a61–b39.

scepticism because a Christian must not only act on but also affirm the truths of faith, including speculative dogmas, and affirm them as being certain[206] even in the face of insoluble objections from reason.[207] In other practical matters and in speculative philosophy[208] he rejects scepticism also, though outside religion he seems to regard it as a rather harmless error.[209] Having accepted that in religion the truths of faith must be affirmed without conclusive evidence, perhaps he saw no reason to withhold affirmation from probabilities in other matters. The distinction between certainty and probability is no longer important; certainty and 'evidence' can be treated as the higher degrees of probability.[210] At all events, while agreeing with the sceptics that all our judgements are fallible, he does not agree with them that wisdom requires that we affirm nothing that may turn out to be false. In all fields we should not only act on but also affirm (though perhaps not as certain, except for the articles of faith) whatever, after due inquiry, seems true.[211]

Since in his later writings he still calls the maxims of reason 'evident' even while emphasising that they conflict with one

[206] Religion requires not the certainty of evidence, but an absoluteness of commitment going beyond evidence. See above, n. 141. This is not necessarily fideism, as I understand that term. The fideist rejects reason in matters of religion because it conflicts with faith, or at least is ready to reject it if it does. Bayle thought that faith and reason are at many points irreconcilable, and that in those cases faith must be preferred; still, he thought that reason approves the commitment of faith (see RQP, 767 a38–43, 770 a26–42), and that faith does not demand that reason be rejected altogether (EMT, 44 b20–49, 45 a7–35, 48 b22–49). It is not clear that he was ready to abandon reason if he had come to think that a choice had to be made. On the other hand, I do not think that he eventually abandoned faith and that his later expressions of adherence to Christianity are insincere. I believe myself that the conflicts between faith and reason which Bayle presents are so severe that a choice must be made and that one must choose reason, but I do not think he thought that the conflict forced a choice.

[207] *RQP* 770 b51–771 a48, *EMT* 42 a40–61. The point of emphasising these conflicts is, I believe, to highlight the nature of faith and the kind of commitment it demands and to produce docility, not to 'ruin' reason or insinuate scepticism. Note that it is not Bayle himself who says he erects faith on the ruins of reason: *RQP* 836 b13, 41–57.

[208] See *EMT* 16 b11–21 (in philosophy we may be unable to decide, or we may declare for the side on which there is the greater weight of reasons).

[209] See *DHC*, art. 'Pyrrho', rem. B, vol. 12, p. 101.

[210] See *EMT* 16 b2–5 on degrees of evidence.

[211] The best analyses known to me of Bayle's position on these topics are Brush, pp. 299–305, 315–320 and James, 'Bayle on Belief', pp. 395–404. Brush calls Bayle a sceptic, but seems to use the term more broadly than I do. To be generally uncertain, and to say that any judgement may be mistaken, is not scepticism in the classical sense unless intended to lead to suspense of judgement. I do not agree with Penelhum that Bayle is a 'conformist' (in his special sense) whose faith is an undogmatic piety (pp. 25–6); see above, n. 141.

another[212] and with truths of faith, what Bayle says in the first chapter of the *Philosophical Commentary* perhaps should not be taken to mean that the natural light shows anything with 'absolute certainty'. In his later writings he says that if scripture clearly teaches something contrary to some apparently evident maxim of reason, then we must believe scripture and reject the maxim as false, at least in that application.[213] This position would allow a possible interpretation of scripture to be rejected because it is not a *clear* scripture teaching and conflicts with one of the maxims of reason, especially one of the more evident ones; it would not allow the simple argument that scripture cannot mean what it seems to mean (perhaps clearly) because that would contradict some (perhaps less evident) maxim of reason.[214] The argument of the early sections of the *Philosophical Commentary* is not really inconsistent with this later position. Perhaps he had already worked it out[215] but did not think it necessary to explain more of it than the argument required, or perhaps he worked out the rest later in thinking about the problem of the origin of evil. At any rate, persecution is not a clear teaching of scripture[216] and the moral principles it violates are among the most evident of the maxims of reason. In the earlier sections of the book he does seem to say that there are infallible maxims of morality, mathematics and metaphysics.[217] Perhaps he says this concessively, since his readers probably believed it and their belief did not have to be challenged to argue the points he wanted to make; or perhaps at that time he believed it himself.[218] In any case it is not an essential

[212] *RQP* 771 a26–38. Perhaps they only seem to conflict: *EMT* 47 b47–48 a4.

[213] *RQP* 763 a34–9, 770 a52–b8.

[214] *RQP* 765 b6–22, 767 a18–31. See above, Essay I, n. 107.

[215] Notice in *CP* pt. 1, ch. 1 the rejection of the position of the Socinians (p. 367, third para.), and the acknowledgement (368 b47–8) that the principle that interpretation of scripture is to be guided by the natural light may require qualification (though not with respect to moral principles—this is perhaps a point on which Bayle changed his mind). He gives examples of the more evident rational principles with which scripture interpretation must not conflict (e.g. p. 367, third para.), as if ready to concede that there may be others less evident which revelation may set aside. Part of his later position on the relation of faith and reason is outlined in pt. 1, ch. 1, at 370 a1–18.

[216] The 'compel them' text occurs in a parable, and this interpretation is against the general spirit of the gospel; see *CP* pt. 1, ch. 3.

[217] See above, nn. 87, 88.

[218] Already in pt. 2 (which I suppose was written not long after pt. 1, ch. 1) he remarks on the conflict of maxims of reason with faith and with one another. See 407

premiss of his argument. He could have argued that the natural light, though fallible, is still a light, and the only light we have when scripture is unclear; and that therefore the interpretation of an unclear scripture text must not conflict with the more evident maxims of morality even if some of them may actually be false. It seems to me, then, that the development of Bayle's thought did not lead, or need not have led, to a repudiation of the argument of the early sections of the book.

'The fallible but absolute judgment of conscience' does not really take the place of the natural light; the two are complementary. The natural light reveals general principles, conscience judges particular cases.[219] Even if the natural light were infallible we would still have to make judgements of conscience applying the general maxims of natural law to particular cases, and such judgements have always been regarded as fallible.[220] According to Bayle conscience is the touchstone of 'truth for me' in practical matters, but this does not mean that I cannot be wrong about my duty. He says that in doing what I mistakenly think is right I may do a good act, but this does not mean that evil may be good or that wrong may be right: it means that in some cases (for example when I do something because I think it is my duty, and in the face of difficulties) the act may deserve praise even though it is in fact contrary to some secondary principle of the moral law.[221] So whether the natural light is infallible or not, the judgement of conscience may be mistaken, and yet 'absolute' in the sense that one must act on it; and the act may be good though wrong.

As for the suggestion that his growing scepticism reduces him in the end to the bare assertion that persecution is a crime, it must be said that he has an argument, in fact a number of arguments, to which the truth or falsity of fallibilism can make no difference. Unless people's consciences are often mistaken there will of course be no serious religious conflict, and there would be no practical point to arguments for toleration. But

a26–30, 415 a41-b4. And see in the *Supplément*, published within two years, *S* 522 b47–523 a8, *S* 546 a55-b64.

[219] See above, n. 88.

[220] See e.g. Thomas Aquinas, *De veritate*, q.16 a.2.

[221] For criticism of positions like Bayle's see Cohen, Goldstick, Govier, 'Conscientiousness', Kordig and Wilcox. It seems to me that Bayle's position escapes these criticisms because of the distinctions between 'good' and 'right' and between the basic commandment and the secondary duties. See above, sect. 3.

how fallible we are is not a question that affects the validity of any of Bayle's arguments. In my estimation Bayle comes reasonably close to proving his main thesis, that persecution is morally wrong. And he recognizes that this thesis and the propositions that those who mistakenly think they ought to persecute have a moral right to try to do so and that they should nevertheless be forcibly stopped are, all three of them, consistent with one another. His position on the rights of conscience is this: those who do what is actually wrong in obedience to conscience do not deserve blame or punishment and should not be tempted *voluntarily* not to do what they mistakenly think they ought to do, but their mistake should be combated by argument, and the act should be forcibly prevented if it threatens the rights of others. They have a moral right to try to do the wrong act, their effort to do it against opposition is praiseworthy, but others may have a moral duty to prevent it even while respecting their conscientiousness.

ESSAY III

Reciprocity Arguments for Toleration

INTRODUCTION

From now on I intend to put aside history and exegesis of texts to take up as philosophical questions some matters which arise from Bayle's argument for toleration. In fact I believe that the main conclusions I argue for in the remaining essays are substantially Bayle's, but I am not concerned to show that they are, and have not adopted them out of any loyalty to him. This third essay is an analysis of the reciprocity argument as a type. I have already discussed Bayle's version, but other versions are possible, and it seems worthwhile to analyse their common structure and consider their limitations. The fourth essay is a discussion of the ethics of belief and inquiry. This topic was touched on in connection with Fr Terrill's views on invincible ignorance (see above, Essay I, sect. 3), and again in connection with Bayle's views on culpable error, prepossession, opinionatedness and temerity (see above, Essay II, sect. 4.2). In the *Philosophical Commentary* see *Supplement*, ch. 17, 'What judgement should be made of those who will not enter into disputes'. But since Bayle's time a good deal has been written on the subject, and a discussion independent of his seems worthwhile. I will therefore put the texts aside and enter upon a consideration of some of the questions they have raised.

Toleration and the open society

Since Bayle's time the idea of religious toleration has been developed and extended into an idea of an open or liberal society, and for the various elements of that idea many arguments have been put forward. Often these arguments do not seem to match the precise conclusions they are meant to establish. It is not enough, for example, to show that a general policy of not punishing people for what they believe will, on balance, generally have good effects. It is necessary to show that not punishing people for what they believe should be regarded as a matter of moral principle, to be followed even in the odd cases when not punishing might on balance have bad effects.[1] Few of the common arguments are even attempts to show that toleration should be regarded as a matter of moral principle.

Is that how toleration should be regarded? Consider the attitude of those who practised or defended what we now regard as religious persecution against the Protestants in seventeenth-century France. Most of them, Arnauld for example, were humane men who believed that conversion ought to result from persuasion, and that mildness is generally more persuasive; still, they were prepared to use coercion, together with persuasion, when they thought that that would be an effective combination; this had also been St Augustine's attitude.[2] This involves occasional toleration, even toleration as a (temporarily) settled policy (for example, during the time when the Edict of Nantes was substantially observed); error is tolerated while mild methods are tried, but coercive methods are kept in reserve. This is not the toleration that Bayle, Locke, Taylor and their successors contended for. What they wanted was a principled abstention from certain methods even when they might work. We may think that these methods never work, or at least are never good on balance. Then toleration means a commitment to principles ruling out such methods even in cases (if there were any) in which they might work, or otherwise be good on balance.

Principles are of different kinds. Some purport to be absolute, exceptionless and conclusive. Such principles, if there are any,

---

[1] Cf. Mill on the 'transcendant expediency' of regarding veracity as a matter of principle, *Utilitarianism*, ch. 2 (p. 223).

[2] In a letter Arnauld remarks that if even half of what is reported about the coercion of the Huguenots is true it is deplorable, and likely to make the Catholic religion odious. But what he deplores is that coercion is being used without adequate provision for instruction. See *Œuvres*, vol. 2, p. 336 (misprint for p. 136). In his *Apology for the Catholics* he adopts St Augustine's opinion that coercion may be justified if it makes people willing to listen and examine (*Œuvres*, vol. 14, pp. 717ff.). Cf. Lecler, vol. 1, pp. 56–7.

are applied by simple deductive argument: 'All acts of such-and-such sort are wrong and not to be done; this act I am contemplating would be of that sort; therefore it is not to be done.' Others are *prima facie* principles.[3] Such a principle constitutes a *prima facie* case for or against some action, but it may in the end be outweighed or overridden by some reason on the other side. *Prima facie* principles are applied by 'deliberation', that is, by 'weighing' in the mind reasons on both sides of the question until the balance seems to come down on one side, until we come to feel convinced that the thing is or is not to be done. Not only moral questions but practical questions of all sorts, for example choice of a house or job, are decided by weighing up pros and cons. There may be 'principles of deliberation' which specify what sorts of considerations may or may not be weighed on the other side. The *prima facie* principle puts a more or less weighty consideration onto one side of the balance, the 'deliberative principles' (if any apply) restrict what can be put onto the other side, and the decision is that 'on balance' this or that is the right or best thing to do.[4]

If something is 'a matter of principle' (and this phrase may represent some narrowing of the notion of a moral principle) then there may be cases in which what it requires is to be done even though, if it had not been a matter of principle, something else would on balance have been better. Consider the principle that promises are to be kept. Suppose I promise you something you want me to promise, in the hope that at some future date you will do something for me. If when the time comes to perform what I promised you have lost the power to be useful to me, then the hope that induced me to make the promise is no

---

[3] Cf. Ross, pp. 19ff. There are also duties of 'broad' or 'imperfect' obligation (e.g. the duty to be generous), which do not require any particular act at any particular time, but require us to do 'a certain amount' over time. Cf. Mill, *Utilitarianism*, ch. 5 (p. 247), and Kant, *Virtue*, pp. 37–8, 48–9. On a particular occasion one may decide that one ought to do something generous, but this 'ought' does not signify strict duty.

[4] The 'weight' due to a consideration of a certain general kind seems to be different in different cases; it is the consideration *as realised in this case* which has to be weighed. This is why intuitive 'weighing' cannot be replaced by deductive application of rules. See Ross, pp. 41–2, and Mill, *Utilitarianism*, p. 259 ('though particular cases may occur in which some other social duty is so important as to overrule any one of the general maxims of justice'). It would seem that considerations of moral duty do not in every case outweigh considerations of other kinds; sometimes a less serious moral obligation may be set aside for the sake of some legitimate but not obligatory purpose. See Foot, pp. 181ff.

reason for performing it. But the fact that I promised is itself a reason. Suppose that in general fidelity to promises is necessary to trust among human beings, and suppose this is a strong enough reason for making it a matter of principle that promises are to be kept. In some cases it may make no difference to trust if I break a promise (suppose the person to whom I made it is dead, and no one else knows of the promise); still, the fact that fidelity is a matter of principle is a reason for keeping a promise even in such cases. The reasons which led me to adopt the principle, or to make the promise, may not be operative, and therefore do not in that case help to outweigh the reasons for not keeping it; but the fact that this is a matter of principle is itself a weighty reason for keeping the promise. Similarly, with other moral principles, there may be cases in which, if no principle had been involved, the balance would have come down on the other side. Arguments for rules which are supposed to be moral principles, such as the principles of toleration, must therefore show not merely that in most cases observance of the rules is the best means of furthering legitimate purposes, but that even in cases (at least, in some cases) in which that is not so the rules ought to be observed. Under some circumstances a reciprocity argument can lead to such a conclusion.

The term 'toleration' has since Bayle's time fallen into disfavour, but for no good reason. One complaint is that to make toleration a virtue suggests that all sorts of evils should be tolerated.[5] But in this context the word means commitment to a certain set of principles: 'toleration' is refraining from certain sorts of actions against certain kinds of things, the actions and things being specified by the principles.[6] Other kinds of action, or actions against other things, are not restricted. For example, one might *argue* as strongly as possible against what one regarded as religious error, one might use physical force to prevent religious fanatics from some dangerous action, and so on. Another objection is that talk of toleration implies disparagement of, and condescension toward, what one tolerates, as being an evil which it would be desirable to eliminate.[7] But

---

[5] See Marcuse, p. 83.

[6] Cf. Benn, 'Privacy', pp. 1–3, on privacy as a 'norm-invoking' concept.

[7] Kant praises the prince who leaves people free to use their own reason in matters of conscience but 'declines to accept the presumptuous title of *tolerant*' (*Enlightenment*, p.58). Tom Paine (p. 107) says that toleration is a despotism which assumes to itself

in the present context, as a term for commitment to certain principles, there is no implication that the thing is evil, but merely that some people might think so. Even in other contexts the word does not always imply disapproval of what is to be tolerated. It is true that if I say, in the first person, that I tolerate something then that implies that I regard it as an evil. But if I call on others to 'tolerate' something there is no implication that I myself regard it as an evil. When there is a tacit reference to principles, even first-person statements do not imply that the thing to be tolerated is evil or that there has ever been any sort of right to repress it. If I say I regard religious toleration (for example) as a matter of principle, that means that even if I thought that some religion were objectionable I would not act against it in certain ways. That I do actually regard some religion as objectionable is not implied.

* * *

Bayle's reciprocity argument for religious toleration turns on the frightful results of wars of religion. Catholics, Lutherans and Calvinists each claim to be Jesus's only true followers and take his words 'Compel them to come in' as a command to persecute the others. If Jesus was divine he must have foreseen the divisions of Christianity, and if nevertheless he commanded his followers to persecute then he is responsible for the resulting shambles. He is responsible even if he meant only his *true* followers to persecute, because he must have foreseen that those who mistakenly think they are his followers would take the command as addressed to themselves. But it is unthinkable that Jesus should be responsible for the horrors of the wars of religion. The words 'Compel them to come in' must therefore not have been meant as a command to persecute. In fact God's law must prohibit persecution, since even without a command to persecute persecution may occur, and God must have foreseen this possibility and provided against it. The prohibition must extend even to those whose doctrines are right: otherwise it would not prevent wars of religion, since it must be applied by fallible beings who cannot distinguish being right from only thinking they are right. The rule against persecution is thus a 'common principle' of morality, in the sense that it applies alike the right of granting liberty of conscience.

to all sects, without distinguishing those who are right from those who are wrong. This common principle makes persecution wrong intrinsically, so that it cannot be justified by its usefulness for the true religion.[8]

Bayle's argument is for religious toleration, and it uses religious premises (for example, that God sees the future); secular versions can be constructed for other conclusions, for example to show that rival political movements should adopt the principles of political toleration, the open society or democracy, or that nations should adopt laws of war or make treaties of disarmament, or that employers and unions should accept an arbitration system. I will use 'sect'[9] for the parties to whom the argument is addressed, and 'persecution' for the sort of behaviour it is directed against (though sometimes another term might be more appropriate—for example 'atrocity', if the argument is meant to establish laws of war, or 'ruthlessness', 'confrontation', 'rough play', etc.). Nothing is called persecution except by those who are against it; people do not claim for themselves 'a right to persecute', though for brevity I will use this phrase (meaning 'the right to engage in what *you* may call "persecution"'). In so far as 'persecution' has a definite meaning it seems to be given by rules arrived at by tacit use of the reciprocity argument (see section 5 below): 'persecution' is what these rules forbid. By 'persecution' I will therefore mean whatever a good reciprocity argument can be directed against, the content of the term being provided by constructing the argument.

There is not just one 'reciprocity argument'. Each rule, disposition or institution to be erected against a certain kind of behaviour needs a particular argument directed to a particular party. I am concerned with what such arguments have in common, with this argument as a type. The idea of reciprocity may come in twice: the argument may begin from what happens (or will happen)[10] when certain actions used by one sect to further its purposes are reciprocated by its rivals; and the conclusion argued for is that such actions should be renounced

---

[8] See above, Essay II, sect. 5.1.

[9] In using 'sect' I do not intend any contrast with 'church'.

[10] The reciprocity argument is not concerned with hypothetical universalisation ('What if everyone did this?'), but with the likely consequences of one's own actions under existing circumstances.

on condition (or in the hope) that the others will reciprocate by renouncing them also.[11] Thus Bayle begins with the evils which result when each of several rival sects takes the saying 'Compel them to come in' as a command to persecute the others; and his conclusion is that the sects should enter into a treaty to outlaw persecution, or that they should leave the right to coerce permanently in abeyance, or acknowledge that there never was such a right.[12]

The argument starts from a consideration of consequences—the bad consequences of persecution, the likely good consequences of renouncing the right to persecute. But it is not a consequentialist argument; that is, it does not presuppose that the goodness or badness of an action always consists entirely in the goodness or badness of its consequences. And it is not merely an appeal to self-interest; the consequences to be considered may include effects on the progress of the true religion, and may not include effects on the worldly interests of true believers or potential converts—what consequences are allowed to count depends on the moral code of those called on to make the calculation. The conclusion may be that some legal or other institutional barrier should be erected; or it may be that someone should adopt rules or cultivate some disposition of character to exclude some type of action as a matter of moral principle, and therefore even when such an action could be done without the bad consequences that motivated the commitment.

The reciprocity argument has no necessary connection with the idea of a social contract, but there are similarities, and the argument may lead to a contract. The classic social contract theorists start from a state of nature in which each person has certain natural rights, and argue that these rights should be renounced or qualified. Different writers postulate different natural rights: to do anything whatever, to do whatever one judges conducive to self-preservation, to enforce the law of nature, and so on. Behind these various particular rights there

[11] It is the second reciprocity that I regard as characteristic of this kind of argument. Perhaps the others will persecute us whether we persecute them or not, but if we renounce persecution as a matter of principle (which is more than simply not practising it), perhaps they will follow suit. The argument is about the likely consequences of committing oneself to a principle when the consequences may include a similar commitment by others.

[12] See above, Essay II, sect. 5.1.

seems to me to be one really fundamental right, the right to act upon our own judgement of what it is morally permissible to do (or obligatory and therefore permissible). The purpose of the argument in social contract theories is to show that we should modify our view of what is permissible, or that we should renounce the right to act on our private judgement of what is permissible.[13] Similarly the reciprocity argument begins by postulating (or at least conceding for the moment) that there is a right to persecute (whether in the state of nature, or in a civil state in which there remains some right to act on our own judgement, or one in which the government is permitted to persecute on behalf of an established religion or other ideology), and sets out to show that that right should be abandoned, or that some institutional arrangement should be made to stop those who think they have it from exercising it. But, as I will later try to show, the renunciation of the right, although it is made in the hope that others will reciprocate, need not be conditional upon their doing so. In some circumstances the argument may lead to a contract, in others it may not.

In this essay I will explore some of the issues raised by reciprocity arguments, to decide how much they can prove and for what circumstances.

I. THE GOLDEN RULE

The sketchiest reciprocity argument simply invokes the saying 'do unto others'. To spell it out a little: relevantly similar cases should be judged the same way; so do not persecute others unless you could (or do) acknowledge that they would be entitled to persecute you if the positions were reversed. Some such argument is implicit in charges of moral inconsistency. Lutherans at first complained against persecution by Catholics, but when they were strong enough they persecuted Catholics and other Protestants.[14] Since they had challenged the established Catholic authorities, how could they then deny the right of others to challenge them? Since they had complained when Catholics persecuted them, how could they rightly persecute others? Their initial challenge and complaints implicitly

---

[13] See my article, 'Locke on Political Obligation'.
[14] See Lecler, vol. 1, pp. 147ff., 242ff.

asserted rights to think for oneself, to disagree with established authorities, to obtain a fair hearing, to preach and practise without penalty; since their later attempts at repression implicitly denied those rights they were morally inconsistent.

One possible reply is that a challenge implicitly asserts, not rights in the full sense, but only liberties, or even less.[15] In the minimal sense, if I have a right to do something you do wrong to blame me for doing it but otherwise you have no correlative duties. In a somewhat stronger sense, if I have a right you have a duty not to try to obstruct or deter my act *intentionally*; you have no duty to help, or even to get out of the way (even if you realise you are in the way), but you do wrong if you get in the way on purpose. Then there are rights in some fuller sense, which impose other duties besides the duties not to blame and not to obstruct intentionally (for example, to help). Suppose we were in a 'state of nature' (at least where ideological conflict is concerned), each of us having a 'natural right' to do whatever we think right to propagate whatever we think true. Such a natural right would not impose any duty except not to blame those who exercise the right. We would have no duty not to try to prevent what we might regard as false teaching, even by force or threats (threats not of punishment, which implies blame, but of damage). We would do no wrong in doing what we thought we should do to propagate truth, or in obstructing one another's propaganda, even intentionally. There may be nothing wrong in trying to prevent something there is no blame in attempting.

Moral consistency requires that when we claim some sort of moral right we must concede that others have a right of the same sort in relevantly similar cases. What sort of right do we claim merely by speaking? A right of the lowest degree. To speak implies (perhaps) that we believe that anyone in like circumstances can rightly speak, without deserving blame, but not that anyone else has a duty to listen, or a duty not to prevent others from speaking. The use and threat of force and

---

[15] See Hart, 'Natural Rights', pp. 56-7. Hart says that a liberty imposes no duties on others. It seems to me that every liberty imposes a duty not to blame, and some liberties (or should we call these rights?) may impose a duty not to obstruct intentionally. Perhaps the duty not to obstruct is imposed by some part of what Hart calls 'the protective perimeter' ('Bentham', pp. 179ff.); but, even so, to postulate a liberty implies some duty, by bringing into play some protective principle.

other disincentives are not blame and do not imply blame. Rules against the repression of speech must therefore have some other basis than the rights implicitly claimed by speaking. Those who challenge established authority may imply that what they are doing does not deserve blame, but not that there is any right to do it in a strong sense of right, and therefore not that they in their turn have any duty not to obstruct, even intentionally and by force, those who may later challenge them.

Another possible reply is that there is no inconsistency because the cases are not similar. Under one description they are similar: established authority is challenged and represses the challenge. But they are not relevantly similar. It is not the case that establishment just by itself, and nothing else, justifies authority. If positions of authority ought to be held by those with genuine knowledge and good intentions (or some other characteristic besides establishment), then a challenge to established authority by some better-qualified group is not relevantly the same as a challenge to a well-qualified authority by others who are not, and repression in one case is not the same as repression in the other.

To some this reply may seem ridiculous: the members of every sect think that they are right themselves and the others wrong.[16] To others it may seem shocking to suggest that truth and error may have the same rights: this sounds like scepticism or indifferentism.[17] But why is it ridiculous to think that knowledge is a relevant qualification for having authority? Is there some argument, not sceptical or indifferentist, to show that knowledge is not a qualification? At a given moment we cannot tell the difference between knowing and only seeming to know, but knowledge is no worse off in this respect than any other qualification. At a given moment we cannot tell whether someone who seems to have any quality really has it, though it is

---

[16] 'If he says that he is to be spared because he believes true, but the other was justly persecuted because he was in error, he is ridiculous. For he is as confidently believed to be a heretic as he believes his adversary such' (Jeremy Taylor, *Liberty of Prophesying*, p. 517). Cf. the quotations at the beginning of Dworkin's article.

[17] 'Right is a moral power which ... it is absurd to suppose that nature has accorded indifferently to truth and falsehood'; 'they ... end at last by making no apparent distinction between truth and error ... [T]he Church ... is forced utterly to reprobate and condemn tolerance of such an abandoned and criminal character' (Pope Leo XIII, in Gilson (ed.), *The Church Speaks to the Modern World*, pp. 72, 78).

possible that further experience may dissipate false appearances; but it is not true universally that a quality about which we may be mistaken is morally irrelevant. We attribute rights and duties for the present to those who at present seem to have the qualities that at present seem relevant, and hope that further experience will correct some of our mistakes. If being right is to be treated as irrelevant as a qualification for authority it must be for some better reason than the possibility that what seems true may not be.

It seems, then, that the simple 'do unto others' argument does not get very far. It needs to be completed by an argument to show, first, that the rival sects (parties, nations) have against one another certain rights in some sense strong enough to rule out some methods of carrying on their conflict (methods we will then call 'persecution', 'atrocity' etc.); and, second, that those rights and duties are not affected by the truth or falsity of their beliefs. These two points cannot be assumed, they need to be proved. That is the purpose of the more elaborate reciprocity arguments.[18]

2. A CONTRACT

Bayle argues from the evils of religious warfare to moral rules against persecution, assuming that God's command is the basis of morality and that God eternally foresees these evils; he argues that God must have laid down rules to prevent them. To construct a non-theological version of the argument let us leave open the question of the basis of morality, assuming simply that the rival sects do have some morality (different moralities, perhaps), and let us set aside God's foreknowledge, and ask whether human beings can deal with the evil when they see it by applying or adapting their existing moralities and institutions. Later I will consider whether it is possible to do without any bilateral or multilateral agreement, but since current moral codes include the principle that voluntary agreements are to be

[18] To 'treat like cases alike' we must know how to decide which cases and which 'treatments' are alike; see Hospers, pp. 286ff. Substantive rules, such as the rules of toleration, help determine which similarities and differences are to be regarded as equivalent. In deciding whether to commit ourselves to such rules we must consider the consequences of 'treating like cases alike' according to the classification implicit in the rules. Which cases and treatments are to count as alike is decided by deciding on the rules.

kept let us explore first the possibility of a reciprocity argument leading to a contract. By virtue of the 'basic' duty to keep agreements the parties would assume 'additional' duties going beyond the duty not to blame or punish implied by the mere liberty to try for a hearing.[19] The terms of the agreement must take no account of the difference between real and apparent truth or orthodoxy (or whatever value is in dispute), not because the difference cannot be discovered or does not matter, but because it is in dispute; an agreement to reduce the evils of conflict will be ineffective if it is framed in terms which are at the centre of the conflict. Thus the two requirements which emerged at the end of section 1 will be met, without scepticism or indifferentism.

Under what circumstances would it be reasonable for rival sects to enter into a contract? I will merely indicate in general terms what sorts of things each sect's deliberations should take into account. First, the sects will have their own, possibly different, moralities, the content of which will affect the possibility of agreement. The reciprocity argument has no practical value unless it can show that even those who now believe they *ought* to engage in (what the other side calls) persecution should nevertheless renounce the right to do so. To take account of their position is not to endorse the belief that they have a duty to persecute. The force of the argument will be this: *even if* it were true that they had a duty to persecute, still in certain circumstances it would be right for them to agree not to do so in future; we may later argue that there never was such a duty, but that will be another argument.[20] The supposed duty to persecute might be regarded as either absolute or *prima facie*.[21]

[19] By a 'basic' duty I mean one directly prescribed by the moral code (even if it could be derived from other rules, it is directly prescribed). By an 'additional' duty I mean one which arises from some action by virtue of a basic duty, e.g. the duty to do something arising from the act of promising to do it by virtue of the basic duty to keep promises, or a duty arising from a superior's command by virtue of the basic duty (if there is one) to obey the powers that be. In different moral codes additional duties may arise in different ways.

[20] A reciprocity argument may thus have some impact on people who subscribe to 'non-neutral' principles. 'Compel them to come in', understood as addressed only to the true religion, is a classic 'non-neutral' principle, one whose 'application to particular cases is a matter of controversy for the parties whose conduct is supposed to be regulated' (Dworkin, p. 492). Bayle's argument seeks to establish 'common principles' which can be applied to regulate conflicts without the need first to decide the questions in dispute (see above, Essay II, n. 163).

[21] On this terminology see above, Introduction.

If it is regarded as absolute then that belief must be contested by some other argument before the reciprocity argument can get under way, since presumably people cannot rightly agree not to do what they believe they have an absolute duty to do.[22] But if they regard it as a *prima facie* duty they may consider reasons against carrying it out. Rules of deliberation included in their morality may exclude some sorts of reasons, or direct that they be given little weight. Perhaps the temporal cost (for example in human suffering) is not to be counted, or is to be taken into account only when other things are equal (for example, if free discussion and repressive methods are apparently equally favourable to the progress of orthodoxy, the sufferings caused by repression may be allowed to tip the balance). Perhaps the sufferings of the saints should be weighed but not those of heretics, or the sufferings of heretics should not be given as much weight; or conversely, perhaps our own suffering is not to be weighed while the sufferings of others should be; and so on. It depends on these and other aspects of the moralities of the sects concerned whether they can agree to renounce persecution without betraying or modifying their principles.

Second, they must consider relative strengths. If one sect (or coalition) is much stronger than the others, then the weaker sects have reason to offer an agreement but the stronger has no reason to accept. The agreement will not be reasonable for all unless the parties are evenly matched, or unless for some other reason the stronger cannot be sure of the outcome. If two sects are found in some other place in communication with this one and the stronger sect here is not stronger there, then both may have reason to make an agreement for both places.

Third, each must consider whether the other can be relied on to keep such promises. Some sects have believed, or have been suspected of believing, that faith is not to be kept with

[22] Very likely they will regard the absolute duty as something intuitively obvious. We might suggest some other formulation and ask them to consider whether it is not rather this that seems to be their duty. Or we might try to invent some analogous case in which their principle loses its intuitive appeal. Or there might be some other principle that could be brought in some cases into conflict with this one. 'When an impudent rascal blasphemes ... the authority who allows such an act and does not punish it severely shares before God in that sin' (Luther, quoted Lecler, vol. 1, p. 156). Could the principle rather be that we must dissociate ourselves in some way (e.g. by protesting), without necessarily inflicting punishment? What about the analogous case of other sins: to avoid sharing in sin must the ruler search out rigorously every sin of whatever sort and punish it?

heretics, or that a promise must be broken if it turns out to be detrimental to God's cause.[23] Some sects may be unconscientious, not taking admitted obligations seriously enough. If a now powerful sect agrees not to persecute it may lose the chance to secure its position only to be persecuted by its rivals later if they do not keep their promise.

It is sometimes said that an agreement made by one generation cannot bind its successors, since we cannot be bound except by our own promise (or by a promise made by an authorised agent). Even if those who make the agreement keep their promises their successors therefore may not. There are various possible ways round this difficulty.[24] Perhaps the agreement can be to do something that one generation can do which will make it difficult or impossible for a future generation to persecute even if they do not believe themselves bound by agreements they have not made. For example, there might be an agreement to teach the principles of toleration as 'basic' rules of morality, or to write toleration into the constitution of the country. But it may be objected that it is untruthful to teach children to regard something as a basic part of morality if you do not yourself regard it as such, and if one generation cannot make agreements on behalf of later generations then perhaps the constitution ought to be rewritten every generation.[25] Another possibility is to rely on the notion of succession.

[23] Catholics were suspected of believing this after John Hus was burned despite a safe conduct. Some Protestants adopted the same maxim. Suspicion over this was an obstacle to the development of toleration. See Lecler, vol. 1, pp. 290-1, 302; and vol. 2, pp. 236-7, 241-2.

[24] This is not the same as the difficulty about reciprocity between generations (see Barry, 'Justice as Reciprocity', pp. 69ff.). The agreement I am concerned with would regulate relations between contemporaries; the problem is whether it will be reproduced into the future. 'As the ends of such a partnership [the State] cannot be obtained in many generations, it becomes a partnership not only between those who are living, but between those who are living, those who are dead, and those who are to be born' (Burke, p. 106). This is not right: there is no partnership between members of different generations. Rather, since the end sought by members of this generation cannot be attained without an agreement which will not be made unless it is expected to last beyond one generation, there must be some assurance that members of new generations will join in the same agreement with other members of their own generation.

[25] 'Each generation ... has ... a right to chose for itself the form of government it believes most promotive of its own happiness; ... and it is for the peace and good of mankind, that a solemn opportunity of doing this every nineteen or twenty years, should be provided by the Constitution' (Jefferson, p. 675). But it is unlikely that a federation could ever be formed unless the parties believed that the constitution would

A successor is bound, not by the predecessor's promise, but by accepting the succession with its attached obligations. Against this it may be objected that later generations may not be successors in every respect. They may succeed the earlier generation as property-holders, for example, and be bound to pay off mortgages, but perhaps they are not bound to keep the promise to practise toleration. Another possibility is to say that they are bound to respect 'vested rights', meaning rights which, because they have existed and been relied on for a long time, cannot fairly be abolished without notice or compensation.[26] But perhaps the rule of respect for vested rights is merely an application of the rule of respect for promises, the promise in such cases being tacit; and if a new generation is not bound by its predecessors' promises it is not bound by their tacit promises. Another possibility is to invoke Rawls's suggested duty of fair play.[27] But this applies only to those who have voluntarily accepted benefits, and a later generation may claim that it had no choice, since toleration was already the practice.

Whether the other parties to an agreement believe—rather, whether their successors believe—that later generations must keep agreements made by earlier generations determines whether the agreement will be enforced by the consciences of future generations of members of the agreeing sects. But other people's beliefs are also relevant. They might be outraged (though for no reason we have been able to discover) if the agreement were repudiated for the reason that an earlier generation cannot bind its successors, and they might help enforce it out of a (possibly mistaken) sense of interest in an unrestricted version of the principle that agreements are to be kept.

Even if it is doubtful that the other party can be trusted or that later generations will feel bound, it may still be reasonable to make the agreement, gambling on the likelihood of some change of belief when conflict diminishes, or on the stability of peaceful habits. If the practice of toleration becomes well

last more than one generation. On binding future generations see Locke, *Second Treatise*, sect. 116; Rousseau, pp. 169-70; Bentham, pp. 494, 501; Paine, pp. 63-4. If (as Hume argues) the practice of promising is based on a sense of its utility, the utility of being able to make arrangements that will last beyond one generation is a reason for rejecting the view that promises cannot bind successors.

[26] See Barry, *Political Argument*, p. 102. 'Prescription' is a similar notion. See also Hume, *Treatise*, vol. 2, pp. 254-5.

[27] On fair play see Rawls, *Justice*, pp. 111-12.

established, the question whether it should continue may not occur to the new generation of a sect even if the balance of power has shifted their way.

There are, then, circumstances in which an agreement to outlaw persecution might not be reasonable: the rival sect might be weak and likely to remain so, one's own moral code might make what others will call persecution an absolute duty, the other party might not be trustworthy, or it may be possible that their successors will not feel bound. In such cases a reciprocity argument might not work, at least not without preliminary argument to change some of the parties' moral or factual beliefs.

3. TREATMENT OF NON-JOINERS

Two or more sects which agree not to persecute one another may still persecute others. If one of the others turns out to be well able to reciprocate it may also be admitted to the agreement, but a non-persecuting sect might not have enough bargaining power to get admitted. What reason might there be to agree not to persecute a non-persecuting sect? The fear of being persecuted is not the only possible inducement to agreement; a milder inducement, which may sometimes be enough, is dislike of being subjected to precautions. There is an important difference between persecuting the intolerant and taking precautions against them. But even if the precautions are really precautions and not disguised persecution, and even if they are carried no further than reasonable fears justify, they may bear quite heavily on members of a feared sect.[28] If a powerful but non-persecuting sect takes precautions against sects which might persecute it, this may be reason enough for the latter to agree with it to outlaw persecution.

[28] On precautions see above, Essay II, sect. 6.3. The exclusion of Catholics and Dissenters from public employment in England until the nineteenth century was defended by some as a reasonable precaution and criticised by others as virtual persecution. See Cobbett, vol. 9, cols. 1047–59, vol. 26, cols. 780–831, and vol. 28, cols. 387–452; also *Hansard*, n.s. vol. 4 (1821), cols. 949–1030; Hoadly, *passim*; Paley, pp. 472–7; Macaulay, vol. 1, pp. 7–9, and vol. 2, pp. 255ff.; Mill, *Prefaces*, p. 151. A similar debate took place in the 1950s about similar precautions against Communists; see Hook, and articles by Hook, Lovejoy and Lowe in *Journal of Philosophy* 48 (1951), and 49 (1952). Precautions may take other forms, such as preventive detention and surveillance.

Suppose now that the terms of the agreement are altered, and the parties promise not merely not to persecute one another but not to persecute anyone, including those who do not join in the agreement and those who join but later violate it, but reserving the right to take reasonable precautions against non-joiners, and against those whose beliefs or behaviour suggest that their adherence may not be sincere. To frame the agreement this way may make it more difficult for the reciprocity argument to succeed. In taking 'reasonable precautions' instead of persecuting there is a sacrifice of security which a sect now powerful enough to persecute may regret if others grow powerful and do persecute. Sects which do not join at the beginning are less likely to join later, since being subjected to precautions is not as strong an inducement as being subjected to persecution. But these drawbacks may be balanced or over-balanced by the fact that an agreement in these terms is likely to be more stable and more effective. Acts of persecution by unrepresentative members of a sect, or a false rumour of persecution, or a real but perhaps temporary relapse, will not be so likely to cause the collapse of the agreement and the renewal of outright warfare; it will lead only to a heightening of precautions, providing an incentive to the erring party to honour the agreement in future. Also, the practice of toleration uniformly toward all, rather than only toward those who join in an agreement, is more likely to develop into an unquestioning habit, which, as was noticed above, may be the best solution to the problem of making the agreement last through generations. As long as some sects are persecuted it is obvious that the toleration of others rests upon voluntary agreement, and the practice of toleration cannot become unquestioning habit.

References to inducements and security do not mean that the calculation is self-interested. It is to be done in accordance with the deliberator's moral code, which will determine the extent to which selfish interests may be taken into account. If all that is allowed to matter is some ideal cause, then security in the relevant sense has been sacrificed if the cause is jeopardized, and the inducement is benefit to the cause. The worldly interests of individual sect members may not count at all.

4. A UNILATERAL GUARANTEE

So far we have considered two kinds of reciprocation. First (in section 2) we imagined an agreement by which one sect promises not to persecute the other, on condition that the other makes the same promise, while each keeps the right to persecute those who are not parties to the agreement. Then (in section 3) we imagined another agreement in which each promises not to persecute anyone at all, on condition that the other makes the same promise, while each keeps the right to take reasonable precautions. Now we come to a third kind, in which a sect or individual, without waiting for agreement with others and without making the promise conditional upon anyone else's promise, undertakes not to persecute anyone, reserving the right to take precautions. The undertaking is unilateral and unconditional, but it looks for some reciprocation.[29] It is made in the hope that others will follow suit, now that they feel less threatened by persecution and can expect some relaxation of precautions against them if they also renounce persecution.

Just as in the second version there is a sacrifice of security in comparison with the first, so in the third there is a sacrifice in comparison with the second: those who renounce persecution without waiting for others may lose a chance to strengthen their position without getting anything in return, since after all the others may not reciprocate. Thus there may be some circumstances in which an unconditional and unilateral promise would not be sensible, in which it would be better to seek an agreement. But just as the second version has an advantage which may overbalance the risk, namely that it is more stable (see above, sect. 3), so has the third, namely that it is easier to bring about. When there are many sects their suspicions may make it difficult to organise an agreement that includes enough of them to secure peace; a unilateral declaration may then be as much as any sect can do toward peace, and may be worth the risk. An agreement as in the second version between some sects is a unilateral declaration on their part in relation to the others. A movement toward toleration may begin with a

---

[29] This is common behaviour. Acquaintances often do one another favours partly in hope of return, but it would be unfriendly and self-defeating to attach conditions in every case, or even to be too conscious of the balance of the account.

unilateral declaration by one sect, or an agreement of the second kind between sects, and be carried forward by unilateral commitments from other sects who wish to avoid being objects of precaution. In fact the movement may be begun and carried forward by individuals. An agreement between sects must be made by representatives able to speak for the sects, and leaders are often unable or unwilling to make new and risky commitments. But unilateral declarations can be made by individuals speaking for themselves. Anyone can announce that he or she will no longer behave in certain ways (and refer to them as 'persecution'), and call on others to renounce such methods also.[30] The practice of toleration can spread without waiting for sect leaders to be convinced, behind their backs or over their heads.

Thus a reciprocity argument need not be an argument for a contract. Under some circumstances it may favour a unilateral commitment. A commitment need not be a promise.[31] In general terms, the argument is meant to show that some sort of guarantee should be given that certain kinds of things will not be done. A guarantee may consist in physical things (as when the French Protestants were allowed under the Edict of Nantes to fortify certain places), or in social arrangements (for example, it may be established by a public promise attaching the sanction of public opinion, or a constitutional amendment attaching legal sanctions). It may consist in a disposition of character, in being the sort of person who can be relied on not to act in certain ways, whose conscience rejects and disapproves such actions; so we might cultivate in ourselves or in others (for example children) a commitment to a certain rule or ideal as a 'basic' duty of morality, or by means of a promise make it an 'additional' duty of morality. A reciprocity argument is an

---

[30] Or, to take a topical instance, we could individually say that we will have nothing to do with nuclear weapons or the materials from which they can be made, no matter what others may do.

[31] 'When this common sense of interest is mutually expressed, and is known to both, it produces a suitable resolution and behaviour. And this may properly enough be called a convention or agreement betwixt us, though without the interposition of a promise'; 'Every member of society is sensible of this interest: every one expresses this sense to his fellows, along with the resolution he has taken of squaring his actions by it, on condition that others will do the same'; Hume, *Treatise*, vol. 2, pp. 195, 202. As the second passage indicates, mere expression of a sense of interest is not enough; what is needed is the expression of a resolution, indeed an undertaking or commitment, though it need not take the form of a promise. And it need not be 'on condition'.

attempt to show that some sort of guarantee should be given on condition that others reciprocate, or in the hope that they will, as a way of ending or reducing the evils which result when several parties exercise or carry out some alleged duty, right or liberty against one another. The argument is that whatever ideal and other ends the moral code requires or allows are best served on the whole if certain actions which might sometimes have been useful toward those ends are renounced as a matter of principle, or made impossible or difficult or costly.[32]

If the guarantee consists in accepting something as a moral duty, then persecution (aggression, atrocity, undemocratic behaviour, or whatever the actions outlawed are to be called) is morally wrong even when it is expedient: toleration (for example) has become a matter of moral principle.[33] Many of the classic arguments for liberal principles are not strong enough to reach this conclusion. For example, Mill's argument in Chapter 2 of *On Liberty* to show that truth is best served by freedom of discussion does not show that an occasional judicious act of censorship (for the sake of truth, or for some other legitimate end) must be morally wrong. The general usefulness of a policy does not make it morally wrong to depart from it even when a departure would be useful. But if a reciprocity argument shows that we should commit ourselves, as a matter of principle, not to practise censorship (for example), and we do make the commitment, then any act of censorship is morally wrong, by virtue of the principle that commitments should be kept. But this is not always the outcome of the argument. There are various possible guarantees besides morality, and various possible ways of setting up a guarantee (for example, contract or unilateral commitment); in some circumstances a reciprocity argument might succeed for some of these possibilities and not for others. There may be some circumstances in which no reciprocity argument works at all.

[32] See my paper 'Utilitarianism and Virtue'. The reciprocity argument is a subclass of the kind of argument explored there.

[33] When liberal Catholics began to favour toleration liberals suspected a strategem, that if the Church ever became strong enough to persecute again it would do so. Archbishop Dupanloup's distinction between thesis and hypothesis seemed to mean that Catholics regarded toleration as right only for the prevailing circumstances; see Vidler, p. 152. 'Eurocommunism' has met with similar suspicion. To count as genuine, the conversion must be to the belief that toleration is a matter of principle.

5. AN HISTORICAL DIGRESSION

Historians sometimes suggest that religious toleration came about first as a 'peace of exhaustion', by a process in which moral principle played little part: the warring sects gave up persecuting when they found that they were making little or no headway at great cost. It is suggested that it was only in later times that toleration and other liberal practices became genuinely a matter of moral principle for all except some who would still persecute if they could. But perhaps moral reasoning played a larger part. Reciprocity arguments might under changing circumstances justify a series of steps such as in fact were taken: religious war giving way to 'non-aggression pacts' between neighbouring sects; these giving way to general toleration, as compacts give way to unilateral and unconditional commitments to tolerate all who are not intolerant, and as more sects and individuals see the advantage of such commitment (the advantage increasing as the party of toleration increases); persecution of the intolerant giving way, especially when the intolerant have been outnumbered, to toleration of all with reasonable precautions against the intolerant; and deliberate adoption and proclamation of tolerant principles giving way to unquestioning acceptance of toleration as a matter of 'basic' morality. In the end, when toleration has been taught as part of morality in many families for several generations, the intolerance of those who lived before the movement toward toleration began will seem immoral and the calculating and bargaining unprincipled. But the process may well have been motivated and guided by reasoning of the sort I have been analysing, starting from a moral code, deliberating in ways permitted by it, and arriving at a revised morality (which may permit other modes of deliberation, leading to further revision, and so on).

The outcome is a complex set of rules regulating conflict arising from religious beliefs, and from beliefs connected with or like religious beliefs, such as moral and political convictions. Some of the rules assert rights or duties—some absolute, others imperfect or *prima facie*—and others are rules of deliberation which limit what can be weighed against these rights and duties. The rights and duties run more or less as follows. Concerning *thought*: people are not to be punished for what they believe, or for changing their beliefs;[34] negligence or self-deception or other faults are not to be inferred merely from what they believe;[35] we all have a *prima facie* right to investigate any question as we see fit;[36] there is to be no compulsory religious instruction.[37] Concerning *expression*: we all have a *prima facie* right to express and advocate our beliefs to any audience and by our own methods, and a right *not* to do what may seem like an expression of belief (an absolute right, if the act is normally taken as an expression of religious belief);[38] we have a duty of imperfect obligation to give a serious hearing to the beliefs of others. Concerning *action*: we have a *prima facie* right to act on our beliefs, and a *prima facie* duty not to tempt others to act against conscience;[39] we have an absolute right not to perform an act normally taken as religious. Concerning *public neutrality* toward religious and similar beliefs: we all have a duty of imperfect obligation to make it easy for other people

[34] Hardly anyone has thought that people can rightly be punished just for misbelief, but many have held that those who have once accepted the true faith can be punished if they abandon it; see e.g. Thomas Aquinas, *Summa*, 2–2, q.10 a.8.

[35] Some have thought that there are errors no one can fall into (e.g. about basic moral principles) without being guilty of negligence or self-deception or some other fault. The principle suggested in the text requires that there be specific evidence of such faults; they are not to be inferred simply from what the person believes. See above, Essay II, sect. 4.2, and Locke, *Third Letter*, pp. 297–9.

[36] Christians have often believed that it would be wrong for them to 'check up' on the truth of their religion. Conservatives have sometimes taken the view that it is blameworthy for ordinary people to pry into the foundations of society. (According to the Bishop of Rochester the Treasonable Practices Bill of 1795 was 'merely directed against those idle and seditious public meetings for the discussion of the laws where the people were not competent to decide upon them. In fact, he did not know what the mass of the people in any country had to do with the laws but to obey them, with the reserve of their undoubted right to petition against any particular law as a grievance on a particular description of people' (Cobbett, vol. 32, col. 258).) Sometimes it is believed that certain inquiries are permissible only if carried on in certain ways (e.g. by asking respectful questions of the authorities). To act on such beliefs oneself, or to persuade others to act on them, is compatible with commitment to toleration (to be tolerant it is not essential to be a free-thinker), but not to enforce them upon others.

[37] Melanchthon defended compulsory attendance at sermons as compatible with liberty of conscience: 'The Prince does not force the spirit, but only the motory faculty [i.e. he makes sure they do not walk out]; he forces people to listen to the true doctrine, and he forbids outward blasphemy; after that, the listener keeps the duty and the power to know the truth, if he wants to' (quoted Lecler, vol. 1, p. 253).

[38] On the right not to express a belief (even if you actually hold it) see Konvitz, *Liberties*, pp. 111–16.

[39] On temptation see above, Essay II, sect. 5.2.

to take part in community life, whatever sect they belong to;[40] minority beliefs should get a fair share of attention in public discussion; members of organisations open to the public have the right to exercise a veto, or to contract out, when the organisation is about to do something against their beliefs; the State and public opinion are not to enforce religious or moral rules as such; public institutions are not to profess or help (intentionally and directly, at least) any religion or similar doctrine;[41] if we make any unfavourable moral judgements of others we must judge them according to their lights;[42] in taking precautions we must not give much weight to the presumption that the members of a sect all think and act alike.[43]

The rules which assert *prima facie* or imperfect rights or duties put a weight into the balance, a heavier weight the higher the ideal of an open society is supposed to come in the scale of values. The rules of deliberation which limit what can be weighed on the other side seem to me to be best stated as *excluding* certain kinds of reasons, rather than as listing what can be given weight.[44] *Rules of deliberation*: Against the rights and duties set out above no weight is to be given to any al-

[40] Ordinary good manners require considerateness toward members of minorities— to acknowledge their existence, to provide food they can eat, to avoid words they regard as offensive, to take account of their religious holidays and so on. Toleration is concerned with such things in so far as minorities are constituted by their beliefs. As requirements of toleration they may have more weight than they have as requirements of good manners.

[41] The State subsidises religion indirectly if it subsidises private hospitals and some of them are religious. The subsidy to religion might be intentional: the policy might have been designed to provide certain religious groups with income. Or it may be unintentional (even if the benefit to religion is known): the purpose might be to extend hospital services. On controversies involving these distinctions see Konvitz, *First Amendment*, pp. 12, 16, 23–6, 60.

[42] See above, Essay II, sect. 3. This applies to unfavourable judgement only. Toleration requires that we respect those who live by their own code, not that we judge them unfavourably if they do not. In any case, their code may be excessively demanding.

[43] The difficulty of predicting what people will do from what they believe was one of Bayle's favourite themes; see *Miscellaneous Reflections*, sects. 135–6, 176, 181. Cf. Fox, vol. 4, pp. 2–4; Macaulay, vol. 1, pp. 7–9. This was one of Macaulay's arguments against excluding Catholics from government jobs; see above, n. 28.

[44] For an example of the method of listing what can be weighed, see McCloskey, p. 221; for an example of the method of listing what is *not* to be weighed see Scanlon, pp. 209, 213. The advantage of the latter is that it does not need a complete list of possible reasons for action. The point of the principles of the open society is to *exclude* certain kinds of reasons for interfering with others. Toleration should not be formulated so as to tie it closely to any particular system of positive values, since people who hold

legation that some belief is bad in itself, or unlike the beliefs of others (against 'community standards'), or that it has practical implications contrary to religion, law,[45] morality or public opinion.

The details of this account of liberal social principles may be disputed, but the point I want to make is that the rules are complex and rather untidy. This is more easily explained if we assume that they are like clauses of a peace treaty worked out under the guidance of reciprocity arguments, reflecting the intensity of various kinds of conflicts and the distribution of power in post-Reformation Europe. The rules of deliberation against giving weight to certain kinds of reasons are directed against the motives which have led in the past to the worst conflict. The absoluteness of rights and duties relating most directly to religion reflects the length and bitterness of the religious struggle. Since so far (perhaps because dissenters have always been outnumbered) there have been no 'wars of morality', except in so far as morality is involved in religion, the rules relating to morality are not absolute. Thus the State is permitted to enforce a socially beneficial rule which is part of morality provided it is not enforced because it is part of morality, whereas the State cannot enforce participation in religious worship or support specifically religious education even when that would improve social cohesion or serve some other legitimate secular purpose. Such features seem easiest to explain on the hypothesis that the rules were arrived at through reciprocity arguments. None of the other arguments for toleration leads to such a complex conclusion.

different systems are all supposed to be tolerant. (Mill's principle of liberty as I understand it—see my article 'Mill on Duty and Liberty'—says what *can* be a reason for interference, namely some violation of duty to others; but in deciding what to regard as duties to others we are governed by the rules of deliberation stated above, which say what *cannot* be a reason.)

[45] I do not myself acknowledge any moral duty to obey the law because it is the law, or because it has majority support. Those who think there is such a duty will think that if the act would be illegal, that counts against the *prima facie* right to act on one's beliefs. But it does not count against the other *prima facie* rights and duties. For example, advocacy (short of incitement) is not to be judged wrong because the belief advocated is that some illegal act ought to be done; people must be free to discuss whether they ought to obey a law.

6. LIMITATIONS OF RECIPROCITY ARGUMENTS

Most people these days seem to regard the principles of toleration as permanently and universally valid moral principles; the intolerance of past ages may be excused by ignorance, but objectively it was wrong. But reciprocity arguments will not justify this judgement. During the Middle Ages in Europe Catholics were much stronger than other sects and had no reason to doubt that they always would be. Communication between Europe and other parts of the world was poor, so missionaries could be sent to distant lands without expecting that they would be excluded or persecuted because of Catholic intolerance in Europe. Given these facts and their beliefs, medieval Catholics could not reasonably have thought it best to commit themselves to toleration as a matter of principle. The reciprocity argument for toleration would not have worked if it had been addressed to them.

But although it would probably not have convinced them, perhaps objectively it would have been a good argument, since it was always possible that the dominance of the Catholic Church would come to an end. Medieval Catholics should have taken account of that possibility, and should have provided for it by adopting the principles of toleration. And it might be argued that, in general, history shows that no group can be sure it will never need the protection of the principles of toleration, so everywhere and always it is wise for everyone to acknowledge these principles. The answer to these arguments is that they make a mistaken assumption about what caution requires. A group (a nation, for example) would not increase but reduce its security if it now committed itself to the peace treaty it might have to accept if it lost its present advantage, no matter how unlikely it is that this will happen soon. It would not have been reasonable for the medieval Church to commit itself to the principles of toleration while its dominance seemed secure. The force of the reciprocity argument is limited. The most it can show, I believe, is that it is reasonable to adopt the rules of toleration when the circumstances are as they have been, and are likely to continue to be, in modern times. From now on they can be treated as part of 'basic' morality, but at the risk of distorting our judgement of the morality and intelligence of people in the past.

John Rawls's theory might seem to provide a way of escaping this limitation. On his account a social contract is agreed upon (the agreement must be unanimous)[46] in ignorance of the relative strength of sects and in accordance with an extreme view of what caution requires. He believes that the contract would provide for equal liberty of conscience, limited only by the interest in public order and security. In the Original Position the contractors do not know whether in ordinary life they belong to a strong sect or a weak one, and do not know what in ordinary life their moral and religious convictions may be. But they know that they *may* have moral and religious convictions that impose absolute obligations. In deciding the rules of justice they assume the worst—that an enemy will assign their place, as Rawls sometimes puts it; so they assume that they will be in a weak position. To make sure that, in a weak position, they will be able to carry out whatever absolute obligations they may believe they have, they must adopt rules which guarantee equal liberty of conscience. But they also agree that the State may regulate liberty of conscience for the sake of public order and security, provided the regulations can be shown to be necessary by 'ordinary' modes of argument. The State has no moral or religious function; its duty is limited to underwriting the conditions of equal moral and religious liberty, which it does by ensuring public order and security.[47]

But even apart from questions about why we should go behind such a veil of ignorance, and about the reasonableness of the cautious decision rule, this argument does not seem to work. It is possible (and presumably the possibility will be known

---

[46] In reality no contract is involved; see Snare and Hampton. The theory is that the rules of justice are those which it would be rational for *any* person to adopt if he or she were ignorant of (or disregarded) certain facts and had to choose the same rules for self and others. Whether there is any actual consultation and agreement makes no difference to what those rules would be.

[47] See Rawls, *Justice*, pp. 205-21. Restrictions on liberty of conscience must be justified by modes of reasoning which are 'acceptable to all', 'ordinary', 'not controversial' (p. 213). There may be none; and the exclusion of some modes of reasoning (e.g. from the bible) may be controversial. The reciprocity argument begins from the existing convictions and ideas about reasoning of each of the parties to whom it is addressed, and (if it succeeds) arrives at rules which may include rules of deliberation limiting the reasons which may be appealed to in certain situations, permitting Rawls's 'ordinary' modes of reasoning (and any peculiar modes not ruled out). What sort of reasons are to be regarded as acceptable is thus decided by the outcome of the argument, not assumed without argument by appeal to a consensus. See above, n. 18.

behind the veil of ignorance) that the moral and religious convictions some people have in ordinary life oblige them to persecute. If the contractors must hold themselves free to act on
their possible moral and religious convictions, then they must
hold themselves free to persecute. Rawls answers that, even so,
the principle of equal liberty of conscience must be agreed upon
if any principle can be.[48] But perhaps none can be. If the
deliberators behind the veil of ignorance must reserve enough
freedom to discharge absolute moral and religious obligations,
and if these may include obligations to persecute, and if they
must follow a cautious decision rule, then they cannot agree
upon any principles. They must leave ideological conflict un-
regulated by rules of right and duty. They will not adopt rules
of toleration, or any rules or institutions which might hinder
intolerant acts which some may think they have an absolute
moral or religious obligation to perform. There will therefore
be no State to underwrite the conditions of equal liberty of
conscience by preserving order and security, since the State
might stop some from carrying out what they may believe is
their duty to persecute. If there is a State, it must be prohibited
altogether from hindering conscientious acts, including acts of
persecution.[49]

If the 'veil of ignorance' lifts partly to allow the original
contractors to discover whether in ordinary life they believe
they ought to persecute, then some will discover that they do.
Unanimous agreement on any rules or institutions will still
be impossible unless they are allowed to discover the relative
strengths of the parties, and it may be impossible even then.
But once the veil of ignorance has lifted so far, the argument is
a reciprocity argument of the sort I have been discussing,[50] and
has the same limitation.

---

[48] Rawls, *Justice*, p. 208.

[49] Such a prohibition would be a considerable restriction of state power. Contrast
Bayle and Locke, above, Essay II, sect.6

[50] Not quite. Rawls's argument is about a hypothetical decision (the rules of justice
are the rules it would be rational to adopt under certain conditions), whereas a
reciprocity argument is a reason for establishing a guarantee, and requires completion
by an actual decision and action; toleration becomes a moral duty only when a
commitment is actually made.

7. REJECTING THE RULES

The old controversies about religious toleration are paralleled today by disagreements over the rules of liberal democracy. These rules impose certain moral obligations: to obey the law until it is changed by the proper parliamentary process, in extra-parliamentary political action to respect the law, to respect the equal political rights of other people, and so on. Some critics of the existing order openly reject these rules. Others say they accept them, but encounter contempt from one side and distrust from the other, just as liberal Catholics did at first. It is suspected that they have abandoned the fight, worn down by the moral pressure of liberal precautions against them and seduced by the prospect of respectability, or that their apparent conversion is just a trick.

As has often been pointed out, the rules of liberal democracy work to the advantage of those who already get most out of the existing social order. The parliamentary process is generally biased against parties of the left, and so are the laws which extra-parliamentary action is supposed to respect. Parliamentary government is in fact one part of a dual regime, the other part consisting in the private oligarchical governments which rule most of the everyday life of most people, namely the managements of business firms, schools and universities. Since private business controls a large part of economic activity, government needs business confidence. Equal political rights for all groups are most beneficial to those who have money and time, since they can exercise their rights more effectively. Everyday life conditions people to take for granted ideas favourable to the existing state of things, so when the critics get a hearing they sound foolish. Even if they are persistent they make no headway. The oligarchs need give no reasons in defence of their power, they only have to sit tight and wait for the critics to give up or die.

Why then should those who believe that the existing state of society is unjust or exploitative accept the rules which regulate ideological competition, and accept them as being a matter of moral principle? To be acceptable to all parties, including the stronger party, rules designed to moderate conflict must reflect the existing distribution of power. The only alternative is to have no rules. Rules supported by a reciprocity argument will therefore on many occasions give certain advantages to the stronger party. Even so, to guarantee obedience to the rules may on balance and in the long run be better for the weaker party or for the cause they represent than the alternative, having no rules. Under some circumstances, therefore, it may make good sense for opposition and other minority groups to make a sincere commitment to biased rules.

Under some circumstances this may not be true. Reciprocity arguments do not always deserve to succeed. Just as those brought up to regard the rules of religious toleration as part of basic morality often cannot see the calculating and bargaining that took place in the past as anything but immoral and unprincipled, so well-brought-up liberals often find it hard to sympathise with those who will not commit themselves to the rules of the open society. But in so far as the commitment rests on reciprocity arguments, people have a right not to commit themselves to obedience if they think that this would, without a good enough reason, stop them from doing things they believe they ought to do; and if they do commit themselves and then come to feel that that was a mistake they should be able to withdraw, with due notice and perhaps with some compensation to those affected by their withdrawal. But of course other people have the right to take precautions against those who refuse or withdraw the commitment, however reasonable (by their lights) that may be.

POSTSCRIPT: RECIPROCITY

Rawls has made several references to reciprocity, but not in my sense. In one place he says that what makes reciprocity 'fundamental to both justice and fairness' is the 'requirement of the possibility of mutual acknowledgment of principles by free and equal persons who have no authority over one another'.[51] Elsewhere he calls reciprocity the propensity in human beings to respond in the same way to kind and fair treatment.[52] The first reciprocity might be compared with the thought that figures in reciprocity arguments, that if we persecute they will too, since they have as much right. The second

[51] Rawls, 'Justice as Reciprocity', p. 256.
[52] Rawls, *Justice*, pp. 496ff.

reciprocity might be a reason for hoping that if we adopt the principles of toleration they may too.

Barry's 'Justice as Reciprocity', sects. IV–VI, is concerned with something like what I call reciprocity arguments, and draws attention to limitations like the ones I point out. He suggests that reciprocity is not a strong argument for foreign aid, since rich countries are not likely to need aid from poor countries. David Richards, also concerned with foreign aid, suggests that the limitations of reciprocity can be overcome if we substitute what he calls 'moral reciprocity' for 'actual reciprocity', moral reciprocity being the idea of 'treating persons in the way one would oneself reasonably like to be treated'.[53] This looks like the golden rule, discussed above in sect. 1. The only way I can see to define how it would be *reasonable* to like to be treated, and what is to count as treating people that way, is to construct a reciprocity argument, which is concerned with *actual* reciprocation (see above, n. 10), and the same limitations would be encountered.

Part of the job in constructing a reciprocity argument is to find the right level of abstraction (see above, n. 18). Individual citizens of a rich country may have reason to commit themselves to the rule that anyone, anywhere, at any time, who needs help to stay alive should be helped (or something similar), and this implies a duty to support foreign aid. More likely they will have reason to commit themselves to some more restricted rule, for example that people in need should be helped by relatives, friends or neighbours; or to a more complicated rule specifying an order in which others are to help—if the neighbours cannot help, then .... . Residents of a rich country might be obliged by this rule to help residents of poor countries when closer help has failed.

[53] D. Richards, p. 278.

ESSAY IV

The Ethics of Belief and Inquiry

INTRODUCTION

One of the arguments used by the Academic sceptics of ancient times, to force general suspension of judgment upon the Stoics, ran as follows: (1) Any proposition, however certain it may seem, may in fact be false; (2) the wise man (according to the Stoics) will not assert dogmatically anything that may be false;[1] therefore (3) we should not affirm anything. Premiss 1 is fallibilism, which to me seems true, and 2 is a proposition of ethics which to me seems false but harmless, if I understand it correctly. If 'assert dogmatically' means assert in a way that implicitly denies the possibility of being mistaken then perhaps 2 is true. But if it means something like 'say is true, and ask others to believe', then it seems false, since there seems nothing wrong with asserting, in that sense, something that seems true even if there is some possibility of mistake. Still, in that sense 2 is harmless, since it would allow us to say that something *seems* true, or seems *probable*, and would allow us to act on such probabilities.

But some sceptics, ancient and modern, have gone on to a further conclusion which seems false and pernicious, namely that we might as well give up serious thinking and do nothing, or act on whatever we happen to believe on instinct or by custom or by accident. Many people seem to find it tempting to adopt that attitude as soon as they become convinced that certainty is unattainable. It might be a reasonable attitude if (as the Pyrrhonian sceptics claimed) what seems true were just

---

[1] Cicero, *Academica*, II.xx.66-7. Perhaps the origin of this thesis was simply the thought that no one is ideally wise who ever makes a mistake. But it does not follow that no one trying to realize that ideal must ever risk making a mistake.

as likely actually to be false whether it is the result of serious thinking or not, or if probability were not enough for action— if before acting we had to be absolutely and infallibly certain, as we never can be. But although it may be true for some people and for some subjects, it does not seem true generally that serious thinking cannot improve our chances of being actually right; and while a high degree of probability (or even in some sense certainty) may be required for some very drastic actions, in most cases a lower degree of probability seems sufficient.

Many members of the academic profession espouse a mitigated scepticism which I think is also false and pernicious. They assert that nothing is to be asserted unless it can be backed by 'good and sufficient reasons'; or, if they distinguish between knowledge and mere opinion in terms of the reasons one must be able to produce to justify a claim to knowledge, they assert that nothing is to be asserted (at least, as being *known*) unless it can be backed by good and sufficient reasons. If they are not fallibilists these mitigated sceptics may say that the reasons have to be good enough to make the proposition certain. But usually they are not as strict as that. In fact they are usually vague about what counts as a sufficient reason; perhaps they think the standard of sufficiency cannot be formulated in the abstract but has to be learnt by association with those who perceive it. But they suppose that there is some standard, the same for everyone, which one's reasons have to meet before one is justified in making any positive assertion, or at least in claiming to know something. As for action, some say that any departure from what they regard as ordinary behaviour has to be justified by good and sufficient reasons, which puts an onus of proof on the innovator; others say that whatever one does has to be justified by such reasons; and others seem to allow action (as the ancient Academics did) on appearances and probabilities, confining their demand for sufficient reasons to an academic context.

My objection to the demand for good and sufficient reasons is that there is no standard of sufficiency. To formulate such standards is supposed to be the business of epistemology or of an 'ethics of belief', but it has not actually been done. Ordinary deductive logic can say that *if* the premisses are true the conclusion must be true, but cannot say whether they are true.

Inductive logic says what makes evidence stronger or weaker (e.g. a generalisation based on many diverse cases is better grounded than one based on a few similar cases), but cannot say whether the evidence is strong *enough* to justify belief. Epistemic logic is supposed to give rules for determining whether the evidence for a proposition is strong enough to justify affirming it, as knowledge or as reasonable opinion, but I have never seen any specimen rules: it remains an unrealised project. Similarly with the 'ethics of belief': there is no way of saying how readily we ought to believe.

In the following essay I will argue for Bayle's position, that it is always right to assert and do what conscience suggests, to act upon whatever has the 'taste' of truth (see above, Essay II, sect. 3.3), and that in some cases there may be no fault in asserting and acting on beliefs we have never examined and for which we can produce no reasons. Instead of an ethics of belief we need an ethics of inquiry. Believing does not need to be justified. The conduct that led to the belief might need justifying, the failure to do anything to test the belief might need justifying, but not the believing itself: just as doing what leads to catching cold, or not doing anything to treat it, may need justifying, but not having the cold.

* * *

Some Christians have held that faith is a duty, one with different implications for believers and non-believers: non-believers ought to investigate until they discover the vital truths, believers ought to protect their belief, if necessary by refusing to investigate.[2] Against this is the view, developed first also by Christians[3] but later taken over by Rationalists as an

[2] The first Vatican council denied that Catholics and non-Catholics have the same duty in matters of belief. Theologians explained that those in the true faith are obliged to be constant and forbidden to doubt, whereas those not yet in the true faith are obliged to seek it, and to doubt their present sect and leave it after inquiry. See Harent, 'Foi', in *DTC*, vol. 6.1, cols. 287-9. See also Thomas Aquinas, *Summa*, 1-2, q.6 a.8, q.19 a.6, q.76 a.2. Contrast Bayle's claim that we must be ready to listen to missionaries even from Australia: above, Essay II, n. 92.

[3] See Hooker, vol. 1, p. 269 ('[I]t is not required nor can it be exacted at our hands, that we should yield unto any thing other assent, than such as doth answer to evidence which is to be had of that we assent unto'); Chillingworth, pp. 293-4 ('God desires that we believe the conclusion as much as the premises deserve, that the strength of our faith be equal or proportionable to the credibility of the motives to it'); Taylor, *Liberty of Prophesying*, pp. 495, 497; Locke, *Conduct of the Understanding*, *passim* (e.g.:

important part of their critique of Christianity,[4] that the duty is not to believe any particular set of propositions, but to inquire seriously and to believe only what the evidence warrants. The Rationalist ethics of thinking, or parts of it, are summed up by various terms: open-mindedness, a critical outlook, objectivity, detachment, intellectual honesty, fair-mindedness, rationality, and so forth. These are ideals which many philosophers and other academics try to advance, sometimes in a crusading spirit.

Since concern for truth is a duty, or something morally good, acts and dispositions are subject to moral evaluation as demonstrating concern for truth, or lack of concern. The part of morality to which such evaluations belong I will call the ethics of thinking, stretching the term 'thinking' somewhat. It has at least three possible branches, dealing with areas in which it might be thought possible to show concern for truth: the ethics of belief, concerned with 'acts' of believing, assenting, suspending judgement etc., and with certain dispositions related to those 'acts'; the ethics of assertion, concerned with the expression of belief, either mentally to oneself or verbally to others; and the ethics of inquiry, concerned with gathering and considering evidence and argument. I will argue that the ethics of belief and the ethics of assertion should be eliminated, or at least relegated to a minor place, and that the ethics of inquiry should take more account of circumstances which are often ignored. This essay is, to put it crudely, a plea for a liberty of dogmatising, a defence of the closed mind. More exactly, it defends ways of thinking which may seem to show lack of concern for truth if circumstances which I believe are morally relevant are overlooked, as they often are. Whether we are justified in believing or asserting something without inquiring further depends not on what evidence we have, but on what we could or should be doing besides inquiring.

'What one of a hundred of the zealous bigots of all parties ever examined the tenets he is so stiff in, or even thought it his business or duty to do so? It is suspected of lukewarmness to suppose it necessary, and a tendency to apostasy to go about it' (p. 381)); Bayle, *CP*, pp. 337, 428, 437, 438.

[4] E.g. Collins, p. 33, Clifford, p. 186, James Mill, pp. 20-1, Kant, *Religion*, p. 124n. ('The shepherds of souls instil into their flock a pious terror ... of investigation ... a terror so great that they do not trust themselves to allow a doubt concerning the doctrines forced upon them to arise, even in their thoughts, for this would be tantamount to lending an ear to the evil spirit.').

1 . THE ETHICS OF BELIEF

The most obvious objection against an ethics of belief is that belief and the other 'acts' in question are not voluntary, and there are duties only where there is voluntary control. Whether belief is voluntary is a question with a long history. The Stoics held that assent is voluntary, although we cannot withhold it when the evidence is clear.[5] This was also the opinion of Thomas Aquinas, William of Ockham, and some other medieval writers.[6] Duns Scotus, however, denied that the will can control belief except indirectly, by diverting attention from one matter to another: otherwise it would be possible, just by willing it, to believe that the number of stars is even—which is not possible.[7] Scotists and Thomists debated the question at the Council of Trent in the sixteenth century.[8] Descartes held that assent is an act of the will, voluntary but necessary when there is intuitive evidence, optional where there is not—but then it ought to be withheld.[9] Most other modern philosophers have adopted the position of Duns Scotus. In Thomas More's Utopia they did not punish false belief 'because they be persuaded that it is in no man's power to believe what he list'.[10] Hobbes also argued in this way for freedom of thought: 'the inward thought and belief of men ... are not voluntary ... and consequently fall not under obligation.'[11] Locke in his writings on toleration

[5] Cicero, *Academica*, I.xi.40, II.xii.37-8, Zeller, pp. 88-9, Stough, p. 121. The Sceptics held that the evidence never is absolutely clear, and that assent should always be withheld. (It is possible that the Stoics and Sceptics held that assent and non-assent are always both voluntary and necessary; see Burnyeat, p. 42, n. 38, and see below, Appendix.)

[6] See Thomas Aquinas, *De veritate*, q.14 a.1. According to Ockham, when there is evidence, assent and the apprehension of evidence are the same thing, but when evidence is absent, belief can be caused by the memory of seeing the evidence or by the will (2 *Sent.* q.25, L, X–Z).

[7] Harris, vol. 2, pp. 285-90. That the stars are even (or odd) was a commonplace example for ancient and medieval writers of a proposition which is inevident and neither probable nor improbable; see e.g. Cicero, *Academica*, II.x.32, xxxiv.110, or Sextus Empiricus, *Against the Logicians*, I.243, II.147, 317.

[8] Sarpi, p. 209.

[9] 'Reason ... persuades me that I ought no less carefully to withhold my assent from matters which are not entirely certain and indubitable than from those which appear to me manifestly to be false' (Descartes, vol. 1, p. 144). See also pp. 175-6, 233. Cf. Cicero, *Academica*, I.xii.45, II.xx.66-8.

[10] More, p. 127.

[11] Hobbes, pp. 500-1; cf. pp. 410, 526, 527, 576, 700.

also used the same argument.[12] In the *Essay Concerning Human Understanding* Locke concedes that voluntary suspense of judgement may be possible when there is little or no evidence,[13] but argues that otherwise the will's influence is indirect, through the control of inquiry.[14] Many other philosophers since the sixteenth century,[15] including most of those who have written on the subject recently,[16] have argued that belief is involuntary.

This is also my opinion; belief is not directly voluntary, it can be controlled only indirectly. Some acts or changes we can bring about in ourselves simply at will; for example, we can open or shut our eyes, speak or be silent. Others we cannot bring about directly, but we may be able to act at will in a way which puts us under the influence of causes from which some change may result. Such indirect control is usually imperfect, since the outcome of the procedure is somewhat unpredictable. Belief is not directly voluntary; I cannot by a naked act of will believe that the number of the stars is even. But it is indirectly voluntary; I can open my eyes, or speak to some one, and what I see or the answer I hear may change my belief,

---

[12] Locke, *Toleration*, pp. 11, 12, 40, *Two Tracts*, pp. 127, 129, Bourne, vol. 1, p. 176. Hobbes realised, but Locke apparently did not, that this argument is not enough to establish religious toleration, since outward acts, including utterances, are voluntary, and may remain under the sovereign's control. Further, as Locke himself admits (see next two notes), beliefs may be voluntary at least indirectly.

[13] Probability lacks 'that intuitive evidence which infallibly determines the understanding' (Locke, *Essay*, IV.xv.5, p. 656). 'Where ... there are sufficient grounds to suspect that there is either fallacy ... or certain proofs ... to be produced on the contrary side, there assent, suspense, or dissent are often voluntary actions' (p. 716; see also pp. 717-18).

[14] After thorough inquiry we cannot help assenting to the side on which probability is greater (*Essay*, pp. 718(7-14), 716(10-11), 716(21-3), 717(1-2), 717(7-17)). 'We can hinder both knowledge and assent, by stopping our inquiry ... if it were not so, ignorance, error or infidelity could not in any case be a fault' (p. 717); 'all that is voluntary in our knowledge, is the employing, or withholding any of our faculties from this or that sort of objects, and a more or less accurate survey of them: but they being employed, our will hath no power to determine the knowledge of the mind one way or other; that is done only by the objects themselves, as far as they are clearly discovered' (pp. 650-1).

[15] Hooker, vol. 1. p. 268, Taylor, pp. 522-3, Whichcote in Tullock, vol. 2, p. 102, Stillingfleet, vol. 4, p. 134, Spinoza, vol. 2, p. 124, Bayle, *CP*, pp. 385-6, Hume, *Enquiries*, p. 48, James Mill, *passim*, J. S. Mill, *Logic*, vol. 2, pp. 737-8, Peirce, *Writings*, pp. 256, 292, 299. For other references see Levy, pp. 313-20.

[16] See Ammerman, Blanshard, ch. 11, Chisholm, 'Lewis', pp. 223-7, Classen, Curley, Evans, Fohr, Govier, 'Belief', B. Grant, Hampshire, pp. 155-8, J. Harrison, Johnson, Kauber and Hare, O'Hear, Penelhum, pp. 43ff., Pojman, Price, Suckiel, Williams, 'Deciding'.

though I cannot predict the change exactly. The most important of the indirect procedures is inquiry, the gathering and consideration of argument and evidence. Other causes besides evidence seem to influence belief,[17] so there are other indirect procedures, for example to live as if a proposition were true or to associate with believers. Some beliefs seem to arise in childhood and throughout life from unknown causes which cannot be manipulated. Some means by which we may affect other people's beliefs, such as reward and punishment, may not be available for modifying our own beliefs. Whether, and how, and to what extent, we can control our own beliefs seem to me questions of fact[18] about which some difference of opinion is to be expected, especially since people may try to control beliefs in different ways and with different degrees of success.[19]

A moral code regulates voluntary behaviour; it regulates directly voluntary behaviour in the first place, and it may thereby regulate certain things which are indirectly voluntary. Precepts about what is indirectly voluntary must be reducible to precepts about what is voluntary directly, otherwise they cannot be carried out. Belief results, without possibility of direct control, from the action of various causes upon a person with certain dispositions; the dispositions include prior beliefs, and other dispositions, some temporary (such as moods or resolutions) and others more or less permanent. Belief can be indirectly controlled by controlling experience and dispositions. These cannot be controlled directly by a simple act of will any more than belief itself can be, but there may be indirect methods of control. If we do certain things which are directly in our power the effects may make a difference to our experience or dispositions, and in turn this may make a difference to our beliefs. The indirect control of experience is the concern of the ethics of inquiry; control of the dispositions would be the concern of an ethics of belief.

[17] James Mill argues that belief is altered *only* by evidence: 'The proof is indisputable, because the view which the mind takes of evidence, and its belief, are but two names for the same thing' (pp. 1–2; cf. Ockham, above, n. 6). This is not what 'belief' means, and Mill's thesis seems false in fact.

[18] Williams, 'Deciding', p. 148, argues that it is a matter of logic that belief is not voluntary. For criticism see Govier, 'Belief', pp. 645–7, Winters, pp. 243–56.

[19] For an account of some indirect methods of controlling belief see Wolterstorff, pp. 148ff.

The traditional ethics of belief includes exhortations to suspend judgement, to be 'indifferent', and to proportion assent to the strength of evidence.[20] These things are not directly voluntary: we cannot stop believing just by deciding not to believe, or stop wanting something to be true or false just by deciding not to want it, or vary the degree of assent just by deciding to do so. These exhortations will have to be dropped unless they can be applied to indirect methods of control. Now there do seem to be indirect ways of putting oneself into a suitable frame of mind: by resolution, by self-exhortation, by reminding oneself of the risk of mistake, by interacting in certain ways with other people, by carrying out certain rituals, and so on. But the judicial frame of mind seems to pertain not to the ethics of belief but to the ethics of inquiry. It is a disposition, perhaps temporary and limited to certain subjects, to attend seriously to evidence on both sides. It does not seem to involve suspending existing beliefs or not wanting them to be true or false. A man or woman who holds a belief and hopes it is true may be sincerely concerned to know whether it really is true, and may seek out and attend to evidence against it. The members of a jury form a tentative judgement early in the case and test it and modify it as the evidence unfolds; without some tentative judgement they might miss the significance of some of the evidence.

Can we do anything to proportion assent to the strength of evidence? Assent can be changed by collecting more evidence, but this is not what is meant. Can we increase or decrease assent *given a body of evidence*? Turning the evidence over in the mind may modify assent, but this is by bringing about an altered perception of the evidence. Can we control our response to a given body of evidence once we have it all in view? Teachers

---

[20] An inquirer should 'put himself wholly into this state of ignorance in reference to that question; and throwing wholly by all his former notions, and the opinions of others, examine, with a perfect indifference, the question in its source' (Locke, *Conduct*, pp. 383-4). 'The surest and safest way is to have no opinion at all until he has examined' (p. 383). 'We should keep a perfect indifference for all opinions, nor wish any of them true' (p. 380). 'In the whole conduct of the understanding, there is nothing of more moment than to know when and where, and how far to give assent; and possibly there is nothing harder' (p. 378. On the proportioning of assent to evidence see Cicero, *De natura deorum*, I.i.1 (quoted by Locke at the beginning of *Conduct*), *Academica*, I.xii.45, Hooker, vol. 1, p. 269, Chillingworth, p. 27, Locke, *Essay*, IV.xix.1, Hume, *Enquiries*, p. 110. Hooker, Locke, Hume, James Mill and others believed that assent is involuntary, but inconsistently made rules about the giving of assent.

try to teach students to be less precipitate in judgement, and perhaps we can educate ourselves in the same way; this may suggest that it is possible to develop a power to control assent. However I do not believe that teaching or self-education can give the power deliberately to control response to a given body of evidence—to size up the evidence and then allow oneself to feel convinced by it to just the right degree; response on a particular occasion seems to be spontaneous, and not subject to direct control. Response to a particular body of evidence may reflect a general responsiveness, and perhaps this disposition can be modified deliberately; education might make us habitually less ready to assent. However the effect of education can be accounted for, partly and perhaps altogether, in other ways not pertaining to the ethics of belief. Education may leave us just as ready to assent and our feelings of conviction may be as strong as ever, but it may make us cautious in certain other ways—more disposed to continue with inquiry (since we know from experience how much difference it may make), more tentative in speech and action. If we are properly cautious in these ways the spontaneous impulses to believe may not matter much.

Even if belief is not itself directly voluntary, and even if we cannot (to any great extent) deliberately modify the dispositions which determine readiness to believe given a body of evidence, still it may be that some degree of slowness to assent is a moral virtue, or at least a valuable quality of some sort. But I do not think we know what degree of slowness or readiness to value. It seems quite possible that those who form beliefs readily and hold them strongly inquire more effectively: they may be more responsive to evidence, more likely to notice and be bothered by conflict of evidence, more fertile in hypotheses. It seems possible that as long as readiness to believe is accompanied by sensitivity to conflict among beliefs, a concern for truth, and a readiness to inquire (which may not be unconnected with one another), quickness to assent may favour, rather than impede, the growth of knowledge. Until we know what to say to such suggestions we do not know which disposition to prefer, readiness to assent or slowness.

I conclude that there is little scope for an ethics of belief.

2. THE ETHICS OF ASSERTION

Since the act of asserting a proposition is directly voluntary, some of the traditional ethics of belief might be translated into an ethics of assertion. For example, the injunction not to believe without sufficient evidence[21] could be reinterpreted as an injunction not to assert without sufficient evidence. Even if we cannot at the moment help believing whatever we believe with whatever degree of assent we happen to feel, perhaps we should refuse to assert or to act on a belief unless it is supported by good and sufficient reasons.

But there is another objection which applies to an ethics of assertion as much as to the ethics of belief, that there is no satisfactory way of specifying how much evidence is sufficient to warrant assertion or belief. It might be said that the evidence is sufficient when it is as much as a reasonable man or woman would require. Perhaps there is some way of saying in the abstract just how much evidence a rational person would require, and then the reference to the rational person is eliminable; or perhaps the standard of sufficiency can only be grasped intuitively through discussing a range of cases with a good judge. In the present section I will argue against various ways of specifying in the abstract how much evidence is sufficient. In section 4 I will suggest that what a good judge is good at is deciding when to break off inquiry to do something else, which is a matter for the ethics of inquiry.

2.1. *Sufficient to guarantee truth*

Is it possible to say in the abstract how much evidence is sufficient? 'Sufficient' invites the question 'For what?' If the aim of thinking is to know or believe the truth, then we might

[21] 'It is wrong always, everywhere, and for anyone, to believe anything upon insufficient evidence' (Clifford, p. 186). Perhaps there are degrees of sufficiency and degrees of assertion, but those who treat this topic often write as if a proposition is either asserted or not asserted and as if the evidence is either sufficient or not sufficient. I will follow this practice. The degree of assurance can be regarded as part of what is asserted: the proposition may indicate the probability of an event, or it may be accompanied by another which attributes to the first a certain likelihood of error. The question is then whether the evidence is sufficient to justify the assertion of such a proposition or pair of propositions.

begin by saying that the evidence must be sufficient to guarantee that the conclusion is true, and that an assertion is permissible only if it is warranted by such evidence.[22] To guarantee that the conclusion is true, the propositions offered as evidence must themselves be true without possibility of mistake. If these propositions must also be guaranteed by evidence, then an infinite series of justifications would be needed before any assertion was warranted, and nothing could ever be asserted. So some propositions must be evident in themselves, or perhaps some pieces of evidence are not propositions; at any rate, justified belief must ultimately rest on something superior to the demand for justification.[23] Unless there is infallible basic evidence there can be no knowledge, and no beliefs or assertions will be warranted.

But there are no infallible propositions, and no conclusions for which there is enough evidence to exclude all possibility of mistake. Experience seems to support fallibilism, the doctrine that an apparently true statement of *any* kind may be false. Perceptual judgements and assertions of logical truth are the kinds that seem least likely to be fallible. But perceptual judgements sometimes have to be revised—we have to concede that we must not have seen what we thought we saw or what we think we remember seeing. Circumstances can be imagined in which we might feel certain about what we think we perceive and yet be wrong. As for truths of logic, propositions which seemed such have sometimes had to be abandoned or revised, for example in the face of antinomies. A necessary truth must be true, but we may be mistaken in classifying something as a necessary truth, or in drawing out its implications, or in applying it to the world of experience. So error is possible with judgements of every distinguishable kind. There are no ultimate premisses permanently beyond question, for which supporting argument is impossible and unnecessary—though it may happen that for the moment we cannot think of any objection or supporting argument.

Further, it seems possible that we may make mistakes which we can never correct, because they never show up in conflicts

[22] The wise man assents only to presentations which are such as no false presentation could be; see Cicero, *Academica*, II.xviii.57, II.xxxi.101, II.xxxv.113, Sextus Empiricus, *Against the Logicians*, I.151-3.

[23] Cf. Aristotle, *Anal. post.*, 72 b5-25, 100 b3-18, *Metaph.*, 1006 a5-12, 1011 a5-15.

among our beliefs, or in disagreements with other people, or in any other way. Some beliefs may be 'incorrigible' and yet false. If we are in the power of Descartes's evil demon we will never know it unless he lets us know, and much of what we think will be incorrigibly mistaken. It cannot be proved that we do make undetectable mistakes; neither can it be proved that we do not. The suggestion is not proposed as a fact, only as a possibility; and it does seem possible. If it is, then we may be mistaken even about things which seem certain, and there is no knowledge, and no permissible assertion, according to this first formulation of the standard of sufficiency.

2.2. *Sufficient to remove actual doubt*

Perhaps knowledge can be defined according to some lower standard, or perhaps we can say that some assertions are warranted if they meet the lower standard even though what they assert is not knowledge. One possible lower standard is this: a proposition can rightly be asserted if it is free from all actual doubt. This is, in effect, the standard put forward by C. S. Peirce.[24] His position is as follows. Any belief may be mistaken, but this possibility does not make any belief actually doubtful; suspicion on general grounds (for example, because it is always possible that what seems true is actually false) is not actual doubt. Actual doubt cannot be summoned up at will.[25] Doubt arises when there is a specific objection, some conflict with another belief, for example with a perceptual judgement, or with the belief of another person.[26] If there is no specific objection and no doubt, then the belief can be asserted without supporting evidence. If there is doubt it may be removed by inquiry, and inquiry is pointless unless there is doubt.[27] Inquiry should continue until sufficient evidence is collected to remove actual doubt. To achieve this it is not necessary to argue from

[24] For an exposition of the relevant parts of Peirce's philosophy see Chisholm, 'Fallibilism'.

[25] Doubt comes from surprise: 'It is as impossible for a man to create in himself a genuine doubt ... as it would be for him to give himself a genuine surprise by a simple act of the will' (Peirce, *Writings*, p. 292). 'The breaking of a belief can only be due to some novel experience .... Now experience which could be summoned up at pleasure would not be experience' (ibid., p. 299).

[26] Ibid., p. 229, *Papers*, 2.160, 5.509.

[27] *Writings*, pp. 10–11.

basic premisses permanently beyond doubt—in fact there are none, since in the course of life anything may become doubtful (though not everything at once); it is enough if the premisses are not doubted at the moment.[28] A belief is as good as a belief ever can be while it is free from actual doubt.

Peirce hopes that experience and discussion will take us toward the truth. 'There is but one state of mind from which you can "set out", namely the very state of mind in which you actually find yourself at the time when you do "set out"—in a state in which you are laden with an immense mass of cognition already formed.'[29] This original stock of beliefs (some of which may be instinctive) is continually enlarged by perception, abduction and testimony.[30] It is also pruned. Conflict among one's beliefs, or with the beliefs of other people, leads to doubt, and this leads to inquiry, which eliminates, modifies or adds beliefs. The logician's hope is that these changes of belief take us closer to the truth. 'Different minds may set out with the most antagonistic views, but the progress of investigation carries them by a force outside of themselves to one and the same conclusion.'[31] 'Reasoning tends to correct itself . . . it not only corrects its conclusions, it even corrects its premisses.'[32] It even corrects its own method and motivation: 'No matter how erroneous your ideas of method may be at first, you will be forced at length to correct them so long as your activity is moved by that sincere desire', namely, to learn what is true. 'Nay, no matter if you only half desire it, at first, that desire would

---

[28] Ibid., pp. 11, 57–8, *Papers*, 5.213f. Peirce rejects the doctrine that anything is 'basic, ultimate . . . because there is nothing beneath it to know' (*Writings*, p. 55). Cf. Popper, *Logic*, p. 111 ('Science does not rest upon rock-bottom . . . . It is like a building erected upon piles . . . . When we cease our attempts to drive our piles into a deeper layer, it is not because we have reached firm ground. We simply stop when we are satisfied that they are firm enough to carry the structure, at least for the time being.').

[29] *Writings*, p. 256.

[30] 'Abduction' is Peirce's term for the inference whereby one supposes tentatively that a proposition is true because it seems a natural way of explaining something that is a fact, though other explanations are possible (cf. Popper's 'conjecture'); see *Writings*, pp. 151–3. A perceptual judgement is a kind of abductive inference, an interpretation spontaneously imposed upon sensation by a process which is not conscious, which one cannot control or criticise because one cannot go behind the perceptual judgement to compare it with the originating sensations; 'sensations emerge into consciousness in the form of beliefs'. See *Writings*, pp. 36, 302–5, *Papers*, 2.140–3, 5.216–37, 5.263. On instinctive commonsense beliefs see *Writings*, p. 293. Another apparently original source of beliefs is the testimony of other people; *Papers*, 7.226. See above, Essay II, n. 112.

[31] *Writings*, p. 38.

[32] *Papers*, 5.575.

at length conquer all others, could experience continue long enough.'[33] Such is the logician's hope and faith: finite experience is not enough to demonstrate that it is true. A sceptic is one whose experience of inquiry has destroyed this hope: but perhaps the experience was not continued long enough, perhaps the despair is premature.

Peirce's approach is attractive. But on one important point I disagree with it. To remove actual doubt is not the sole purpose of inquiry; another purpose is to reduce the chance of mistake. The suspicion that a belief may be mistaken arises from (a) conflict with other beliefs—i.e. there is an argument against this belief from premises which also seem true; (b) disagreement with other persons—if they give reasons using premises which seem true then there is also conflict with one's other beliefs, but even if they give no reasons the mere fact that they disagree is disturbing; (c) the possibility that further experience or discussion may reveal conflicts or disagreement—a belief not much tested or discussed is under suspicion even if no actual conflicts or disagreements are known; (d) the possibility that some false beliefs may be incorrigible—for example, because our minds are controlled by an evil demon. Inquiry cannot remove (d), and this possibility therefore cannot affect the order of priorities among possible inquiries, and it cannot affect action since the error will never show up; it is a bare possibility about which nothing can be done. It is in this sense an 'idle' hypothesis, but it might nevertheless be true. Inquiry can reduce suspicion (c) by testing and discussion, and (a) and (b) by the construction of arguments. If argument sometimes resolves conflict or disagreement, instead of extending it, some beliefs must 'outrank' others, in the sense that conflict leaves the former unshaken and eliminates the latter. When that happens we do not just coolly 'reallocate truth values' but undergo a change of belief. Perceptual judgements seem to be high-ranking. A proposition which conflicts with a perceptual judgement will probably cease to seem true—or, perhaps we should say, if a perceptual judgement is one of a set of seemingly true

---

[33] Ibid., 5. 582. For a treatment of moral reasoning similar to Peirce's of empirical reasoning, see Wellman. Peirce explains the convergence of empirical belief by postulating real objects constraining agreement, at least among those capable of perceiving them. If discussion leads to convergence of ethical judgements, should we postulate moral objects constraining ethical intuitions? See Quinn.

but apparently inconsistent propositions, at least one of the others will cease to seem true. Perceptual judgements may not be the only high-ranking beliefs.[34] A high-ranking belief is not immune from suspicion, and may itself in the end be eliminated if it ceases to seem true. But argument is useful even when its premises are not all high-ranking; it may reduce or shift suspicion, or at least it may extend the conflict and articulate the problem. To a great extent inquiry is the construction of arguments from premises which are low-ranking and themselves under suspicion.[35]

'Actual' doubt is suspicion under heading (a), or perhaps (b); but there is at least one other heading, namely (c), to which inquiry may be relevant. Since even what is not actually doubted may be suspected of being mistaken, it is *not* pointless to investigate what is not actually doubted. A belief which is free from doubt after investigation is better than one which is free from doubt but has never been investigated.[36] But since it is impossible and uneconomic to question everything, the agenda of inquiry must be selective. An obvious criterion of selection is the importance for theory or practice of being right. Some actually doubtful matters may not get onto the agenda because they are not important, and some important matters may although they are not actually doubtful. If it is important to be right, evidence which removes actual doubt may not be sufficient.

2.3.   *Sufficient as being unrefuted*

More recent authors have put forward theories which resemble Peirce's in allowing a proposition to be asserted with no, or little, supporting evidence provided there is no serious specific

[34] On the 'hierarchies of forcefulness' see Wolterstorff, pp. 173-5. In moral thinking the counterpart of perceptual judgement is intuitive judgement of the moral character of a particular action. But such judgements do not clearly outrank ethical generalizations: sometimes consideration of some ethical principle leads to abandonment of the particular judgement.

[35] I use 'inquiry' also to cover the collection of new evidence, and the consideration and reconsideration of evidence and argument already collected. Moral inquiry includes collecting and considering cases.

[36] Peirce sometimes says this himself; see *Papers*, 5.451. Cf. the distinction made by Carneades between the 'probable' and the 'probable *and tested*' (Sextus Empiricus, *Outlines*, I.xxxiii.227, and Bury's introduction to his edition, p. xxxvi).

objection. For example, if I believe (or conjecture), without evidence, that there are Martians, I can assert (or entertain) this proposition unless there is evidence that there are no Martians. Thus Popper allows testable conjectures to be entertained pending refutation, and to be believed if they resist refutation. Chisholm regards a proposition as 'acceptable' provided its contradictory is not 'adequately evident'. Lehrer says that belief in a proposition is completely justified provided we believe that the proposition has less chance of being false than any objection against it. Pollock says that we are justified in believing some propositions without reasons, and others for which the former constitute *prima facie* reasons, in the absence of good reasons for disbelieving.[37] From some points of view the differences between these theories may be important, but they all alike set an easy standard of justified assertion. This might be (and by some of these authors is) accompanied by a more demanding ethics of inquiry. It is the ethics of inquiry which does the real work.

How important it is to make sure that an assertion is true depends on how it connects with other thought and action. To assert to oneself is to formulate and acknowledge one's belief, which is the first step toward reflecting on and criticising it, and acting on it. To assert to others is also a way of testing one's belief and may be part of acting on it (which may involve persuading other people). Apart from some such connections with further thought or action assertion is trivial, and would hardly need to be regulated by moral or other standards. How much supporting evidence or inquiry is sufficient depends on what the assertion will lead to, in theory or in practice. In lawcourts, for example, the standard of proof is higher in criminal cases than in civil because the judgements have different practical implications. So let us adjourn the attempt to decide how much evidence is sufficient to justify assertion and consider some of the connections between belief and action.

3. BELIEF AND ACTION

If a belief may be mistaken, as any belief may be, then it is appropriate to act on it with caution: with the more caution the greater the likelihood of being wrong and the greater the

[37] Popper, *Conjectures and Refutations*, p. 228, Chisholm, *Perceiving*, pp. 8–9, Lehrer, pp. 189–92, Pollock, pp. 30–1, 40–1, 44.

importance of being right. Caution can take several forms; for example, we may delay while we make more inquiry, we may keep open lines of retreat. Caution costs something: to delay or to keep open a line of retreat is profitable only if the cost is likely to be exceeded by the benefit of reduced risk; there is an optimal degree of caution which may be less than the greatest possible. The forms of caution may supplement one another, or one may substitute for another: for example, the less it costs to provide a good line of retreat the less need there is to delay.

Since there are various kinds and degrees of caution, which can be adjusted, roughly, to the chance of mistake, it seems unnecessary to refuse to act on a belief which falls short of some single fixed standard of certainty. Such a refusal would be a kind of caution, but a simple-minded and rigid kind. A more graduated and discriminating caution is actually more cautious, since there is some risk in disregarding any pro- position that seems true and relevant—it might, after all, *be* true. This is what is wrong with scepticism. It is often said that universal suspense of judgement would mean inaction, or action at random, to which the sceptic can reasonably reply that if any proposition we can act on is as likely to be false as true then we might as well do nothing or act at random. Another objection is that universal suspense is unnatural and impossible to maintain in practice; but that does not show that it is ever reasonable to judge and act on our judgements, only that some- times we cannot help it. The objection I am making is that to me it does not seem true that every proposition that seems true is just as likely to be false (those to whom this does seem true will properly be sceptics). It seems safer, more prudent, more reasonable, to take into account in thought and action *every*- thing that seems true, even if it is uncertain—taking into ac- count also the apparent likelihood of error. What seems true may be true—indeed we believe that it is (unless experience has led us to total mistrust of seeming truth); if it seems true, and if it may be true, then it is risky to disregard it simply because we cannot show that it is true with absolute certainty, or to some other standard of sufficiency. It is perhaps strange to say 'it seems true, and I believe that it may indeed be true', but it is reasonable to say this when we adopt a critical attitude toward what seems. The sceptic says 'it seems, but just as likely it is not'; I say, 'it seems, and—sometimes at least—it seems probable that it really is as it seems, though it is always possible that it is not'; and if I am right, then it is incautious to think and act as though what seems true (though it may not be) is just as likely to be false.

When we act on a belief cautiously we are acting on other beliefs as well: about what else might be done instead, and the advantages and disadvantages of each option, about what can be done to salvage the situation if some belief turns out to be wrong, about the chances of being wrong, about the costs and benefits of further inquiry, and so on. Among the beliefs involved two kinds are noteworthy. First, there are higher-order beliefs about how to apply other beliefs to practical decisions. They may require us to act as if we do not believe certain things we do believe, or as if we believe certain things we do not—for example, as if we trust someone whom in fact we distrust.[38] Beliefs about the appropriateness of caution in some situations, and about the form it should take, are among these higher-order beliefs. Second, there are beliefs about the likelihood of mistake. An estimate of the chance of being wrong may be based on the strength of the feeling of assurance, or on the experience of testing similar beliefs, but usually it is a spontaneous belief for which little or no support can be offered. Usually the estimate is too rough to represent as a numerical probability. Sometimes no estimate is possible; but to be cautious in action we must be able to pair at least some of the beliefs involved with an estimate of the chance of being wrong.[39] In view of the role of these two kinds of beliefs, and others, it might be better not to speak of acting on a belief as if in isolation, but of acting on the ensemble of one's beliefs, or at least on the relevant subset.

What I propose, then, is that we should reject the view that lack of justifying evidence or argument is itself an objection

[38] To say that a higher-order belief may require us to act *as if* we believe *p* although we do not is to say that when we act on the ensemble of our beliefs a person ignorant of certain of them (namely the higher-order belief) may mistakenly infer from our action that we believe *p*. For example, I may act towards a person in such a way that he observes nothing from which he can infer that I do not trust him, and will naturally suppose that I do. So strictly speaking we act only on the set of propositions which we do believe.

[39] As I indicated above, n. 21, I take a statement of partial belief as a conjunction of two statements, '*p*' and 'There is such-and-such a chance that *p* is false'.

against a belief (for some people this would be a mental re-volution—it is very common to assume that if we find that we cannot justify a belief we should therefore abandon it), and that we should acknowledge (assert) and act on all our beliefs, including those for which we can find no credentials ('spon-taneous' or 'intuitive' beliefs—I call them such without im-plying that there is any special infallible faculty of intuition). Spontaneous beliefs arise perhaps from instinct, or from (other) occult causes. Abduction and deliberation[40] are important thought processes which lead to spontaneous belief. In most departments of thought little of substance would be left if in-tuitive beliefs really were excluded, and without guesses about the chance of being mistaken and about the likely yield of various possible inquiries cautious action and planned inquiry would be impossible. The point, however, is not that we cannot get on without them, but that it is imprudent to ignore anything that seems true and relevant, if it might indeed be true.

4. THE ETHICS OF INQUIRY: FIRST VERSION

The possibility of mistake calls for caution. In a particular case considered by itself it might seem worthwhile to postpone action for further inquiry; the improvement in decision and the reduction in the risks of action might seem likely to make up for what is lost by delay. But the decision whether to make further inquiry cannot be made in isolation. The time and resources needed for more inquiry might be more urgently needed elsewhere. We must decide by balancing not two things, the benefit in this case of inquiry against the cost of delay, but many competing possibilities; and we must decide not project by project but across many projects at once. To adjust the competing demands of many projects is a typical problem of economics, so as a first step toward an 'ethics of inquiry' it may be useful to sketch out an 'economics of inquiry'. To bring the

---

[40] When we deliberate we consider and reconsider the pros and cons until a con-viction forms. Unless a conviction forms spontaneously we cannot 'make up our mind'; we can decide to do the contemplated act, but not to believe that it is the right thing to do. The only way to check the outcome of deliberation is to reconsider, to do it again. The pros and cons are not deductive arguments: to reject the arguments on one side is not to imply any doubt about their premises, or about the validity of arguments of that type. Deliberation is common in moral and other practical thinking, and also in choice of theories.

two together I will assume (for this section) that we have only one moral duty, to do as much good as possible. I will also assume that there are other goods besides truth, that we therefore engage in other activities besides inquiry, and that sometimes inquiry may help one of these other activities. The problem is to decide when we have carried an inquiry far enough for the time being.[41]

We will do our duty if we allocate our time and resources in such a way that any reallocation which would have a better outcome in some respects would have a worse outcome in other respects, and the losses would equal or exceed the gains.[42] Now it is important to notice that allocation includes timetabling. The right quantities of time and resources must be allocated in the right order, at the right times. An inquiry or other activity which generally goes well may run into trouble, or a generally difficult one may open out, and then attention should switch from the one to the other. Progress along one line may presuppose progress in another. Some necessary resource may not be available for the moment; some practical matter may for a time take priority over speculation. In practical matters opportunities and deadlines are set by outside causes, and may be ordered and spaced out in various ways. To do as much good as possible we must judge well when to switch from one project to another.

[41] My sketch of an ethics of inquiry will concentrate on this question because it will focus attention on the matters in which I believe the rationalist morality of thinking is most mistaken. But the ethics of inquiry is also concerned with other things; e.g. it might lay down a duty (of imperfect obligation) to cultivate a judicial frame of mind. Other branches of morality may also include rules about thinking, e.g. 'In thinking about whom to appoint to a university lectureship pay no attention to the candidates' religious beliefs'; such rules are not part of the morality of thinking in my sense since they are concerned not with truth but with other values.

[42] In saying that our duty is to do as much good as possible I do not mean that we should try to maximise our subjective satisfaction; I mean we ought to do what really is good, whatever that may be. To decide whether reallocation leads to more loss than gain, we must be able to compare outcomes and decide which is really preferable. If there are several kinds of intrinsic goods (things good in themselves, not merely as means), the decision will be an intuition arrived at through deliberation (see above, n. 40). I believe that there are several kinds of intrinsic goods, and that we ought to seek several kinds; we cannot concentrate exclusively on what we do best. I believe, with Aristotle, that the intrinsic goods include some kinds of knowledge, and also some kinds of action; the outcomes to be compared are not only the consequences of action, they are the outcomes of allocating time and resources to various activities some of which are valued for themselves. However, these points are not assumed by the argument of the text.

The timetabled allocation can be thought of as a plan of action. What we are doing now should be the first stage of a plan, or of a number of possible plans, than which there is none better. The plan should allocate some time to reconsidering ends and means and to revising the plan, but not too much, since the return on revising such plans is especially uncertain. The plan is based on various beliefs which could themselves be investigated; the decision whether to investigate them is also based on beliefs which could be investigated; and so on, indefinitely. But we are not obliged to investigate every belief on which we act. We investigate only when it seems likely that investigation will yield a good return. Since no plan will be carried right through, the later stages can and should be left vague. The plan should make sense starting from scratch at this moment. Perhaps something was not done that should have been done, but this does not mean that it should be done now, or ever, since opportunities pass and new needs appear. Perhaps something was done in the past to prepare for something to be done now, but that does not mean that it should now be done, since by now it may be possible to do something better.

An inquiry has been carried far enough for the time being when a properly drawn-up plan directs a switch to something else; it will do so when the likely gain from more inquiry now is exceeded by the likely loss from not doing something else instead. This provides an answer of a sort to the question earlier adjourned, of how to decide when the evidence is sufficient to warrant assertion or other action. If we want to continue to talk about evidence being sufficient, let us say that we have to make do with the evidence we have, we must regard it as enough for the time being, when the moment comes to adjourn the inquiry. The evidence is then sufficient not forever, and not by some logical or epistemological standard which is the same for everyone,[43] but in relation to the inquirer's particular circumstances at the time—his or her purpose in inquiring and

---

[43] C. I. Lewis's 'critique of cogency' (as described by Chisholm, 'Lewis', p. 228) is an attempt to formulate canons which will tell us what we have a right to accept, and these canons refer to the character of the evidence, not to the circumstances of the inquirer. Chisholm views the matter in the same way: 'If you ask me to defend some conclusion of mine which you may think unreasonable, I will present evidence which I take to be such that, for *anyone having that evidence* (and no additional relevant evidence), the conclusion is a reasonable one to accept. Here, too, my justification may be formulated in a "practical syllogism"; the major premise will say that *anyone having just*

other purposes, the time and resources available, the sequence of opportunities.

4.1. *Some implications*

Justifying believing something is not the same as justifying the proposition believed. A proposition is justified, to some extent and provisionally, by testing and argument.[44] But what about the believing? If belief is not directly voluntary, then the 'act' of believing does not need to be justified morally, whatever the belief. If belief is the indirect result of some reprehensible directly voluntary act or omission in the past (for example, neglect to inquire) then that act or omission, but not the belief, is reprehensible, and would be even if this belief had not resulted.[45] It seems to me, then, that believing is not itself the sort of thing that requires or can be given justification. What about allowing a belief to stand, without subjecting it to (further) inquiry—when is that justified? That depends on our 'plan'; if the plan does not direct us to investigate the belief now, then whatever evidence we have for it (if any) must be deemed sufficient for the time being for whatever assertion and other action our plan envisages, and we are justified in allowing the belief to stand. Perhaps we ought to have investigated it in the past and did not, but this does not mean that we should investigate it now or in the future. Different people should have different plans, because of their different starting-points, talents, deadlines and opportunities. Two conclusions follow: (1) a body of evidence which suffices for one person, given his or her circumstances, may not be sufficient for another; and

the evidence in question is warranted in accepting the conclusion; the minor premise will say that I am in the position of having just that evidence; and these premises will imply that I am justified in accepting the conclusion' (ibid., p. 226, emphasis added). Cf. Kornblith, 'Beyond Foundationalism', pp. 599–602, on what he calls the 'arguments-on-paper' thesis. (Kornblith argues that the circumstances relevant to the justification of a belief include what other beliefs the person holds: I say, and also the person's purposes, opportunities, resources.) I agree that if one person is justified another person similarly placed will also be justified. The disagreement is over what has to be justified and which similarities and differences are relevant. I maintain that what needs justifying is not belief, but inquiring or (especially) not inquiring, and that the relevant circumstances include the likely returns from other possible uses of our time and resources.

[44] See above, p. 149.

[45] See above, Essay II, n. 109.

(2) in some circumstances we may be justified in letting a belief stand for which we have no evidence at all—even if we have never examined it, even if it conflicts with our other beliefs, even if other people reject it. I do not mean merely that this sort of behaviour may be excusable—that if they have acted by their lights in a difficult situation those who violate the morality of thinking in its rationalist version should not be blamed. I mean that by the standards of a more reasonable version they may have done no wrong, objectively.[46]

5. THE ETHICS OF INQUIRY: SECOND VERSION

The argument of the last section assumed that we have only one moral duty, to do as much good as possible. But this view of duty is not correct. It is in some ways too lax, in others too demanding. I want to leave the content of the moral code as open as possible (without implying that one code is as good as another), but it seems that a correct code will probably not include a general duty to do as much good as possible, and probably will include special duties some of which are of strict obligation, to be carried out whatever the effect on all or some other legitimate projects. What is left after the strict duties are done need not be devoted entirely to the service of a set of compulsory goals; some goals will be optional, some good acts will be supererogatory. The duty to further a goal seems generally to be of imperfect obligation; that is, it requires a reasonable effort over time, but no particular act at any particular time.[47] Within the field of optional activities there are differences of better and worse. The maximising plan described in the last section, modified to allow for the demands of special duties, would show the best way of allocating time and resources, and this would provide a reference point for judgements of better and worse. But to do what is better is not an obligation, and not essential to being rational.[48]

[46] We may objectively meet the standards of a revised morality of thinking, and yet action based on our beliefs may violate the standards of some other department of morality. And other people might possibly have the right to deter this act and similar acts by threatening and inflicting penalties.

[47] See above, Essay III, n. 3.

[48] It is sometimes said that action is 'practically' rational only if the agent has conclusive reason for doing just that act, or only if he believes that there is no better way of furthering his ends. For a discussion of such conceptions of rationality see Benn

Perhaps there are duties of inquiry (either strict duties, or duties of imperfect obligation), some of which may go with certain roles (as member of a jury or of a commission of inquiry, examiner, etc.). In optional inquiry we do better or worse depending on how closely we conform to a version of the maximising plan, modified to allow for the demands of duty. We can say that in optional inquiry sufficiency is judged in relation to the plan, except that 'sufficiency' is too strong a word—any amount of inquiry is morally sufficient when there is no duty. Perhaps the right word is zeal. Due concern for truth does not require the greatest possible zeal. How zealous someone is for truth can be judged by reference to the maximising plan. A given degree of zeal for truth will not require the same inquiries from everyone, since their plans ought to reflect their different circumstances, and it is compatible with not examining even uncertain beliefs which one holds and acts upon. In fact the conclusions drawn at the end of the last section still hold: it may be that of two persons having the same belief and the same evidence, one may reasonably let the belief stand while the other should subject it to inquiry, and it may in some cases be rational to let a belief stand entirely without supporting evidence and without ever examining it. To exclude these conclusions it would be necessary to adopt a code of duties so comprehensive, exacting and undiscriminating as to leave no room for optional inquiry or for differences of duty corresponding to the individual's particular circumstances and projects. I do not imagine it would ever be reasonable to adopt such a code.

So whether the truth lies with some maximising ethic, for example some form of utilitarianism, or with some kind of deontology, in either case it will not be easy to decide whether someone is properly zealous for truth because of the difficulty

and Mortimore, p. 4. I suggest instead something like this: an action is rational if it does not conflict with the agent's beliefs. To work this out it would be necessary to decide what is to count as conflict; perhaps there are degrees of conflict and degrees of rationality. There is clear conflict if we believe that it would be wrong not to do a certain act on a certain occasion and then do not do it. There is clear conflict if we believe that it would be wrong ever to do less than our best, and then on some occasion do less than our best. But if we do not believe in such an exacting duty then we do not need conclusive reasons, and do not need to suppose that no better act is possible. Unless our code of duties is comprehensive and exacting, or unless 'conflict' is taken very widely, our beliefs will often leave open a range of possible acts none of which would be irrational (though they might be open to criticism in other ways).

of knowing enough about the relevant circumstances. '... you will perhaps think this is a case reserved to the great day, when the secrets of all hearts shall be laid open; for I imagine it is beyond the power or judgment of man, in that variety of circumstances, in respect of parts, tempers, opportunities, helps etc. men are in, in this world, to determine what is everyone's duty in this great business of search, inquiry, examination; or to know when anyone has done it.'[49]

6. SCIENTIFIC INQUIRY

Methodology is like a morality of scientific thinking, a combination of an ethics of assertion and an ethics of inquiry.[50] According to Popper, belief is irrelevant to science, which is an object, an artefact, constructed by scientists but existing independently of their minds.[51] A methodology is a set of rules controlling changes to this artefact. The attempt to control construction from the foundations up has been abandoned, since there are no foundations. We begin with theories already provided by instinct or tradition (the source does not matter), test them, and change them when they fail. We need creative imagination to devise tests and revisions, but some possible changes are excluded by methodological rules which, ideally, it should be possible to apply mechanically, without exercising intuitive judgement. The ideal set of rules would exclude all possible changes but one, so that competent inquirers would all agree. A theory is not objective unless it can be tested by public, 'intersubjective', repeatable observations;[52] otherwise agreement could not be attained. But the ideal rules have not

---

[49] Locke, *Second Letter*, pp. 103–4.

[50] Different methodologies set different 'standards for intellectual honesty', according to Lakatos, p. 122.

[51] 'I am not a belief philosopher: I am primarily interested in ideas, in theories, and I find it comparatively unimportant whether or not anybody "believes" in them' (Popper, *Objective Knowledge*, p. 25). 'I wish to distinguish sharply between objective science on the one hand, and "our knowledge" on the other' (Popper, *Logic*, p. 98). See also *Objective Knowledge*, pp. 73–4, 106–12, 121–2; and see Haack. A reason given for the elimination of belief is that 'Our subjective experiences or our feelings of conviction ... can never justify any statement' (Popper, *Logic*, p. 44). But 'justify any statement' is ambiguous. The statement, i.e. the proposition stated, is not justified by the fact that I believe it, but my stating it is justified by my believing it. See above, sect. 4.1.

[52] See Popper, *Logic*, p. 56.

yet been devised, and agreement must sometimes rest on convention.[53]

I disagree with this view of science at several points: the elimination of belief, the claim that concern for agreement is essential to objectivity, and the elimination of intuitive judgement from methodological decisions.

(1) A theory can be regarded as an artefact independent of its constructors' beliefs; a fundamentalist Christian might make useful contributions to the theory of evolution, an atheist might be a theologian. But the point of work on these artefacts (at least the ostensible point—the real point may be to advance someone's career) is to provide means of knowing and understanding[54] and guidance for action. Explicit knowledge and understanding involve belief, and a theory can reasonably be acted on only if it is thought to be true—that is, believed. There is therefore no point in elaborating a theory unless it is at least 'potentially credible', that is, unless someone (not necessarily the constructor) might believe it.

(2) Thinking is objective if it has certain characteristics which make it likely to lead to truth. I will not try to specify the characteristics, or to analyse the notion further; the essential point is that objectivity is connected with truth, not with agreement.[55] Disagreement is a reason for suspecting falsity,[56] but it is not a conclusive reason, nor the only reason; it would not be absurd to suppose that some people can see truths to which others are congenitally blind, or, on the other hand, that the human race may unanimously and forever agree upon something false. Thus there is no necessary connection between truth and agreement, nor, therefore, between concern for agreement and objectivity. So there seems no reason to believe, and I

[53] Cf. Lakatos, pp. 106–12, 125–31.

[54] 'We use objective knowledge in the formation of our personal subjective beliefs' (Popper, *Objective Knowledge*, p. 80). 'Subjective' presumably means here not 'arbitrary' or 'unfounded', but 'in a subject'—cf. Essay II above, n. 47. I would add that it is only because we use it to form subjective beliefs that objective knowledge, i.e. the artefact, can be called 'knowledge', the primary reference of which is to something someone knows.

[55] Peirce defines the truth as the opinion upon which all inquirers would agree if inquiry were carried indefinitely far (*Writings*, pp. 38–9, 240, 247–8, 257–8). This is not acceptable. If the external world does not exist then the belief that it does is false even if every inquirer (or the only inquirer) holds it and will always hold it; some false beliefs may not be corrigible.

[56] See above, p. 149, point (b).

do not believe, that science cannot be objective unless it is 'intersubjectively testable'. Much of physics is not intersubjectively testable, if this means actually testable by everyone, because some people are deaf and blind; if the race evolved so that human beings normally were blind then optics might come to seem mystical except to a sighted minority, but it would not for that reason lose its objectivity. On the other hand, if the principle means testable by those capable of appropriate experiences then it is vacuous.[57]

Nothing in the nature of science, therefore, forbids work on a theory by those who think they understand it and regard it as potentially credible, even if most other people regard it as mystical or quite incredible. It may be that questions about the use of common resources or the conduct of educational institutions will require collective decisions, and this may lead to political activity some of which may be quite legitimate; for example, there might be academic political activity aimed at taking away resources or room in the curriculum from some theory or subject which most members of the scientific community regard as mystical or incredible. But nothing in the notion of scientific inquiry itself requires consensus, spontaneous or imposed.

Perhaps the notion of a scientific community engaged in certain kinds of co-operation requires concern for agreement. Two kinds of co-operation can be distinguished: (a) discussion, and (b) management of common resources and common projects other than inquiry (teaching, for example). The first kind is part of inquiry. Discussion does not presuppose agreement, or even aim at it (the aim is knowledge of the truth—of course if all the participants attain that aim they will, incidentally,

[57] 'Some mystics imagine that they have such a method [whereby beliefs are determined by reality, by an 'external permanency'] in a private inspiration from on high. But that is only a form of the method of tenacity, in which the conception of truth as something public is not yet developed. Our external permanency would not be external, in our sense, if it was restricted in its influence to one individual. It must be something which affects, or might affect, every man' (Peirce, *Writings*, p. 18). 'Or *might* affect' destroys the force of this passage. Mystics do not say that their revelations are essentially private, restricted necessarily to one individual; they might affect everyone except that some people lack the necessary receptive capacity, just as some people are blind or deaf. (Two incidental comments: Truth is neither public nor private, but something independent of what any person, or all persons, may think. And it does not follow that something restricted in its influence to one person is not (in the relevant sense) external.)

agree). The second kind may presuppose some agreement. If we decide to call people scientists only if they are members of a community based (in part) on the second sort of co-operation, then agreement may be an essential concern of science.[58] But I do not think use of the word 'science' should be restricted in this way, and if it is, that will merely determine what certain activities should be called, not what people should do or how they should do it. Agreement is neither a presupposition nor an aim of the search for truth.

(3) No plausible methodology yet formulated can do without intuitions, hunches, guesses and the like. For example, there are no rules which say that in specified circumstances a rational inquirer must definitively abandon one paradigm or research program for another.[59] The multiplication of research programs alarms some, delights others. 'We *must* find a way to eliminate *some* theories. If we do not succeed, the growth of science will be nothing but growing chaos.'[60] 'Knowledge...is... an ever increasing ocean of mutually incompatible (and perhaps even incommensurable) alternatives.'[61] Economic considerations make some sense of both attitudes, and suggest that each may be appropriate in different circumstances: when one programme is clearly more promising the others should be eliminated or adjourned, but when no programme seems very promising many programmes should be tried. A programme abandoned now may be revived later, if the rival programme which now seems more promising runs into difficulties. Since difficulties cannot always be foreseen, it may be sensible to keep several programmes going simultaneously—but not too many, only those whose chance of yielding credible theories seems good enough to justify the costs of carrying them on.[62] Just as

---

[58] Kuhn sometimes uses the word this way, for example at p. 159(19).

[59] This seems to be the outcome of the discussion in Lakatos, pp. 154–177; cf. Feyerabend, pp. 185-7. 'There is no neutral algorithm for theory-choice, no systematic decision procedure which, properly applied, must lead each individual in the group to the same decision' (Kuhn, p. 200). The choice is made by deliberation. See Kuhn, pp. 199(37) and 204(1-2); cf. above, n. 40. The failure of attempts to substitute the mechanical application of clear criteria for intuitive judgement is also clear in Hempel, pp. 27(34-40), 30(7), 32(1-3), 36(23-5), 41(31), 57(41-3), 60(41-2), 65(20), 75(21-2).

[60] Lakatos, p. 108.

[61] Feyerabend, p. 30.

[62] According to Kuhn, an approach which has some striking success, so that it seems much more promising than its rivals, may become paradigmatic for almost all work in

a firm occasionally reviews its projects and eliminates or reduces those which seem least promising, so an inquirer should occasionally abandon or shelve the programmes which seem least likely to yield credible theories.[63] This is an investment decision made under uncertainty, and for such decisions there are no rules sufficient to eliminate intuition and guesswork. The inquirers need not all make the same investment decision,[64] although some collective decisions may be needed.

If these three points are right, then from the standpoint of the morality of thinking there is no difference between scientific and other inquiries, and what was said earlier about inquiry in general applies also to scientific inquiry. There is no reason in the nature of science why scientists should not conduct their inquiries according to their own beliefs, including intuitive beliefs for which they have little or no evidence, even if other scientists disagree.

7. DISCUSSION AND TEACHING

The norms of intellectual honesty in discussion and teaching are part of the morality of thinking, or closely allied to it. We can show concern for truth not only in the interior dialogue of our own thinking but also in dialogue with others. I will indicate briefly how the line of thought I have so far followed extends into these areas.

the subject; but if later on a crisis develops and it no longer seems so promising, competing schools of thought appear again until another paradigm is found. This makes good economic sense. To concentrate investment on the most promising approach is especially sensible when work in the field is costly, requiring expensive equipment and materials and highly trained personnel, and, on the other hand, costly research is justified only when the programme seems promising. For both reasons some correlation is likely between what Kuhn calls 'maturity' and costliness; the 'immaturity' in this sense of a discipline in a field like philosophy, in which inquiry is relatively cheap, does not mean that nothing worthwhile is being accomplished.

[63] 'In developing their research programs they act on the basis of guesses about what is and what is not fruitful, and what line of research promises further results in the third world of objective knowledge. In other words, scientists act on the basis of a guess, or, if you like, of a subjective belief (for we may so call the subjective basis of an action) concerning what is promising of impending growth in the third world of objective knowledge' (Popper, *Objective Knowledge*, p. 111). Cf. Kuhn, pp. 157(26)–158(7).

[64] It may be good that some people are willing to make investments which others consider too risky (Kuhn, p. 186(24–9)). (Kuhn's account of science is reminiscent of Adam Smith, in that an 'invisible hand' guides individually narrow-minded scientists in ways which bring the scientific community closer to Popper's ideal of the self-critical scientist; see e.g. pp. 24(31), 64(30)–65(20).)

One of the premisses of J. S. Mill's argument for freedom of discussion is that our best means of coming to know the truth is to listen to all that can be said against our beliefs by persons of every variety of opinion.[65] The obvious objection is that life is not long enough.[66] Since time is scarce the inquirer must choose some inquiries and some ways of inquiring instead of others, and must judge when to switch from one to another. To listen to other people is only one way of inquiring, and there are many people who might be listened to. It would be inefficient to discuss everything with everyone through to the end; we must decide when to stop listening and switch attention elsewhere. Special duties attached to certain roles may require us to go on listening even when it might seem a waste of time, but it is unlikely that the list of such duties will add up in practice to anything equivalent to Mill's recommendation.

In deciding whom to listen to, or what to read, we are guided by beliefs about the likely returns on time spent in this and other possible ways. Such beliefs may be based on advice, for example from a book reviewer. We may be unlucky in our advisers, but if time is very short we may still do better to act under fallible guidance than to leave the allocation of time to chance. Though book reviewers are fallible, it is not sensible to read books through to the end in just the order in which they happen to come to hand.

Teachers are advisers in the planning of inquiry, who advise students on what to read and whom to listen to. A reading list may be more useful if it is selective. If the teachers' advice is followed the effect may be much the same as censorship. There is obviously a risk in this, a risk which is increased when the same advisers help select books and articles for publication and help select people for jobs, and in particular when they select and train and appoint their own successors. To give all these tasks to the same people saves time and resources, but it is risky. On the other hand, even if these advisers are only moderately reliable, *not* to accept their guidance may be wasteful and therefore harmful. There is risk either way.

In relation to teaching, the main point of the academic ethics is to reduce the risk that the teacher may censor and repress.

---

[65] Mill, *On Liberty*, p. 232.

[66] Mill acknowledged this himself; see 'The Spirit of the Age', pp. 40–4.

This is the point, for example, of the rule that good marks should be given for well-argued papers whatever the opinion expressed. But examiners must rely on their own opinions about which propositions have a fair chance of being true. It is not arguing well merely to avoid self-contradiction and validly derive some improbabilities from others. Arguing well means knowing what is unlikely and needs support and what can be taken for granted, which objections are strong and which are too improbable to need an answer. If the argument is that an hypothesis must be true because it is the only good explanation of the data, then the arguer must be able to distinguish a good explanation from others which are possible but unlikely. In judging whether someone argues well we must therefore rely tacitly on our own sense of what is likely.[67] We can think that a proposition has a fair chance of being true without believing that it is true, so it is possible to judge that someone argues well while disagreeing at many points. Still, a student whose opinions about what is likely to be true are too much at variance with the teacher's cannot reasonably be given good marks. The problem would arise even in Utopia. If jobs were more equal the teacher's power would be less; but as long as people would rather be selected for one social role than another, for whatever reason (selfish or not), and as long as selection is based (to save time and resources used in selecting) partly on performance during education, there will be a risk that teachers may censor and repress, perhaps unwittingly. The economies may justify the risk.

Students and members of the public also assess the reliability of teachers, experts and other leaders, and their assessments also reflect what they think likely to be true. Which leaders

[67] Something similar can be said about clarity of thought and expression. Members of a circle of like-minded people will congratulate one another on being the only clear thinkers. A line of thought seems unclear if it is hard to tell how to continue it to answer other relevant questions, or if it seems to suggest unlikely answers. What seems relevant depends on what theories seem possible and likely; new possibilities raise new questions, and what formerly seemed clear may come to seem obscure. In judging clarity of thought we therefore rely on our sense of likelihood, in judging clarity of expression we assume that some words and ideas are familiar and clear and others in need of explanation. A line of thought can never be made absolutely clear; the most that can reasonably be asked is that it be made clear enough to those concerned for present purposes. Deciding who is concerned, what purposes should be envisaged, and how clear is clear enough, is part of the planning of inquiry, and can be covered by what was said in sects. 4 and 5 above.

people choose or willingly accept therefore depends on the quality of existing public opinion. Since discussion and other forms of inquiry begin from and are guided by the inquirer's existing beliefs and by advice given by leaders whose influence depends on the existing state of opinion, discussion in a community in which ignorance and error are widespread may merely strengthen the authority of pseudo-experts and confirm and disseminate false beliefs. People much superior to the rest might serve the cause of truth best by forcibly displacing the existing leaders, defending their position by means of censorship, and using their influence to spread true opinions. If this produced a more enlightened state of public opinion free discussion might then become the best means of further improvement; but until then authoritarian methods might be better.[68] Thus Mill's argument for freedom of discussion assumes some degree of general enlightenment, as he acknowledged;[69] it will not, and should not, convince those who believe that very many people are seriously mistaken on matters of importance.

8. THE ACADEMIC MORALITY

I have argued not merely that we cannot (directly) help believing whatever we believe, or that it may be reasonable to have beliefs which may be mistaken, but that it may be reasonable in some cases to assert and act upon possibly mistaken beliefs without further investigation; and I have suggested how we might decide in a given case whether that is reasonable. At the beginning I said that, crudely, this essay is a defence of the

[68] There could be some freedom of discussion within the élite group, and some 'right of petitioning' for people outside the group (that is, a right to make representations to the élite); compare Plato, *Laws*, 634e. Mill's arguments in *On Liberty*, ch. 2, will not seem so strong if the possibility of a graduated and stratified repression is taken into account.

[69] 'The early difficulties in the way of spontaneous progress are so great, that there is seldom any choice of means for overcoming them .... Liberty, as a principle, has no application to any state of things anterior to the time when mankind have become capable of being improved by fair and equal discussion' (Mill, *On Liberty*, p. 224). See also *Representative Government*, pp. 418-20. (However, a reciprocity argument may support freedom of discussion even when discussion may disseminate and confirm error; other things count besides truth, such as peace. It seems to me that some reciprocity argument is the best basis for freedom of discussion, not the dubious claim that it furthers truth.)

closed mind. This is how it may seem to those who hold the position I have attacked, namely that it is immoral to hold a belief and act on it without sufficient evidence. But more exactly I am proposing to reinterpret parts of the ethics of belief as an ethics of inquiry and of action under uncertainty. Under the proposed reinterpretation, whether we are justified in acting on our beliefs without further inquiry does not depend upon whether our evidence is sufficient by some standard unrelated to our projects, talents, opportunities, etc. but on how else we could use our time, given our circumstances. It does not seem possible to say exactly how it depends on circumstances, so as to reduce the decision to rule. The relevant circumstances will usually be known in detail only to the person him- or herself. We should therefore be pretty slow to say that someone else has a closed mind; on the other hand, we cannot be too sure that we ourselves have not. Sometimes (for example, in helping to choose someone for public office or for a job) we need to judge other people's devotion to truth, but in most disagreements it is enough simply to urge on them what we may think they would have seen if they had looked further, without suggesting that they should have done so. Instead of passing judgement it is better to argue. But of course none of this means that in intellectual matters there are no duties and no moral differences of better and worse, or that one opinion is as good as another, or that it is wrong to criticise—indeed, it is part of respecting others to take their opinions seriously enough to criticise them, and to credit them with willingness to listen to criticism frankly expressed.

The common academic morality dismisses 'unfounded' opinions (especially in religion and politics), and discourages people from asserting and acting on beliefs they cannot justify. Against this I claim that our assertions and actions may and should take account of all of our beliefs, including opinions, intuitions, and other beliefs for which no credentials can be shown. Philosophers since Plato have disparaged mere opinion, holding that while opinions may be unavoidable and in some ways useful they are no part of philosophy. Modern philosophy has tried to base thought and action on principles which are certain, and to devise criteria and rules of thinking which can be applied mechanically to give authoritative conclusions. These attempts have not succeeded. The principles are merely spontaneous beliefs under another name; criteria are revised if they give intuitively unacceptable decisions; the proposition that thought and action should be based only on certain principles cannot be justified in its own terms (since it is not self-evident or provable); the theoretical structure grows too slowly for the needs of action, and a gap opens between theory and practice—everyday life is based on opinions which are not part of the justified system, and the opinion that it is all right to live this way is not part of the system either.[70] The academic ethics ends up as an armoury of weapons to be used selectively against unpopular creeds.

The policy which I advocate is at least self-consistent and practicable: to assert and (with due caution) act upon all the propositions which seem true and relevant, whatever their source and credentials, examining them if and when this is opportune, not claiming for any of them—even after thorough examination—any infallibility or authoritative status.[71] This policy does not guarantee that a false belief accepted with no credentials except that it seems true will eventually be eliminated. No policy for the conduct of the understanding can guarantee this, since it seems possible that some false beliefs may be incorrigible. But as long as it does not seem true that what seems true has an equal chance of actually being false, there seems to be nothing more rational we can do than to act on what we believe even when we cannot prove it.

POSTSCRIPT: EPISTEMOLOGY

Epistemology and the ethics of belief are two parts[72] of a wider enterprise without a name, the response to scepticism. The term 'epistemology' refers to the Platonic contrast between *epistēmē* and *doxa*, knowledge (in a strong sense) and mere opinion.[73]

---

[70] Cf. Descartes's provisional code of morals, adopted 'in order that I should not remain irresolute in my actions while reason obliged me to be so in my judgements' (vol. 1, p. 95). In ancient times Carneades set standards for knowledge so strict that no belief could meet them, and then allowed action to be based on probability; see Cicero, *Academica*, II.xxxi.99-100, xxxii.104.

[71] This is equivalent to Bayle's policy of following conscience. See above, Essay II, sect. 3.3.

[72] On their relationship see Firth.

[73] See Plato, *Meno*, 97-8.

Academic sceptics deny that we have knowledge, epistemology defines knowledge and tries to answer the question whether we have it. The Academic denial has its place in an argument like that which was presented above at the beginning of the introduction to this essay: (1) Any proposition, however certain it may seem, may in fact be false; (2) we should not affirm anything that may be false; therefore (3) we should not affirm anything. Instead of (2) the Academic may say: '(2a) We should not affirm anything we do not know.' If we cannot, in the strong sense, *know* anything unless it is true, then, once more, conclusion (3) seems to follow. My response to such arguments is to concede (1), but deny (2) and its analogues, and deny (3). But others avoid (3) not by denying (2) outright but by substituting: '(2b) We should affirm nothing of which we are not at least reasonably or justifiably sure' (although it may in fact be false). Thus epistemology comes to concern itself not only with knowledge in the strongest sense, but also with the broader notion of justifiable belief.[74]

The response to scepticism—the attempt to work out what really does follow, for theory and for practice, from the considerations which move the sceptic, and in particular from the possibility that whatever seems true may actually be false—is a necessary undertaking. But in my opinion epistemology, like the ethics of belief, is a mistaken project and should be scrapped—though much of what is at present classified as epistemology might still be useful in responding to scepticism. In my opinion there is no philosophical importance in the distinction between knowledge and mere opinion, and no proper notion of epistemological justification. Much work in epistemology manages to avoid the question of what it means to say that a belief is epistemologically justified. For example, the definition of knowledge classic in epistemology is that we know a proposition if (a) it is true, (b) we believe that it is, and (c) our belief is justified. Is some fourth condition needed, to rule out a claim to know in a case in which we have a justified but false belief which implies another belief that happens to be true?[75] To discuss this question it is not necessary to say what

[74] Justifiable, that is, *epistemologically*, as being an approximation to knowledge. (Some epistemologists, however, give the term an ethical interpretation—see Kornblith, 'Justified Belief'.)

[75] For an account of the discussion arising from Gettier's article see Dancy,

'justified' means, although the term occurs on every page. In the same way many other questions of epistemology can be discussed without giving any account of this central concept. Now I challenge epistemologists to say, before they pursue those other questions any further, how we are to judge whether an affirmation is justified in the epistemological sense, and what that sense is.

Some will say that we are epistemologically justified in affirming whatever seems true. I agree that we are justified in affirming whatever seems true, but what is the point of 'epistemologically'? I say we are justified not epistemologically but morally, against those who say that we have a moral duty to affirm only what we know or are reasonably sure of: we are justified simply because there is no such duty. To say for this reason that it is justifiable to affirm whatever seems true is to *reject* the pretensions of epistemology, not to provide an account of 'epistemological justification'.

The epistemologist may in turn challenge me to say what I mean by knowledge, as distinct from mere opinion ('I don't just think it, I *know* it'), and what I mean by the justification of a proposition (since I do refer to such justification—see above, sect. 4.1). I will begin with justification. A proposition is justified *to someone's satisfaction*, and *for the time being*. If I believe that a certain proposition is true, test it, look for evidence and argument for and against it, and at the end of the time available for this investigation I still believe it—or if you assert something, and in response to my demand for justification produce evidence, arguments, results of testing, which in the end cause me to share your belief—then it has been justified to *my* satisfaction, not necessarily to anyone else's; and the end of the process is always in principle an adjournment because it is time to do something else, not an absolutely final conclusion. There is no question of measuring the evidence against epistemological canons, which in any case do not exist.

As for what I mean by knowledge, my account is as follows. In formulating the conditions for correct application of the term 'know' we need to distinguish two kinds of cases, namely those in which I claim that I have knowledge, and those in which I ascribe knowledge to someone else, for example to

pp. 25-40.

you.[76] If I claim that I know something, then (i) I must believe it, and (ii) I must estimate as pretty low the likelihood that it is actually false. If I say that you know some particular proposition, then (i) I must believe that you believe it, (ii) I must also believe it, (iii) I must estimate as pretty low the likelihood that it is actually false, and (iv) I must think that it is not just by chance that you got it right.[77] Two questions arise. First, when I say you know something, must I think that *you* estimate as pretty low the likelihood that it is actually false? I am not sure, but I think not: it seems possible to say that you know something you do not know you know—or even think you do not know—as long as you believe it. Suppose I believe that you have second sight, but you believe there is no such thing and try to ignore these fearful expectations that unaccountably come upon you, though you cannot help believing that your fears will come true: then I may regard as knowledge beliefs of yours which you quite reasonably regard as highly suspect. 'You did know, after all,' I may say when things turn out as you could not help fearing they would. Second, if I claim to know, must I believe that it is not just by chance that I am right? Again I am not sure, but I think not: it seems to be enough if I am confident that what I claim to know is not actually false. If I thought my belief was an accident I might have no confidence in it, but I may be confident without knowing why, without my confidence being based on anything. Condition (iv) must be satisfied if I say that you know, because otherwise I can ascribe knowledge to you simply because you believe something I believe I know. The point of claiming that I know seems to be to give others my assurance (for whatever they think it is worth) that the thing is true,[78] whereas the main point of saying that others know seems to be to say something about *them*.

[76] More attention to this distinction might clarify the disagreement between 'internalism' and 'externalism' (see Bonjour): to be justified in claiming knowledge for myself I must believe that I know, but I can ascribe knowledge to another person who does not know that he knows, and even thinks (even for good reasons) that he does not know, and even to one who has not done his duty under the 'ethics of thinking'.

[77] See Unger. To be justified in ascribing knowledge to you I need not know *why* I think, or whether I have any reasons at all for thinking, that you are not right by chance. 'Causal' and 'reliabilist' theories sketch kinds of reasons I may have when I have reasons, but are not part of the analysis of what knowledge is.

[78] See Austin, pp. 67ff.

None of this involves any reference, even tacit, to epistemological canons, or to justification under the ethics of thinking. If I claim knowledge I do not imply that my belief is justified under the ethics of thinking, and I do not imply that yours is if I ascribe knowledge to you. What I recognize as knowledge depends in the first place on what seems true to me. I cannot claim to know p, or ascribe knowledge of p to you, unless to me p seems true. It may not be true. I must estimate as pretty low the possibility that it is actually false. 'Pretty low' is vague and cannot be made precise; it cannot be measured against canons valid always, everywhere and for everyone. When does a house count as a 'big house'? That depends on the social circles you move in, and on many other things. Similarly, in some circles, and in some contexts, people claim or ascribe knowledge more readily than in others. To make the best use of others' advice we need to develop a sense of how readily they claim to know; to communicate our views properly we need to develop a sense of how they will take our expressions of doubt and claims to know. In the expressions that convey these nuances there is no ideally correct standard of usage. Philosophers careful never to claim to know or to be certain will often seem more uncertain than they really are—without upholding any philosophical standard, because there is none.

When someone asserts or claims to know something, I do not think we should conduct any inquest to see whether he or she has enough evidence to justify making such a claim. We should simply ask, is it true? To answer that question we may want to know what evidence the asserter has, but we should not then try to decide whether it is enough to satisfy the canons of epistemology, or whether the asserter was justified in making an assertion on the basis of such evidence: instead we should simply look for more evidence, for and against, for as long as it seems reasonable to continue the inquiry. Sometimes we need to assess the reliability of other people. That does not depend on how readily they claim knowledge (though we may need some sense of that to interpret what they say), but on how likely they are to be right—which, in turn, does not depend on their epistemic standards, but on their general background knowledge of relevant matters, their intelligence, and how much study they have made of the matter. It has nothing to do with reluctance to believe.

CONCLUSION

Sincerity and Being Right

The case for toleration as Bayle presents it seems closely tied to the proposition that if we do what we sincerely think right then we do a morally good act, even if that act is actually wrong. The prominence of this proposition in his book would have made it seem unpersuasive to some of the people most important to convince, namely those who followed 'the principles of St Augustine'. Arnauld, for example, rejects the Jesuits' thesis that an act cannot be morally bad unless we do it in the belief that it is wrong, for reasons that imply rejection of Bayle's thesis that an act must be morally good if we do it in the belief that it is right. In fact, neither proposition is needed as a premiss in Bayle's main argument for toleration, but the difference over this matter is a suitable starting-point for reflection on some of the features of Bayle's moral theory.

I. BAYLE'S MORAL THEORY

Bayle identifies moral goodness with deserving praise and badness with deserving blame and punishment; he distinguishes between goodness and rightness and between evil and wrongness, and holds that a wrong act may deserve praise; it follows that an act may be both morally good and wrong. Arnauld does not identify goodness with praiseworthiness, but holds that to be praiseworthy an act must be morally good, and that it cannot be good unless it is right; and he holds that an evil act deserves blame and punishment; it follows that a wrong act cannot be good and must deserve blame and punishment. Arnauld admits that a wrong act done in ignorance may be excused, but much of the ignorance or mistaken belief that

Bayle would regard as excusing or justifying wrong acts Arnauld classifies as ignorance inflicted as punishment, which he holds does not excuse. According to Arnauld an excuse does not transfer the act into the category of morally praiseworthy acts, but merely wards off blame and punishment.

Through these disagreements runs a common concern with desert or merit, with what ought to be praised, blamed, rewarded or punished: what is deserved or merited is either reward or punishment, and praise and blame are thought of as species of reward and punishment. This concern with desert, sometimes under the rubric of 'moral responsibility' (thought of as liability to punishment), is in fact characteristic of most European moral theory until at least the end of the eighteenth century.[1] In this tradition morality is often thought of as being like the law of a State, as being part of God's government of the universe. Moral judgement is an anticipation of God's judgement on the last day. God will then reward praiseworthy acts and punish blameworthy ones—not as an incentive or deterrent but retributively.[2] (By 'retributively' I mean just because it is deserved, without any other reason.) Our moral judgement meanwhile is the recognition that the act merits reward or punishment, or praise or blame thought of as kinds of reward and punishment. Arnauld opposes the idea of purely philosophical sin precisely to keep the link between moral judgement and God's distribution of eternal rewards and punishments.[3]

Concern with merit leads to another preoccupation of many writers in this tradition, namely with what these days is often called 'contra-causal' freedom,[4] called in Bayle's time 'liberty of indifference'.[5] This is the idea that my choices (some of them, at least) are free in the sense that at the very moment when I

---

[1] Even Kant thought that morally valuable acts must be rewarded, and argued that we must postulate God to guarantee that they will be. See *Critique*, pp. 638–41.

[2] I am using 'retribution' to include reward as well as punishment.

[3] Arnauld and other Catholic Augustinians do not reject the idea of merit. Where they differ from the Pelagians is in holding that after Adam's sin all deserve punishment and can be saved only by unmerited grace. Once grace is given merit begins again: on the last day God will 'crown his own gifts' by rewarding the meritorious acts grace has made possible (see Augustine, *Ep*. CXCIV.v.19 (*PL*, vol. 33, col. 880)).

[4] See Campbell, p. 117. For criticism of this term see van Inwagen, pp. 14–15.

[5] Arnauld criticised this term, and preferred the expression *facultas ad opposita*; Labrousse, *Pierre Bayle*, vol. 2, p. 396, note 38. This is an echo of Duns Scotus' term, *potentia ad opposita*, 'power for opposites'.

am choosing to do something I also have complete power to choose not to do it, no matter what the antecedent events and circumstances may be—in particular, no matter what my character and present impulses may be. Thus choice is not determined by the antecedents: I can choose either way. Such a conception of human freedom was unheard of, I believe, before Duns Scotus.[6] But whoever originated it, during the fourteenth century it became, with some variations, the common doctrine of the Franciscans,[7] and later of the Jesuits and of Catholics generally. Earlier moralists, such as Augustine,

[6] '[A] manifest power for opposites accompanies this freedom. . . . For there is in it a power to will after not willing, or to will a succession of opposed acts. . . . But there is also another [power] without any succession which is not so manifest. Take a will created such as to have its existence only for a single instant, and which performs a particular volition in that instant. It would not perform this necessarily. . . . For a cause is not contingent only because it exists before the instant in which it causes and as pre-existent could cause or not cause. . . . There is thus a power of this cause for the opposite of that which it causes, without succession being involved' (Duns Scotus, in Hyman and Walsh, pp. 593-4). See Harris, vol. 2, pp. 283-300, 308-18, and Bonansea. Thomas Aquinas would have agreed that there is power to choose either way, but I think not that both powers are complete at the moment of choice: his conception of free-will involves succession. According to St Thomas, no created good can be completely satisfactory, as there is always some limitation or drawback; consequently we can always find a reason on the other side if we look for it, and this is why we have free choice: see *Summa*, 1-2, q.10 a.2, and q.13 a.6. This does not mean that we do always look for reasons on both sides, or that we can choose against the balance of reasons as we perceive it.

[7] For the views of the Franciscan William of Ockham see Clark, especially pp. 132-49. As Scotus does, Ockham contrasts will with natural agency. '[A] natural cause, while it remains the same, always does the same. . . . [Whatever] it does at one time it does at another, unless there is some variation on the part of the patient, or of the agent, or some other impediment.' But a contingent power 'produces some effect, and, *with nothing changed* on its part nor on the part of anything else whatever, has it as much in its power not to produce as to produce, so that of its nature it is determined to neither'. That the will acts contingently has three possible meanings. First, that 'the will existing at a time before instant A, in which it causes, can freely and contingently cause or not cause in A: and this is true, if the will does thus preexist. Second, that in the very instant in which it causes it is true to say that it does not cause: and this is not possible, because of the contradiction that would follow, namely that it causes in A and does not cause in A. Third, it can mean that the will causes contingently in A because, freely, *without any variation or change* coming upon it or upon another cause, and without the cessation of another cause, it can cease from its act in another instant after A—so that in instant A this would be true: "The will causes", and in another instant after A this would be true: "The will does not cause"' (my translations of texts quoted by Clark, in his nn. 45, 47 and 53; emphasis added). Cf. 'Can we say, then, of the wilful wrongdoer that his wrong choice was "free", in the sense that he might have chosen rightly, not merely if the antecedents of his volition, external and internal, had been different, but supposing these antecedents *unchanged*? This, I conceive, is the substantial issue raised in the Free Will controversy' (Sidgwick, p. 59, emphasis added).

also thought that morality is concerned with voluntary action, and that deliberation is a choice between possible courses of action. But it did not occur to them to think that human action is not voluntary unless at the very moment of choice the agent has complete power to choose the opposite of what he *is* choosing: in their view a voluntary action is simply one that is done by choice.[8]

Many modern philosophers have rejected the Scotist conception of the voluntary, but many have adopted it. Part of its attraction is that it seems to harmonize ideas of fairness with moral responsibility, understanding this as a matter of fitness for some sort of punishment or reward. One argument is that I cannot justly be blamed or punished except for my own act, and an act determined by antecedents not all in my power would not be my own act. Augustine and his followers reject this argument: the act is my own if I choose it, whether I could have chosen otherwise or not. Another argument is by analogy: just as I cannot justly be punished for what I *physically* cannot help, that is, for something that happens whether I want it to or not, so I cannot justly be punished for doing what I cannot help wanting to do. Augustine and his followers reject the analogy: 'internal compulsion' is not morally on a par with external compulsion. According to Arnauld, God makes allowance for the effect of adverse external circumstances, but not for internal compulsions: the strength of an inclination to choose what is wrong makes the act more voluntary, and does not reduce the punishment deserved (see above, p. 39). Further, they argue, necessity of choice is no excuse when it is itself a punishment. According to Arnauld (see below, Appendix), since Adam's fall desert supposes only a 'metaphysical' and not 'effective' power of opposite choice. Before the fall Adam had effective liberty of indifference; our reduced freedom is a punishment for Adam's abuse of his full freedom.

Bayle rejects the theory of reduced freedom as punishment (see above, Essay II, sect. 4.2), but otherwise it is not easy to

---

[8] '[A]nyone who says that a stone sins when it is carried downwards by its own weight is, I will not say more senseless than the stone but, completely mad. But we charge the soul with sin when we show that it has abandoned the higher things and prefers to enjoy lower things. What need is there, therefore, to seek the *origin* of the movement whereby the will turns from the unchangeable to the changeable good? We acknowledge that it is a movement of the soul, that it is voluntary and therefore culpable' (Augustine, in Morgenbesser and Walsh, pp. 14–15, emphasis added).

say just where he stands on these questions.[9] In many places, usually in connection with the question whether freedom can be reconciled with God's foreknowledge,[10] he describes the controversy between those who say that our will is 'endowed with free choice (*franc arbitre*) properly so-called', and those who say that it is not, though we are free in another sense.[11] (Notice that the term 'free choice' has been appropriated by one of the parties, although the other also holds that human beings are free and that the will cannot be forced.) As members of the first party he mentions Jesuits, Molinists, Remonstrants or Arminians, and Socinians.[12] Freedom of choice as they understand it is 'liberty of indifference', the 'proximate power not to act, and to choose even the contrary of what we choose',[13] an ability to choose even when the motives on both sides are evenly balanced.[14] According to them, we are 'self-determining', 'masters of our own acts of will'.[15] The other party consists of the various kind of Augustinians; he mentions Thomas Aquinas, the Dominicans, Calvin, the Calvinists of the Synod of Dort, Luther, the Jansenists. They hold that an act is free if it is 'spontaneous'—or, more precisely, if it is not due to external constraint and is done with knowledge and deliberately, that is, out of conscious choice;[16] and that freedom in

[9] My source on this topic is Labrousse, *Pierre Bayle*, vol. 2, pp. 387ff.

[10] Molinists, Jansenists and Arminians were concerned to reconcile human freedom not so much with God's foreknowledge as with his grace; see above, Essay I, Introduction. For some of the ancient and medieval sources of the controversy about freedom and foreknowledge see Cicero, *On Fate*, Augustine, *City of God*, V.8-10, Boethius, *Consolation of Philosophy*, V, Ockham, *Predestination*; see also Bayle, *HCD*, art. 'Paulicians', rem. F, pp. 181-4.

[11] *RQP*, p. 781 b22-6.

[12] He does not mention the Franciscans, who had been the first to claim that we have *potentia ad opposita*.

[13] *RQP*, pp. 791 a33-5, 852 b43-4. 'Proximate' power is what I have called 'complete' power. I could light a fire if I had a match (since the kindling is all ready), but since I do not have one (though I could go and get it) the power is remote, not proximate.

[14] Ibid., p. 780 a40-6.

[15] Ibid., pp. 853 a9, 856 a34. Those who hold this theory envisage 'an absolute empire established in the soul of man, independent of all the rest of the universe: objects may excite the passions, reason may advise a thousand things, the will may be disposed thereby to turn from one side, but nevertheless it retains a full authority over its determinations .... Human liberty is therefore something with no connection with general laws, it is detached from all the rest of the world' (*EMT*, p. 65 a36-55).

[16] *RQP*, pp. 662 a157, 791 a32-3, 852 b45-7.

this sense is not inconsistent with determination of our choice by God's grace, or by vice, or by some other cause.[17]

It might be expected that Bayle, as a Calvinist, would adopt the second theory, but in fact he seems to adopt the first, that of the Jesuits and Arminians—that human beings have liberty of indifference. He does not think, however, that this theory can be established by philosophical argument. The testimony of consciousness is not enough, since occasionalism, or some theory of psycho-physical parallelism and physical determinism, or the Augustinian or Thomist theories of God's action upon human will, could all be reconciled with the phenomena of consciousness.[18] Not psychological reflection but 'morality and religion ought to be the resource of the hypothesis of Mr Jaquelot', that is, of the Arminian theory.[19] But morality does not furnish a decisive argument,[20] and neither does the practice of punishing wrongdoers for the sake of reformation and deterrence.[21] What seems to prove that we have liberty of indifference is the religious revelation that God punishes retributively. 'The revelation of a hell … is the only good proof of our liberty.'[22] Only those who postulate liberty of

[17] Ibid., p. 782 a61-b7.

[18] Ibid., pp. 785 b46–786 a25.

[19] Ibid., p. 786 a59–60.

[20] 'Molinism has some advantage at the tribunal of morality. . . . Its main forces consist in the consequences which follow if man were always to act necessarily. It must be confessed that these consequences are indeed terrible, but a philosopher who was not a Christian would weaken them greatly, either because he would not admit what scripture teaches on the penalties for sin, or because he would delete from the list of sins many actions which Scripture includes. The patrons of philosophic sin, and those who maintain that to sin one must know actually that one is sinning [in a footnote he refers to Arnauld's *Denunciation*], would open for themselves the way to a notable reduction; but sound theology puts before them invincible obstacles—which would not be insurmountable to a pure philosopher. That is why he would more easily maintain the definition Luther and Calvin gave of human liberty [i.e. as 'spontaneity']' (*RQP*, p. 782b).

[21] 'The punishments human law inflicts on malefactors do not suppose they have liberty of indifference: we would destroy disturbers of public peace as we destroy wild beasts even if we believed they had no free choice' (ibid.). On this last point see art. 'Rorarius', rem. F: in some places they hang wolves or crucify lions to discourage the others; 'They would then flog a pickpocket, even if they knew that he had no free will, provided that experience had taught them that by whipping certain people they restrain them from continuing certain actions' (*HCD*, p. 230).

[22] Quoted Labrousse, *Pierre Bayle*, vol. 2, p. 397. (But is this Bayle's own opinion? He is reporting the opinion of the author of a book he is reviewing). To postulate that we have liberty of indifference does nothing to solve the problem of evil: in fact, it aggravates it, since it has to be explained why God gave mankind such a dangerous gift (*HCD*, art. 'Paulicians', pp. 177ff.).

indifference can engage in praise, blame, reward and punishment (when it is retributive, at least) without inconsistency.[23]

Assuming, then, that free choice in this sense is a presupposition of moral merit and demerit (understood as entitlement or liability to praise or blame, reward or punishment), and assuming that moral goodness and evil are the same as moral merit and demerit, and that the effect of external causes on what we believe and on the outcome of our attempts to perform an external act is morally like compulsion, Bayle argues (see above, Essay II, n. 64, and sect. 4.1) that being right and doing the right external acts are morally neither good nor evil: nothing is good or evil morally except the very act of free choice. Provided we choose to do what we sincerely believe is right, it does not matter whether we can actually do it, or whether it is actually right.[24] Merit depends on the reason for the choice, on the reason as we see it; it is as if we freely choose to accept some particular reason, for the deeper reason that this reason seems to have a certain moral quality which we deem good; the deeper choice is the decision to value this quality, and the deepest choice is to love whatever we see as good. Merit arises from the intensity of this basic commitment to the good.[25]

But is this basic commitment, and the intensity of it, freely chosen? An affirmative answer sets off an infinite regress, unless that choice is undetermined: and if it is, if it is made for no

[23] Cf. *CPD*, p. 402 a10–53. But his argument here may be *ad hominem*, and he does not restrict what he says to retribution.

[24] This line of thought, if taken further than Bayle himself took it, leads to some paradoxical conclusions (see above, Essay II, n. 109). Present choices may be determined or influenced by past choices (which may have led, for example, to ignorance or error, or to bad inclinations). If we regard the effects of past choices as a constraint on present choices similar to the influence of external causes, we may conclude that such conditioned choices should therefore be discounted. Thus all moral merit and demerit will belong to original, unconstrained choices, not conditioned by past choices, innate temperament or anything else.

[25] This would explain the connection between merit and difficulty: doing the right thing despite difficulties manifests strength of commitment. According to some scholastics there need not be any actual difficulty; there is merit if love of God is so strong that it would overcome difficulties and distractions if there were any. Cf. 'Paley held ... that our place hereafter would be determined ... by the balance, not of our good and evil deeds, which depend upon opportunity and temptation, but ... by the intensity and continuity of our *will* to do good; by the strength with which we have *struggled* to be virtuous' (Mill, 'Sedgwick', p. 70).

reason, and not out of love of goodness, why is it meritorious? Suppose then that the answer is negative. Suppose that the basic commitment is a matter of innate temperament, that each of us has a finite 'given' amount of moral energy, strength of will or power of right choice, a certain degree of concern to do good (it need not be the same all the time, or the same from one person to the next, and it may be possible to use some of it to develop more). Then we would not deserve praise or reward for the strength of our commitment to the good, because there seems no reason why merit should depend on what is merely 'given'. That would not be fair, since it depends on an external cause, which might give different people different amounts: merit would then depend on luck. Desert can therefore depend on strength of commitment only in so far as that results from self-development. But then it is on a par with any other result of choice, and desert after all depends not on a basic commitment but on the particular choices, discounted to allow for differences in the original endowments of goodwill. Discounting would be no simple matter. If our endowment of moral energy is finite, then someone faced with many hard decisions coming close together will not be able to avoid bad choices altogether. Fairness would seem to require that, in assessing moral desert, allowance should be made not only for our different initial endowments of moral energy but also for the different degrees of rigour with which the world tests our goodwill—for differences in the sequence of problems and temptations and in their order and timing. Only God will know how to make all the allowances fairness requires. Human beings will have to give up assessing one another's moral merits, and their own.

These are paradoxical conclusions, which it would be better to avoid if we can. Against Bayle and others in this tradition, then, I will suggest that merely retributive punishment is wrong, that in relation to moral assessment praise and blame are not kinds of reward and punishment, that praiseworthiness and moral goodness are not identical, that morality does not presuppose liberty of indifference and that sincerity is not enough for moral goodness. Moral assessment is for some other purpose (when it has a purpose) than justifying reward or punishment.

2. MORAL GOODNESS

Bayle's reduction of all moral value to the praise or blame due
to voluntary acts is in my opinion a serious oversimplification.
Morality is indeed concerned in one way or other with voluntary acts—with such acts themselves, and with the dispositions which cause them: but it is not concerned with
dispositions only as caused by voluntary acts. The goodness of
a person, which consists in having good dispositions, must be
defined separately from the goodness of an action, and each is
something complex.

The goodness of an *action* seems to have at least two aspects
(of which Bayle focuses exclusively on the second). To be simply
good an action must both (a) be morally right, and (b) be done
for a morally good or right reason or motive. The action is (a)
morally right if it is not contrary to any moral rule of duty,
that is, if it is permissible. It need not be required as a duty; it
is enough if it does not violate any duty. Duties are not so
numerous and comprehensive as to leave no freedom; often we
have a choice among possible courses of action none of which
is a duty. Duties are of various kinds and can be violated in
various ways (see above, Essay III, Introduction). What violates a deliberative principle (if such a principle lays down a
duty) is not an outward act but some forbidden manner of
deliberating; a duty of imperfect obligation is not violated by
any single act or omission but by not doing enough over time;
and so on. As for (b), that supposes that morality is not merely
a set of rules which restrict what we can do to further our
purposes whatever they are—as if morality said 'Do what you
like, as long as you don't break any of the following rules'—
but is concerned also with the evaluation of purposes and other
reasons for action.[26] Some reasons may be forbidden by moral
principles, for example by principles of deliberation. Some reasons are merely permissible, while others are positively good,
and some are better or best. A right (that is, permissible) act
done for a merely permissible reason is morally good in the
minimal sense that it is not evil; if the reason is positively good,

[26] The goodness of ends sought is another goodness besides that of persons and
actions and reasons for acting. The goodness of an end makes conduciveness to that
end a good reason for doing something. 'Good' is a term with a number of related
meanings; see Aristotle, *EN*, I.6, 1096 b27-30.

and better than others, then the act is morally good, and better than others. It is not a duty always to act for the best.

The moral goodness of a *person* consists in having dispositions which prompt right acts and inhibit wrong ones, and prompt action for good reasons and inhibit action for bad reasons. There are many such dispositions. They include moral virtues, qualities of temperament and certain beliefs, at least beliefs in general terms about what is right and good.[27] Some such dispositions are acquired voluntarily, by deliberate self-cultivation, but others are not: they are acquired accidentally, or are innate, or develop spontaneously. Bayle's mistake here is to say that only dispositions due to deliberate self-cultivation are morally good or evil (see above, Essay II, sect. 4.1). A disposition may be morally good or bad because of the actions it gives rise to, and not because of the actions that gave rise to it. In choosing friends, in considering whether some person is truly worthy of respect, in deciding whether someone can be relied on in certain ways, and in many other cases in which we make what I think can be called moral assessments, we are not concerned to know which of the dispositions which give rise to good actions were due to self-cultivation. And while in some cases self-cultivation may be prompted by a self-cultivated disposition, that cannot be true *ad infinitum*, and it seems unsatisfactory to say that the dispositions which give rise to the first cultivation of moral virtue are not to count as moral dispositions.

Conscientiousness is an important disposition, but it is a mistake to try to reduce the goodness of persons to conscientiousness. Conscientiousness or goodwill is the disposition to do what is morally good because of its goodness. If Christians do something because it seems the Christian thing to do, that shows their Christianity. But if they do the same act in the belief that it is morally good (perhaps because they believe that what Christianity suggests always is morally good), and do it precisely because they believe that it is good, and otherwise

---

[27] What distinguishes moral from other good dispositions is that the former are dispositions to do *morally* good actions. Thus intelligence is not a moral disposition but justice is. I cannot say what distinguishes norms of moral right and wrong from other norms, or what constitutes the goodness of morally good reasons, motives or ends. Assuming that we can somehow recognise moral norms and morally good reasons, I am trying to define the moral goodness of actions and persons.

would not do it, then that shows both Christianity and concern for goodness as such—conscientiousness. The strategic import-ance of conscientiousness is that if we lack other qualities necessary to goodness this disposition may prompt effort to acquire what we lack. For example, if we happen to realize that some morally important general belief may be mistaken—perhaps the belief that what the Christian tradition re-commends is always morally good—then concern to do what is good prompts inquiry. Inquiry does not necessarily lead to correct beliefs; given our existing beliefs and opportunities for checking them it may even lead us further astray. But under fortunate circumstances a concern to do what is good may lead to the correction of false beliefs about what is right and good. Similarly, if we notice some general defect in our character, or if changing circumstances call for some change of disposition (for example, if the present situation calls for more patience), then if we are concerned to do what is good we may try to acquire the appropriate disposition. Conscientiousness is both a determination to do what at present seems good and a source of growth, correction and adaptation to circumstances, and is thus a key virtue.[28] But it is not the only virtue, and is not by itself enough to make a person good. A conscientious person with false beliefs or too little patience will sometimes do wrong, or do the right thing for a bad reason. If goodness consists in being the sort of person likely to do the right thing for the right reason, then conscientiousness is not enough to make a person good.

What if one of the two conditions of the goodness of an act (being right, and being done for a right reason) is met but not the other? Bayle would say that the act is good if and only if the second condition is met, and that to satisfy the second it is enough if the reason *seems* good (see above, p. 68). Arnauld would say that unless both conditions are truly met the act is evil: *bonum ex integra causa, malum ex quocumque defectu* (see above, Essay I, n. 181). I think we should reject both of these answers. To meet just one condition is not enough to make the act simply good, and failure in any one condition is not enough to make

[28] Govier, 'Conscientiousness', takes conscientiousness as doing what we believe to be right, and argues that it is a virtue (if at all) only when the belief is correct. I take it as including a concern to make sure that what we believe to be right really is right, which is a virtue even when our current beliefs are wrong.

it simply bad. Suppose it is done for a good reason but is in fact wrong; and suppose the reason is good in the sense that, although what the act is meant to bring about is actually something pernicious, the agent sincerely believes that it is good. In such a case we ought to say that the act was done for what the agent sincerely but mistakenly believed to be a good purpose, but was in fact wrong. We should resist any demand for a single summary judgement, a 'Yes or No' answer. If someone asks, 'Well, was it good or not?' we must say 'It was, in so far as it was done sincerely, and it was not, in so far as it was wrong and misdirected.'

Similarly with the goodness of a person. Some conscientious people have erroneous beliefs, for example that Calvinists ought to be 'dragooned' into the Catholic Church, or that Catholics should be left unemployed and poorly housed until they become Protestants. People with such beliefs are not simply good, and conscientious people are not simply bad. Again we must insist on the whole story, and say that they are conscientious people who hold certain false and pernicious beliefs. For some specific purpose we may need to sum up in a single 'on balance' judgement, and then the purpose will suggest the weight to be given to the various virtues and defects (and for some purposes a very conscientious person labouring under an error may be worse than a somewhat unconscientious person under the same error). But summary judgements should not be made with no particular purpose in view; if the judgement is simply 'for the record', it must mention the good and bad aspects of the act or person separately, without trying to reduce them to a single measure.[29]

So much for the complexities of goodness. Are praiseworthiness and moral goodness the same, as Bayle assumes? The idea of goodness is complex, but perhaps that of praiseworthiness is too, and they might match. It might be thought that to say that the reason for an act is good is simply to say that it is a praiseworthy reason, that the goodness of the disposition to act for good reasons consists in its being praiseworthy, and so on. There does not seem to be any single strong reason for denying that goodness is praiseworthiness, but for

---

[29] Cf. Feinberg, pp. 15–16, 53–4. 'The record' is our accumulation of impressions of the person's character. On another 'record' see below, sect. 4.

several reasons it seems better to say that they are not the same. Some morally good acts are not praiseworthy or blameworthy but just good (those which merely fulfil a duty, without being difficult to perform). Those which are praiseworthy are not good precisely because they are praiseworthy; praiseworthiness presupposes goodness of some sort, so cannot constitute it. If we suppose that they are the same some some dubious conclusions follow. Praiseworthiness has some connection with difficulty, and on that supposition goodness will have too. A good act will merit praise (which on this hypothesis constitutes its goodness) if it is done despite difficulty; a bad act will deserve blame (which is its badness) if it would have been at least possible to do the right thing, and deserves more blame (and is worse) the easier right action would have been. If outward acts are morally indifferent, and only the act of choice can merit praise, then merit will come from the difficulty of making the right choice. But then good dispositions will diminish merit by making right choices easier, and vice will diminish blame by making them harder. Then people who develop good dispositions in one area of behaviour, to go on meriting, will need to transfer their efforts to some other area. Continuing progress in virtue achieved through struggle against bad inclinations merits praise, but if perfect virtue were ever attained merit would cease. The 'Holy Will' Kant speaks of[30] could not merit, and if goodness and praiseworthiness were the same could not do a morally good act. A good act would be better for being done by someone with evil inclinations: Peter Abelard, whose moral theory in some ways anticipates Bayle's, seems to think that having bad inclinations is lucky because of the merit which that makes possible.[31] These dubious conclusions are avoided if we deny that praiseworthiness is the same as goodness, though some of them could perhaps be avoided in other ways.

Praise and blame are not the only kinds of moral evaluation. Praise seems to be always for an action, or the result of action. Praise for a disposition assumes that the disposition is an achievement, the result of action. But respect (which is not the same as praise—and the expression of respect is not praise) is for good dispositions, without any assumption about how they

[30] *Groundwork*, p. 107.
[31] Abelard, p. 13.

were formed. If someone seems to have developed good dispositions without effort we may wonder whether he or she has the strategically important quality of conscientiousness, and the doubt may temper our respect, but otherwise it should make no difference: that someone's good qualities came easily is not itself a reason for diminished respect. In deciding whom to respect we judge according to our own lights, and there is no reason to try to do anything else. Sincerity[32] or conscientiousness is a morally good disposition, so we should respect anyone who has it. But since it is not the only virtue, we may respect someone for conscientiousness but in other respects assess him unfavourably.

3. LUCK AND RETRIBUTION

On the view of morality I am suggesting dispositions not acquired by deliberate cultivation may count as morally good or bad. This means that moral goodness, and entitlement (if that is the word) to praise and respect, are partly a matter of luck— of having good innate dispositions and being brought up well, perhaps of receiving grace. If there were retributive reward for goodness and punishment for wickedness, especially the dreadful punishment of hell, then it would be morally objectionable that goodness should depend on luck; this is why the doctrine of predestination is morally revolting. Bayle's preoccupation with justice in retribution explains both the leading features of his moral theory and his long struggle with problems of freewill and predestination.

But it seems to me that retributive punishment cannot rightly be inflicted in this life or in the next. It is not right to inflict pain or other damage upon someone for no other reason than that he has done something wrong; and this is true whether we have freewill or not. That the person punished has done wrong is necessary, but not sufficient, to justify the punishment.[33] As

---

[32] 'Sincerity' means purity or genuineness: that the person really does have some disposition (in the present context, conscientiousness), not overlaid by contrary qualities.

[33] Cf. Mill, 'Hamilton', pp. 62–5. The Utilitarian view (which I share, without being a Utilitarian) is that punishment, like warfare, is itself an evil which can be justified only by reducing other evils. But evil cannot be inflicted just whenever that would do good. There are restrictions, themselves justified by their good effects. (This is a 'rule utilitarian' theory—see my article 'Utilitarianism and Virtue'.) The re-

for reward, it seems obvious that to expect praise or reward for a morally good act would be the wrong attitude. Good action is not even 'its own reward'; the notion of reward is simply inappropriate. To be morally good an act must be done for the right kind of reason. The wish to attain, or even to deserve, reward, and to avoid, or not to deserve, punishment are not reasons of the right kind. In other contexts (when teachers or superiors, for example, give praise and recognition as a reward, or give other rewards, to children or subordinates) praise, blame, reward and punishment have a place as incentives and disincentives not related to moral desert. If in some such context something has been held out beforehand as an incentive then those who qualify may be entitled to it as a matter of justice, which is a requirement of morality. But morality does not require reward for morally good acts as such. The doer of a morally good act cannot complain of injustice if there never is any recognition or reward for moral goodness.

4. BLAME AND RESPONSIBILITY

Moral goodness and badness do not, then, consist in, or imply, entitlement to praise or blame, reward or punishment. Moral assessment is not essentially an attempt to make a fair estimate of reward or punishment deserved. Further, the expression of a moral assessment is not itself a kind of reward or punishment. Praise, respect, admiration, liking and their opposites, may be deserved (meaning 'well-founded') or undeserved—but not as reward or punishment, and not as an entitlement in justice. There is such a thing as moral responsibility, but it is not a being called up for reward or punishment. To illustrate what I mean I will offer some observations on blaming.[34]

strictions may provide (for example) that no one is to be punished unless he has been convicted of doing something forbidden by certain rules, and convicted by some reliable procedure. Such restrictions have good effects by giving us all some protection against excessive and misdirected infliction of evil. The terminology of desert alludes especially to the restrictions (or to some of them): punishment is 'deserved' only if they are satisfied—only if the person to be punished has been properly convicted of some forbidden act. Thus there are two conditions necessary for the moral justification of a particular infliction of punishment: it should do good, which is the point of punishment, and it should satisfy the restrictions upon infliction of evil that good may result. Retributivist theories overlook the first condition, and mistake the restrictions for the point.

[34] This is a topic about which much has been written. See Brandt, Beardsley, Kenner, Squires, Feinberg, Holborow, Henderson.

Blaming may be explicit ('I blame you . . .'), but more often we blame without using the word: 'That was wrong', 'You did it to spite him', 'It was cowardly', and so on. Let us call this 'implicit' blame. It involves some sort of explicit moral assessment, but it is only by what it implies that it is blame. There are different kinds of moral assessments, corresponding to the various kinds and conditions of goodness distinguished earlier, so people are blamed for various sorts of things: for doing something wrong; for acting for some bad reason (for example, out of spite); for acting in a way that shows some bad disposition (for example, cowardice). A person is blamed 'for' something (always for voluntary action, or for the result of such action, I think), in view of some morally significant aspect it has (that it is wrong, spiteful, cowardly); the action (rather than the person) is said to be 'blameworthy'.[35]

It seems that any kind of unfavourable moral assessment can count as implicit blame, provided it is understood to be for a voluntary act or for something of which some voluntary act of the person blamed is a cause.[36] If this proviso is not satisfied the moral assessment stands, but no longer counts as blame. Since we differ about what is voluntary, and about what causes what, and perhaps about what sort of causation is relevant, we may not all take the same utterance as implicit blame. If we think, for example, that some bad emotion or disposition a person displays is not due to voluntary action on his part, then we will not count as blame a remark attributing this emotion or disposition to him;[37] but the remark still stands as an un-

[35] See Henderson, p. 53. Hume says that praise and blame are always in view of the motive or disposition of which the act is a sign; see Raphael, vol. 2, pp. 24-5. Not always, I think. People are sometimes blamed on account of the wrongness of their action. Praise and blame due in view of different aspects is not commensurable; see Beardsley, 'Worth', and cf. Feinberg, above, n. 29.

[36] Feinberg, pp. 187ff., Kenner.

[37] See R. M. Adams, Schlossberger, Holborow, pp. 91-2. Against a position like Bayle's (see R. M. Adams, pp. 11ff. and 19, and cf. above, Essay II, sect. 4.1), Adams maintains that people can be blamed for emotions and dispositions, even apart from blame for voluntary acts which caused them. People may be evaluated unfavourably for emotions and dispositions, but they are not blamed: the terms blame, sin, obligation and responsibility apply only to voluntary acts or omissions. (See Beardsley, 'Blaming', p. 581.) Schlossberger says that we are responsible for emotions, since persons who experience certain emotions would be morally better if they did not. 'Whether or not they are chosen, one's emotions express and partially embody one's values, one's moral outlook on the world' (p. 41). '[W]e are not really concerned, when making moral evaluations, with the *causes* of an agent's actions. We are concerned rather with the

favourable moral assessment. If we think that no one ever voluntarily causes anything in the relevant sense (for example, if we think that blaming implies that the person is an absolutely originating cause,[38] and that determinism is true), then we will think that no one can ever be blamed for anything. But that would be no reason to stop making the assessments that on the assumptions usually made count as implicit blame.

Blame may be an attitude of mind, or something expressed.[39] Perhaps an attitude cannot have a purpose, and the expression of an attitude may have no purpose. But in so far as blaming has purpose, various purposes are possible, since we have various purposes in making and communicating moral assessments. One purpose is to understand, perhaps as a preliminary to something else. I may consider in my own mind what disposition you showed in some action ('Was that really as selfish as it seemed?'); I may talk to you about it, to check and improve my understanding—and you may take some of what I say as blame; I may discuss it with someone else—who may take what I say as blame of you, even if I do not use the word. Trying to understand, even when it involves unfavourable evaluation, may be part of friendship. A friend's character is of interest in itself, and we may wish to understand so that we can help. In other cases we may want to understand so as to know what to expect in future. Sometimes the purpose (especially when the assessment is addressed to the person blamed) is to bring about a change.

But blaming may not be concerned with dispositions and future behaviour. We may blame someone precisely for a particular action without caring whether it was in character, or out of character.[40] Sometimes this is a spontaneous expression of resentment or indignation, without purpose. Sometimes its

moral character of the agent' (p. 46). I agree that moral evaluation is, sometimes, of character, without being concerned with what caused it; but, since responsibility is for some voluntary act or omission, people are not responsible for emotions they have not in some way caused. Schlossberger uses the word in another sense: 'When I say that A is morally responsible for x, I ... mean that ... any moral taint or lustre possessed by x applies as well to A' (p. 37).

[38] In fact blaming does not imply that the agent's choice is the absolutely originating cause, but merely that it is a cause, perhaps one link in a chain of causes reaching far back.

[39] See Beardsley, 'Deserts'.

[40] See Beardsley, 'Blaming', p. 580, Henderson, pp. 50-2, Holborow, pp. 93-6.

purpose is to get the offender or someone else to make up for what has been done. Let us call this 'protest' or 'complaint': it is explicit or implicit blame which is intended not to stigmatize, nor to modify the disposition which the act displayed, but to get some sort of compensation. Holborow has suggested that in blame there is an element of 'holding something against someone' (the opposite of which is forgiveness), that we may decide not to hold a lapse against a person with an otherwise good record, and that 'the record' is concerned not always with the person's general reputation but sometimes with the particular action, even if it is out of character.[41] I think this is right, except that 'holding against' and forgiving are elements not of blame generally, but specifically of complaint. When we think we have grounds for complaint we make a mental note of the fact that compensation is due, and keep a record of what has been done to pay the debt. We may forgive people whose behaviour is generally good without insisting upon compensation, since they do a lot of good anyway, or we may just cancel the debt. A prompt apology mollifies not because it settles the account but because it gives assurance that the offender is willing to settle it. The account is not a record of what blame and punishment is due, but of what the person blamed should make up for.

Responsibility by its etymology implies some obligation to make answer.[42] To hold someone responsible is to require him to answer a complaint, either showing that it is not well founded (and, incidentally, that any blame implied is not deserved, that is, not well founded), or admitting that it is and undertaking to make up for what is complained of. If he is willing to answer then he accepts responsibility. If he acts so as to be able to answer satisfactorily, then he behaves responsibly. Accepting responsibility need not mean voluntarily accepting punishment; that may be appropriate in some cases, if it is required by commitment to some social arrangement established to guarantee that certain things will not be done: but accepting

---

[41] Holborow, pp. 88-9, 92-6.

[42] On responsibility see Feinberg, p. 188, Baier, pp. 58-68. Utilitarians often treat responsibility as being precisely liability to punishment, of which they regard blame as a form: 'Responsibility means punishment. When we are said to have the feeling of being morally responsible for our actions, the idea of being punished for them is uppermost in the speaker's mind' (Mill, 'Hamilton', p. 62). I reject this analysis.

responsibility may mean simply answering, or making compensation, undoing the damage, or something else. On the
other hand, being punished involuntarily is not accepting responsibility, nor even being held responsible: a person may be
punished because he will not answer, or has no excuse, or will
not make compensation. 'Responsible' has at least one other
sense. Just as blame is for voluntary acts or their result, so
'responsible', when synonymous with 'to blame', implies voluntary causation: the person responsible and to blame is the
voluntary cause of something complained of. Similarly, we may
say that an inanimate thing is (metaphorically) responsible if
it is the (involuntary) cause. A person who has not voluntarily
caused something, who is not in that sense responsible for it,
and not to blame for it, may nevertheless be responsible for it
in the former sense, that is, in the sense that he is obliged to
answer for it: thus a minister may be responsible for the acts
done by members of his department without his knowledge
or consent. A person responsible in the second sense will be
responsible also in the first.

The answer made by the responsible person may include
excuses, which may be accepted. An excuse is intended to fend
off an unfavourable assessment. Since there are various kinds
of unfavourable assessments and various ways of replying, there
are different sorts of excuses. The excuse of external force removes blame altogether (though perhaps not an obligation to
make compensation): since blame implies that the person is
relevantly the voluntary cause of the thing complained of,
then an excuse that refutes that causal hypothesis removes
the blame. Sometimes an excuse replaces one unfavourable
assessment with another, less unfavourable or perhaps just different (there is no all-purpose scale of degrees of un-
favourableness). 'No, I don't hate the human race, I'm just
irritable on Monday mornings' substitutes one unfavourable
assessment for another. If in excuse I suggest that my irritability
is not a moral vice but a matter of unfortunate native temperament, I may not be blamed for it, since I am not the cause
of it, but the judgement that I have such a temperament is
still an unfavourable moral assessment. I may say that I have
struggled heroically to correct my native irritability, but without success, since I am by nature exceptionally irritable. This

may show that I am exceptionally conscientious, which is a good thing—but still the unfavourable assessment stands, that I am exceptionally irritable.

The excuse of diminished responsibility does not seem to mean that the choice was necessitated. In some cases perhaps there was really no choice at all (rather than a choice which was necessitated). Where there was a choice the point of the excuse seems to be to block certain inferences about the agent's character that might otherwise have been reasonable. A tantrum on the part of someone subject to violent fits of uncontrollable rage does not show the callous disregard for the interests of others that similar behaviour on the part of someone else might show in similar circumstances. Still, such a characteristic is a defect. If it is not caused by voluntary act then the excuse removes blame, but an unfavourable assessment remains.

Expression of blame is sometimes intended (in my opinion wrongly) as retribution, and sometimes as reformative or deterrent punishment, but blame is not essentially a species of punishment.[43] Blame, and other communications of unfavourable assessment, may cause pain, and the pain may sometimes be a means intentionally used to effect change. But this is not always the intention. To say to someone that his behaviour was deceitful may cause him pain, and the purpose in saying it may be to get him to be more honest in future. But the critic may intend to achieve that purpose not by causing pain but by appealing to his general desire to be honest, or to his general conscientiousness, or (at the lowest) to his desire to be thought well of. The criticism pains him because he does have one of these desires. The pain may be not the end, nor a means, but only a side-effect. Similarly, unfavourable moral assessment causes a conscientious person pain even if there is no suggestion that he is 'responsible' in the causal sense, that is, even when the assessment is not blame.

Moral responsibility, then, and moral assessment do not relate exclusively to reward and punishment, praise and blame, and a disposition which was not voluntarily acquired may be the object of some sorts of moral assessment, though not of blame. Actions, however, in contrast with dispositions, must be

---

[43] See Squires; cf. Beardsley, 'Disapproval'.

voluntary to be subject to any sort of moral assessment. Now we must consider the sense in which the actions subject to moral assessment are voluntary.

5. FREEWILL AND DETERMINISM

Does moral responsibility presuppose liberty of indifference? And do we actually have liberty of indifference? Or is determinism true? It seems obvious that if responsibility presupposes freewill in the sense of liberty of indifference, then, since determinism is incompatible with liberty of indifference, determinism is incompatible with moral responsibility.[44] But it seems to me that moral responsibility, and for that matter liability to punishment, does not presuppose freewill in that sense, and is not incompatible with determinism. To hold a person responsible in the first of the senses distinguished above—that is, to call on him to explain and justify his actions and to make up for harm he has done—does not presuppose that determinism is false. As for responsibility in the other sense, implying liability to blame, if determinism were true, and if blame implied liberty of indifference, we would have to give up explicit blaming; but there would be no reason to give up making and communicating the unfavourable assessments now usually taken to imply blame. Blame, however, does not imply liberty of indifference; it implies merely that the person's choice is a cause of the thing complained of, not that it is an uncaused cause, or that, with antecedents identical, he could have chosen the opposite.[45] It may be true that 'ought implies can', but it is not self-evident that the 'can' must mean 'can, no matter what the chooser's dispositions'. When we blame someone for choosing in accordance with an evil desire, we imply that the desire to do right should have been stronger. Do we therefore think that (no matter what the antecedents) it *could* have been

[44] See van Inwagen, chs. 3 and 5. By freewill he seems to mean liberty of indifference; see p. 8.

[45] Philosophers who have held that determinism and moral responsibility are compatible have sometimes, perhaps, seemed to say that we should still bestow what we pretend to mean as praise and blame, and other rewards and punishments, as long as this has a good effect. But since at least implicit blame does not presuppose liberty of indifference there need be no pretence.

stronger? I do not think so, and have never heard any argument to that effect.[46]

Though it is compatible with moral responsibility determinism of course may not be true. I do not know whether it is or not, but I am pretty sure that what is usually regarded as the alternative theory, that volitions are uncaused, is not true. There is, in fact, besides determinism and the theory of liberty of indifference, another possible position, which I will call the 'motives' theory. Let us distinguish between the doctrine that each of my decisions is determined or caused by some motive or other reason,[47] and the doctrine that my motives are determined by a chain of causes extending out of consciousness indefinitely into the past. I will call the former the 'motives' theory and the latter the 'chains' theory. I think the 'motives' theory is correct, and compatible with the view that some actions are voluntary: an action done for a reason is a voluntary act. Now it seems likely that each reason (or other motive) is attached to a chain of causes. Reasons occur to us in various ways: some are brought home to us by another person (who is part cause); others arise out of perception (of which some external object is part cause); others occur spontaneously, coming into consciousness from we don't know where, but perhaps as a result of some physical or psychological cause. What reasons occur and how strong they seem depends on background dispositions, such as character, mood and beliefs, which may be determined by various physical and social causes. It is thus very likely that chains of antecedent causes determine what reasons I see and how I see them. But whether absolutely every motive is so chained, and whether every chain extends back

[46] Broad (pp. 194-5) attributes this position to Sidgwick, and remarks that he can himself make no sense of the 'could'. In fact Sidgwick (pp. 65-6) says something different: that while I am deliberating I find it impossible not to think that I can—I take it he means if I go deliberating long enough in the right way—choose rightly, no matter how strong the opposite impulse, and that its strength is not a reason for choosing wrongly. This is reminiscent of Mill (*Logic*, pp. 840-1), and is consistent with determinism.

[47] I am leaving open the possibility that some decisions are determined by motives that cannot be called reasons. On the other hand, I mean reason in a minimal sense: a perception of some possible action as desirable or undesirable. Perhaps all motives are reasons, in that sense. To see something as a good thing to do is a reason for deciding to do it, distinct from the decision to do it, but for something to seem true is not a reason for believing it distinct from the belief. Thus, while it may be true that every decision has a reason (if all motives are reasons), it is not true that there is a reason for every belief, if we believe some things simply 'because' they seem true.

forever, or to a First Cause, and whether absolutely everything that happens is similarly chained—that is, whether determinism is true—I do not know. The 'motives' theory, however, without help from any version of the 'chains' theory, already implies rejection of the doctrine of liberty of indifference. A voluntary act is something we do because we have decided to do it, and although it is possible, and I think quite likely, that deciding is an act, not just a being moved by reasons,[48] what we decide is determined by the reasons as we apprehend them, given our beliefs, moods and character. At a given moment, until some new thought occurs or some disposition changes, the decision cannot be other than it is.[49]

As Mill pointed out, the thesis that our choices are all caused by motives does not mean that that we are merely passive, or that we must do what is fated no matter how hard we try to do something else.[50] Even if whatever happens is predetermined, our choices and efforts are among the things predetermined, and are among the causes of what will happen.[51] Further, we can deliberately act upon the dispositions which condition our future decisions.[52] We can change our dispositions if we decide to do so—not simply by deciding, and usually not immediately, sometimes not at all, but sometimes by some course of voluntary action which in time causes some change. Of course the decision to try to change is determined. We decide to change only if we have a strong enough motive for doing so.

We are active also in deliberation. Deliberation is a succession of voluntary acts directed by a succession of minor decisions, or decisions 'by default'[53]: we decide to deliberate,

[48] Cf. the scholastic distinction between a velleity and an elicited act of will; Harris, vol. 2, p. 283.

[49] Van Inwagen argues that freewill (meaning, I think, liberty of indifference) is presupposed by deliberation, since if we deliberate we must believe we can choose either way (pp. 154ff.). When we begin to deliberate, and while we continue, we must believe this ('can choose' at least in the sense that we do not yet know what we will choose). But perhaps by the process of deliberation (including any last stage of adopting a method of deciding arbitrarily and carrying it out—e.g. tossing a penny) the final choice is determined, so that at the moment of decision it is no longer true (if it ever was) that more than one choice is open.

[50] Cf. Mill, *Logic*, pp. 934-6.

[51] Cf. Cicero, *On Fate*, xiii.29-30. It is therefore not true that 'If determinism is true, no one has any choice about anything' (van Inwagen, p. 106).

[52] See Mill, *Logic*, pp. 840-1.

[53] See Bach.

decide how to deliberate, decide to give serious consideration to some aspect, decide when to stop deliberating. Some of the sub-decisions are themselves the outcome of a sub-deliberation, but since there cannot be a regress to infinity of deliberations about whether and how to deliberate, others must be spontaneous or 'indeliberate'. (By 'indeliberate' I mean determined by some motive, such as a reason in the minimal sense, that is, a perception of some possible act as desirable, but not preceded by consideration of opposing reasons or other possibilities.) After a sub-deliberation, or impulsively, we may decide to consult someone, or to look something up, or to go somewhere and look or listen. Thus deliberation may involve (or be served by) physical activity. It also involves mental activity, to some extent under conscious direction (we can direct not only our bodies but also our minds): when we deliberate many thoughts come unbidden, but others come because we look for them. We can decide to think about some subject, to try to remember, to search for reasons, to attend to something more closely, to set irrelevant or improper considerations aside. Thus spontaneous thoughts and indeliberate decisions lead to physical or mental activities which give rise to more thoughts and decisions, while yet others occur spontaneously. The decisions and sub-decisions, spontaneous or deliberate, are all motivated,[54] all in that sense determined by causes. Various causes (such as spontaneous thoughts) make me decide to do some things (such as search my memory, ask advice) which may bring to bear some other cause (for example, an adviser). That the process is determined by causes would be clear if deliberation were always like being buttonholed and given unasked advice by other people; the difference is that when we willingly seek advice and search our own minds, some of the causes of these actions are our own spontaneous thoughts.

The thought of doing something may spontaneously occur to me and I may without hesitation decide to do it. But another thought may occur to make me hesitate and deliberate—the thought, for example, that sudden decisions may lead to disaster, that I do not know enough, that I should not act in anger, that I could do something else instead. It may then occur to

---

[54] Scotus speaks as if the will can turn the intellect's attention in any direction; see Harris, vol. 2, pp. 289, 295. I think we can direct our attention to this or that only if something motivates us to do so.

me to try to think of objections, to ask advice, to wait until the situation becomes clearer, to try to calm my anger (for example by reflecting on other possible interpretations of whatever angered me). Eventually the thought may occur that I have deliberated enough, or that the time has come when I must decide, or that further deliberation is not likely to discover any better reasons for choice than I have already.[55] If when time runs out there still seems nothing to choose between the alternatives I may decide to choose arbitrarily. But arbitrary decision is not an exercise of liberty of indifference. My decision to decide now must have some motive, so must my decision to decide arbitrarily, so must my choice of decision method. It may occur to me to toss a penny: I may hesitate to do that, but then the thought occurs that this is as good a way as any; so I decide to stop deliberating about how to make the arbitrary choice I have decided is necessary. Or some rival method of deciding arbitrarily may occur to me: to do what I had first thought to do, before deliberating, or to do what I usually do, or to do something different for a change. If I think about it too much I may be unable to decide how to decide arbitrarily. But probably not forever: if I have come to the conclusion that I must decide arbitrarily, and that there is nothing to choose among several methods of deciding, then if I later find myself thinking 'Let me toss a penny', then this time I have no reason for hesitating to do so. Perhaps Buridan's ass did die of starvation between two equally desirable bales of hay, but if he did he was an unlucky beast.[56]

---

[55] Reflection is sometimes not to decide what we should do but to get ourselves to decide to do what we know we should do (or, in some cases, what we know we should not do), by directing attention toward or away from reasons we expect to strengthen or weaken some inclination. This process is often mixed up with deliberation, but it may be separate.

[56] Bayle says that when the reasons on both sides are in equilibrium we can decide by lot; *DHC*, art. 'Buridan', rem. C. But we may not see anything to choose between choice by lot and other methods of decision. J. S. Mill says that the ass might starve 'if he remained all the time in a fixed attitude of deliberation; if he never for an instant ceased to balance one against another the rival attractions, and if they really were so exactly equal that no dwelling on them could detect any difference. But this is not the way in which things take place on our planet. From mere lassitude, if from no other cause, he would intermit the process, and cease thinking of the rival objects at all: until a moment arrived when he would be seeing or thinking of one only, and that fact, combined with the sensation of hunger, would determine him to a decision' ('Hamilton', p. 67). So if you get stuck, distract your mind from the problem, for example by getting absorbed in something interesting: unless you are unlucky, the

Thus *deliberate* choice is under our control, as the Scotists and Molinists claimed all choices are, but only as belief is, indirectly (see above, Essay IV, sect. 1), and indirect control is possible only because there are spontaneous thoughts and indeliberate choices to prompt and guide deliberation. Deliberating and inquiry are alike. The conduct of inquiry requires decisions, deliberate or indeliberate, and so does deliberation; inquirer and deliberator both take actions which put their minds under the influence of agents they think likely to improve their current beliefs or impending decisions; just as inquiry is guided by spontaneous beliefs, so is deliberation by spontaneous thoughts and indeliberate choices. Theoretical and practical thinking both originate in thoughts we do not choose to have, which may lead to voluntary action, physical or mental, which we expect to result in more thoughts—thoughts in this sense chosen, but not chosen in particular. What we eventually believe, or decide, is not in particular a matter of choice; it is whatever as a result of these voluntary activities comes to seem true, or right.

It seems, then, that both the fact of moral responsibility and the phenomena of voluntary decision-making are compatible with the 'motives' theory, and indeed with thoroughgoing determinism (though I say again that while I think the 'motives' theory is true I do not know whether determinism is). Perhaps we must all answer 'Nothing' to Paul's question 'What hast thou that thou didst not receive?' (1 *Cor.* 4:7), but we will be no less responsible—in the sense of 'obliged to answer', and (when the action is bad and voluntary) also in the sense of 'to blame': but we will not be entitled or liable to retributive reward or punishment. Bayle was therefore mistaken in thinking that our moral responsibility implies liability to retribution, and that this proves that we do have liberty of indifference.

Human beings are free, at least sometimes, in other senses. I may be physically free, free from physical constraint, so that I can do what I want to do. If I decide without being influenced

memory of having realized previously that there is nothing to choose should stop you from being drawn into considering alternatives to what happens to be uppermost in your mind when you return to the problem. As a donkey-lover, I like to think that Buridan's ass had the wit to escape from his predicament by listening attentively to one of his master's early morning lectures on Aristotle, and then having breakfast suddenly.

by some serious threat, then I act 'of my own free will': but this does not imply liberty of indifference. If I decide under threat I do not act of my own free will, but I am nevertheless responsible (obliged to answer) for what I do, though the threat may be a complete or partial excuse, warding off (some sort of) blame. As for internal constraints, the Augustinians were right, I think, not to regard them as simply equivalent to physical constraints.[57] If someone lies because he is a coward and a liar, and for that reason just cannot help lying when cornered, that is no excuse.[58] We do not need to know whether he developed this character in any sense voluntarily. (We might need to know if it were a question of inflicting retributive punishment; but if that is out of the question—if the question is, say, 'Should we trust him?'—we do not need to know.) The freedom I am suggesting is enough to make a person subject to moral assessment is, then, not liberty of indifference, but the 'spontaneity' of the Augustinians: if the act is done willingly, by a choice made by the agent (determined by the balance of reasons), then it is a responsible act, though given the person's background dispositions and the thoughts that have actually occurred to him he has no power to choose differently.

6. TOLERATION

Against the kind of moral theory Bayle represents I have suggested that making moral assessments is not a matter of trying to discern what use has been made of free choice, discounting for moral luck—for differences in innate temperament, in upbringing, in opportunities and temptations, and in help or hindrance by external causes. Moral assessment is not oriented toward retribution. We are all tempted at times to punish someone just because he deserves it, but the temptation should be resisted. Moral assessment has various other purposes, for which we may need to decide what moral qualities a person

[57] Though perhaps we should accept that *some* kinds of internal constraints cancel or diminish moral responsibility. Sidgwick (p. 65) and others have said that some internal compulsions (e.g. those of the alcoholic) excuse while others do not.

[58] Contrast: 'If someone charges you with, say, lying, and if you can convince him that it was simply not within your power *not* to lie, then it would seem that you have done all that is necessary to absolve yourself of responsibility for lying' (van Inwagen, p. 161). Some ways of its being not within your power do not constitute an excuse.

has, but not whether they are innate, accidental or deliberately acquired.

But even if we reject these various items of Bayle's moral theory—the preoccupation with retribution, the thesis that only the exercise of liberty of indifference has moral worth, the thesis that for goodness sincerity is enough—almost all he says about the rights of conscience and toleration will still stand. It was a mistake on his part to present his argument for toleration as if it depended in any way on whether the heretic persecutor commits a sin for which he will be condemned on judgement day. Essays III and IV are in effect restatements of Bayle's position independently of the items in question. In Essay IV I argue that we should affirm and (with whatever caution seems appropriate) act upon what seems true, even if we cannot prove it, and even if there are objections against it. This amounts to saying that we should follow conscience. As Bayle recognised, this does not mean that an act done in accordance with conscience cannot be wrong, that it cannot be criticised, that it cannot rightly be prevented, that the person doing it cannot be criticised (by anyone who knows the relevant circumstances) for negligence or other faults in inquiry. Where I differ with Bayle is in denying that whoever follows conscience necessarily does a good act.

In Essay III my starting point is like that of the classic social contract theories, a right to act on our own judgement of what it is morally permissible to do (see above, Essay III, sect. 1). This is a right in the minimal sense of a liberty; it means that we cannot be blamed for trying to do what we think right, though others might not be to blame if they tried to prevent us from doing it. This is equivalent to the right to follow conscience. What if conscience tells us that it is permissible, or even a duty, to prevent others from advocating or acting on their false beliefs? A reciprocity argument may provide a reason for renouncing the (at least apparent) natural liberty to obstruct other people in acting on their beliefs, and for committing oneself to the practice of toleration as a matter of principle. As I argued in Essay IV, action ought to be tempered by some estimate of the likelihood of being mistaken. The various sets of beliefs that have led to persecution and civil wars, such as Christianity or Marxism, are in my opinion not true (Marxist

criticism of our society seems true enough, though not dis-
tinctive—but not its prescriptions and predictions); and it
seems to me that those who do believe in such doctrines ought
to acknowledge that they are quite likely to be mistaken. None
of them seems certain enough to justify any very drastic repression of opposing ideas.[59] But tolerance based on doubt is
not the principled toleration advocated by Bayle and others; it
is quite compatible with an occasional act of cautious repression
or discrimination. And, as Bayle would point out, it is useless
to call on persecutors to desist because their beliefs are uncertain. They feel certain, or may think they must pretend they
do. To make them doubt we would have to lead them into the
'ocean of controversies', which they may be quite determined
(even as a matter of duty) not to enter. What is said in Essay
IV, then, about the need to allow for the possibility of being
wrong is not enough to establish the principles of toleration, or
to moderate the violence of those who feel sure they are right.

The 'reciprocity' argument, however, addresses doubter and
believer alike, and leads (if it succeeds) to commitment to
toleration as a matter of principle. The doubter will hardly
doubt that wars of religion, and their modern equivalents, are
a great evil, and believers can see that too, though they may
think they see a great good to be achieved through all the evil.
Argument is of no use unless the persecutors will listen long
enough to take it in, but they will feel the force of the reciprocity
argument sooner than they will come to doubt their whole
system of beliefs. If they commit themselves to the principles of
toleration they will still act according to their own lights, although the practical implications of the ensemble of their beliefs
will have been modified by the commitment and their beliefs
may also have been modified at some points. But to accept the
reciprocity argument they need not abandon the substance of
the religious or political creed that motivated persecution, or
regard it as any less certain. Once there is peace there may be
time to explore the ocean of controversies, and toleration may
in time come to be reinforced by what may loosely be called
scepticism—a sense that on contentious questions of religion,
ethics and politics it is very difficult to be sure of being right.

[59] 'To kill men: there is required a bright-shining and clear light.' 'When all is done,
it is an over-valuing of one's conjectures, by them to cause a man to be burned alive'
(Montaigne, vol. 3, pp. 284, 286).

APPENDIX

Arnauld on Freewill and Necessity

According to Arnauld, if we cannot help acting in some way, that is either (1) because external forces or obstacles leave no alternative, or (2) because we cannot help wanting to act that way; and that may be (2a) because we have absolutely no power to want anything else, or (2b) because the power we have is quite insufficient to overcome the inclination to act that way. This gives three kinds of necessity, corresponding to (1), (2a) and (2b).[1] What is necessary in the first way happens whether we will it or not, by physical constraint; in that case the opposite act is not in our power and not possible even if we will it. What is necessary in the second and third ways happens only because we will it, but we cannot help willing it. Because it happens if and only if we will it, it is in our power and voluntary[2]—it is both voluntary and necessary. What is done willingly is voluntary even if we cannot help being willing. In the third case the act is 'effectively' necessary: the opposite action is possible conditionally, if we will it, but it is not effectively possible because inevitably and infallibly we will not will it, though in some sense we have the power to will it. In this case the possibility of willing differently is 'metaphysical', not

---

[1] *Jansen*, pp. 238-49, *Denunciation* 2, p. 123 (based on *Apology*, p. 582). Arnauld quotes or refers to the following passages of St Augustine: *De civitate dei*, V.10, *Enchiridion*, xxviii.105, *De natura et gratia*, xlvi.54. He refers also to Thomas Aquinas, *Summa contra gentiles*, III.138, *De potentia dei*, q.10 a.2 ad 5, *De veritate*, q.22 a.5 ad 1, ad 3, ad 4, q.23 a.4 c, ad ult., q.24 a.1 ad 20, *Summa*, I, q.82 a., 1 ad 1. He quotes many texts from other medieval authors (*Jansen*, pp. 244-9). For the distinction between necessities in Luther and Calvin see Wendel, pp. 190-1. Arnauld at first, like most of his sources, did not generally distinguish the second kind of necessity from the third. For the threefold distinction see *Disquisition*, p. 635(1-17).

[2] According to Augustine a thing is in our power if we do it if we will. On this point Arnauld refers (*Apology*, p. 584 and elsewhere) to *De spiritu et littera*, xxxi.53, *De civitate dei*, V.10, *De libero arbitrio*, III.iii.7-8, and *Retractations*, I.22 and II.1 (*PL*, vol. 32, cols. 620, 630). For Aristotle on 'in our power' see *EN*, III.5, 1113 b2-1115 a3; the concept was much discussed in antiquity. For a definition of liberty like Augustine's see Hobbes, p. 262.

'effective'.[3] If an act is necessary in the first sense, it is neither voluntary nor free; if it is necessary in the second sense, it is voluntary
but not free and not subject to moral evaluation;[4] if it is necessary in
the third sense, it is both voluntary and free, and morally either good
or evil.

The distinction between 1 and 2 Arnauld got from Augustine,
between 2a and 2b from Jansen.[5] According to Augustine, an act of
the will is always free, since we will if and only if we will.[6] But an act
of will may be necessary in the sense that the willer cannot help
willing as he does; for example, God necessarily wills his own goodness,
human beings necessarily will their own happiness.[7] According to St
Thomas, such acts are determined by natural necessity, 'natural'
meaning not by the general order of the universe but specifically by
the nature of the will. When an object is presented which corresponds
perfectly to the nature of the will we simply have no power not to
will it, but if the good presented is in some way imperfect we have
power to will it or not.[8] Thus the beatific vision (i.e. the vision of

[3] *Jansen*, pp. 181-4. In Arnauld's French the distinction is made with the term
effectivement, or with the contrast between *il peut* and *il peut arriver*; in Jansen's Latin,
which Arnauld quotes, the contrast is between *posse facere* and *posse fieri*. For similar
distinctions see above, Essay I, n. 142.

[4] An act is not good or evil unless it is free; see *Liberty*, p. 620(12-22), *Love*, pp.
678(35-6), 679(16-20). See also Arnauld's collection of texts from St Thomas, *Disquisition*, pp. 632-4.

[5] The point of Jansen's distinction is to effect a (perhaps merely apparent) reconciliation between Augustine's doctrines and the doctrine of 'liberty of indifference'
(to which the Catholic Church was by then deeply committed); see above, Conclusion,
sect. 1. Since after the fall liberty of indifference is merely metaphysical, not effective,
Augustine's analysis of freedom is what effectively applies. The third of the Five
Propositions attributed to Jansen is that 'to merit or demerit in the state of fallen
nature, man need not have the freedom which excludes necessity; it is enough to have
freedom from constraint' (Denzinger, p. 445, no. 2003). The distinction between the
two kinds of necessity obviates this condemnation. The Jansenists can say, with at least
apparent orthodoxy, that to merit we need the freedom which excludes not only
constraint but also the second kind of necessity.

[6] Augustine, *De civitate dei*, V.10. He means, I assume, not that there must always
be two separate acts of will—so that one cannot will without first willing to do so,
which would generate an infinite regress—but that an act of will necessarily satisfies
the definition of something in one's power, namely as something that happens if and
only if one wills and not whether one wills or not. See Jansen, *Augustinus*, vol. 3, 622AB.
The argument is an equivocation: the definition is of something that happens if and
only if one wills it, and the 'it' cannot simply be disregarded.

[7] 'We dare not say that because he cannot will to sin God's justice is due not to will
but to necessity', i.e. in the first sense (Augustine, *Enchiridion*, xxviii.105, quoted *Jansen*,
pp. 238-9; cf. *De natura et gratia*, xlvi.54). Indifference cannot be of the essence of
freedom, or God and the blessed would not be free; *Jansen*, pp. 242-3. For a similar
argument from Stoic sources see the quotation from Alexander of Aphrodisias in Long,
p. 183. Duns Scotus also regarded indifference as inessential to freedom; see Bonansea,
pp. 93-7, and Hyman and Walsh, pp. 595-6. Compare Descartes, vol. 1, p. 175.

[8] *Liberty*, pp. 615(37)-616(2), 619(40)-620(4).

God 'face to face' in heaven) is voluntary but necessitated, since the presentation of the most perfect good leaves no power of rejection.[9] In this life we do not meet with anything that corresponds perfectly to the nature of the will. We necessarily will happiness, but since we cannot be completely happy with any particular action we always have power to will that action or not.

Arnauld followed St Thomas on these points. In his later writings he decided to restrict the term 'free' to the indifferent, so that voluntary acts determined by natural necessity are not free.[10] Since in this life we do not meet with any perfectly satisfying object we always have power of opposite choice, that is, freedom 'of indifference', both of contrariety (to do good or evil) and of contradiction (to do or not do this act).[11] But—Arnauld emphasises—free choice does not presuppose that the opposite choices are equally possible, nor that they are both effectively possible; an act is free as long as it is not determined by external constraint or by natural necessity, that is, as long as some (even merely metaphysical) power of opposite choice remains.[12] Choice of any of the imperfect goods we encounter in this life is therefore always free, even when the power to reject it is inevitably and infallibly overborne by desire for it.[13] Thus grace is

[9] Ibid., pp. 617(28)-618(16). *Disquisition* is a collection of texts from St Thomas's *Summa* supporting this thesis. See e.g. 1, q.82 a.1, q.5 a.4, 1-2, q.10 a.2, 1-2, q.13 a.6. For Arnauld's summary in geometrical form of St Thomas's arguments see *Disquisition*, pp. 638-9. Duns Scotus had rejected St Thomas's position on this matter: 'The will wills nothing necessarily, and therefore does not have to will necessarily that by reason of which it wills all other things (if there were anything such)' (*Opera*, vol. 2, p. 99). But Arnauld does not seem to be aware of any controversy.

[10] *Liberty*, pp. 619(22)-620. He says that this is the usage of Thomas Aquinas; see *Disquisition*, p. 635(24-33). But Thomas Aquinas sometimes follows Augustine's usage (perhaps in earlier writings, or when he is commenting on Augustine's words), e.g. in the texts quoted *Jansen*, p. 240 (e.g. *De potentia*, q.10 a.2 ad 5), and in *Summa*, 1, q.82 a.1 ad 1 (see *Love*, p. 684(29-31)). To define free choice Arnauld gives what seems to be a new turn to Augustine's phrase that the will wills because it wills (see above), as if it meant that there is free choice if there is or can be two acts of will, one causing or inhibiting the other (cf. Scotus, in Bonansea, p. 88). The act is free because one wills to will it, or at least does not will not to will it.

[11] *Jansen*, pp. 181-2, 241-3. Notice that we have freedom of indifference even under the influence of grace (*Jansen*, p. 182(1-2)). As will be explained shortly, this does not mean that we are equally able to choose either way. On the distinction between indifference of contrariety and indifference of contradiction see *Jansen*, pp. 181(20-4), 260(3-8), 242(24-5). Jansen refuses to *define* freedom as implying indifference (see above, n. 7), but this does not imply that human beings in this life do not have freedom of indifference.

[12] *Liberty*, pp. 615(37)-617(5) ('the power of the will is not entirely exhausted, so to speak'), 617(38)-618(9). Contrast the position ascribed to the Jesuits, that freedom requires *equal* power for either choice; *Denunciation* 1, p. 7(33-5).

[13] Arnauld sometimes uses the word 'determine' for necessity of the third kind. See e.g. *Jansen*, pp. 182(18), 184(20), and *Liberty*, p. 615(19).

efficacious without destroying liberty: even when the will is infallibly moved by grace or by concupiscence to choose good or evil we always have, metaphysically, both the power to choose good and the power to choose evil.[14] Similarly the blessed inevitably but freely will whatever God wills, and Jesus on earth infallibly but freely willed whatever the Father willed.[15] What is done willingly is voluntary, and, if there is at least a metaphysical power of doing the opposite, free.

After Adam's sin human beings, unless helped by grace, are under an inevitable necessity of sinning. No particular sin is inevitable, but our will-power is so weak in comparison with the strength of concupiscence that, in any situation of choice, if we do not commit one sin we will inevitably commit another, at least the sin of not choosing out of love of God (see above, Essay I, sect. 5). Nevertheless we are free (i.e. have the metaphysical power) to do or not do any particular act,[16] and to do good if we will—but without grace we cannot will it, and the good act is not effectively possible. Similarly we always have power to do evil if we will, but under the influence of grace we cannot will it and sin is not effectively possible; grace is not constraint, however, since its first effect is willingness.[17] Thus we always have the power to sin or to do good, but in every case one or other choice is not effectively possible. The act is always free, since we do it because we will it, and since the opposite act is always (metaphysically) within our power, always in that sense possible, even when actually to do it needs grace, and even when that grace is not given.[18]

[14] *Jansen*, pp. 182–4. The second of the Five Propositions attributed to Jansen is that grace is irresistible. The Jansenists held that it is effectively irresistible, but a 'metaphysical' power of resistance remains. For an analysis of Arnauld's attempt to reconcile efficacious grace with freedom and a discussion of its consistency with the rest of Arnauld's philosophy, see Lennon, 'Jansenism' and 'La logique'. See the latter article on the distinction between *in sensu composito* and *in sensu diviso*. Compare Jansen, *Augustinus*, vol. 3, 825A–27B, 870D–71B, 872CD, Aristotle, *Soph. el.*, 4, 166 a23–37, William of Sherwood, pp. 140–4, and Duns Scotus, in Hyman and Walsh, pp. 594–5. The distinction between the two senses seems to come to this: to say that both choices are possible does not mean that they can both be made at once; but although the opposite acts cannot coexist, the opposite powers can coexist, and each power can coexist with the opposite act. If Socrates has both the power to sit and the power to stand but cannot do both at once, then if he sits he cannot at the same moment stand: but not because he has lost the power. This does not help Arnauld's argument much. His thesis is not merely that Socrates cannot do both things at once, but that morally speaking he is too weak to stand by himself at all, and that when God offers him help he cannot refuse.

[15] *Liberty*, p. 618(17–27).

[16] *Jansen*, pp. 259–60.

[17] Ibid., p. 233(17).

[18] *Apology*, pp. 585(23)–586, in which Arnauld quotes Bellarmine, and *Denunciation* 2, p. 124, in which he quotes Thomas Aquinas: 'If "in human power" means apart from the help of grace, then human beings are obliged to many things not possible

An act which is necessary in either of the first two senses cannot be a sin. Necessity in the third sense does not excuse. To be morally good or evil the act must be free, but acts necessary in the third sense are also free. Since an unavoidable sin is a free act, which we could

avoid 'if we chose' (only we cannot so choose), according to Arnauld it is imputable. But if a naturally necessitated act deserves neither praise nor blame because there is no power to choose otherwise, then it seems that powerlessness excuses, and there seems to be no difference morally between a merely metaphysical power which is infallibly ineffective and no power at all. So why does necessity of the third kind not excuse? Perhaps because this necessity is a penalty for sin (see above, Essay I, sect. 4): what makes the difference morally is the reason for the necessity. Before the fall Adam had 'liberty of indifference', and it is for that reason that Adam's sin deserved punishment (see above, Essay I, n. 137). Among the punishments thus deserved by Adam (and his posterity) is that of being subject to necessity of the third kind—and to punishment for the sins that then become effectively necessary.

without healing grace: for example, to love God and one's neighbour and to believe the articles of faith. But with the help of grace these are possible. This help, if it is given from heaven, is given in mercy; if it is not given, that is in justice, as a penalty for previous sin, at least original sin, as Augustine says' (*Summa*, 2-2, q.2 a.5 ad 1; quoted also in *Excuse*, p. 672, *Difficulties*, p. 374). Compare *Summa*, 1-2, q.109 a.4 ad 2.

BIBLIOGRAPHY

Abelard, Peter, *Ethics*, ed. and trans. E. Luscombe (Oxford, 1971).
Abercrombie, Nigel, *The Origins of Jansenism* (Oxford, 1936).
Adams, Marilyn McCord, 'Hell and the God of Justice', *Religious Studies*, 11 (1975), 433-47.
——and Wood, Rega, 'Is to will it as bad as to do it? The Fourteenth Century Debate', *Franciscan Studies*, 41 (1981), 5-60.
Adams, Robert Merrihew, 'Involuntary Sins', *Philosophical Review*, 94 (1985), 3-31.
Alflatt, Malcolm E., 'The Responsibility for Involuntary Sin in St Augustine', *Recherches augustiniennes*, 10 (1975), 171-86.
Ames, William, *Conscience with the Power and Cases thereof* (London, 1633).
Ammerman, Robert R., 'Ethics and Belief', *Aristotelian Society Proceedings*, 65 (1964-5), 257-66.
Arnauld, Antoine. See Note on References.
Austin, John L., *Philosophical Papers* (Oxford, 1961).
Bach, Kent, 'Default Reasoning: Jumping to Conclusions and Knowing When to Think Twice', *Pacific Philosophical Quarterly*, 65 (1984), 37-58.
Baier, Kurt, 'Responsibility and Freedom', in Richard T. De George (ed.), *Ethics and Society* (New York, 1966).
Baird, Alexander W., *Studies in Pascal's Ethics* (The Hague, 1975).
Barry, Brian, 'Justice as Reciprocity', in Eugene Kamenka and Alice Ehr-Soon Tay (eds.), *Justice* (London, 1979).
——*Political Argument* (London, 1965).
Baudrillart, Henri, *Dictionnaire d'histoire et de géographie ecclésiastique* (Paris, 1930).
Baudry, Léon, *Lexique philosophique de Guillaume d'Ockham* (Paris, 1958).
Bayle, Pierre. See Note on References.
Beardsley, Elizabeth L., 'Blaming', *Philosophia*, 8 (1979), 573-83.
——'Moral Disapproval and Moral Indignation', *Philosophy and Phenomenological Research*, 31 (1970-1), 161-76.
——'Moral Worth and Moral Credit', *Philosophical Review*, 66 (1957), 304-28.
——'A Plea for Deserts', *American Philosophical Quarterly*, 6 (1969), 33-42.

Benn, Stanley, 'Privacy, Freedom, and Respect for Persons', in James Roland Pennock and John W. Chapman (eds.), *Privacy* (New York, 1971).

——and Mortimore, Geoffrey, *Rationality in the Social Sciences* (London, 1976).

Bentham, Jeremy, *Anarchical Fallacies*, in *Works* (Edinburgh, 1843), vol. 2.

Beylard, Hughes, 'Le péché philosophique: quelques précisions historiques et doctrinales', *Nouvelle revue théologique*, 62 (1935), 591–616, 673–98.

Blanshard, Brand, *Reason and Belief* (London, 1974).

Bonansea, Bernardine M., 'Duns Scotus' Voluntarism', in John K. Ryan and B. M. Bonansea (eds.), *John Duns Scotus, 1265–1965* (Washington, 1965).

Bonjour, Laurence, 'Externalist Theories of Empirical Knowledge', in Peter A. French *et al.* (eds.), *Midwest Studies in Philosophy V: Studies in Epistemology* (Minneapolis, 1980).

Bourne, Henry Fox, *The Life of John Locke* (London, 1876).

Boyle, Joseph M., '*Praeter intentionem* in Aquinas', *The Thomist*, 42 (1978), 649–665.

Brandt, Richard, 'Blameworthiness and Obligation', in A. I. Melden (ed.), *Essays in Moral Philosophy* (Seattle, 1958).

Broad, C. D., *Five Types of Ethical Theory* (Paterson, 1959).

Brush, Craig, *Montaigne and Bayle* (The Hague, 1966).

Burke, Edmund, *Reflections on the Revolution in France* (London, 1907).

Burnaby, John, *Amor Dei* (London, 1938).

Burnyeat, Myles F., 'Can the Sceptic Live his Scepticism?', in Schofield *et al.*

Bury, R. G., 'Introduction', in *Sextus Empiricus*, vol. 1 (London, 1967).

Calvin, John, *Institutes of the Christian Religion*, trans. J. T. McNeil Philadelphia, 1950).

Campbell, Charles A., 'Is Freewill a Pseudo-Problem?', reprinted in Bernard Berofsky (ed.), *Free Will and Determinism* (New York, 1966).

Ceyssens, L., 'Autour du péché philosophique', *Augustiniana*, 14 (1964), 378–425.

Chadwick, Owen, *The Reformation* (Harmondsworth, 1972).

Chéné, J., 'Le péché d'ignorance selon Saint Augustin', in *Œuvres de Saint Augustin* (Paris, 1962), vol. 24.

Chillingworth, William, *The Religion of Protestants a Safe Way to Salvation*, in *Works* (London, 1704).

Chisholm, Roderick, 'Fallibilism and Belief', in Philip Wiener and F. Young (eds.), *Studies in the Philosophy of C. S. Pierce* (Cambridge, Mass., 1952).

——'Lewis' Ethics of Belief', in *The Philosophy of C. I. Lewis*, ed. Paul Schilpp (La Salle, 1968).

——*Perceiving* (Ithaca, 1957).

Church, Ralph W., *A Study in the Philosophy of Malebranche* (London, 1930).

Clark, David W., 'Ockham on Human and Divine Freedom', *Franciscan Studies*, 38 (1978), 122-60.

Classen, H. G., 'Will, Belief and Knowledge', *Dialogue*, 18 (1979), 64-72.

Clifford, William, 'The Ethics of Belief', in *Lectures and Essays* (London, 1879), vol. 2.

Cobbett, William, *Parliamentary History* (London, 1806-).

Cohen, Brenda, 'An Ethical Paradox', *Mind*, 76 (1967), 250-9.

Collins, Anthony, *A Discourse of Free Thinking* (Stuttgart, 1965).

Curley, Edward E., 'Descartes, Spinoza and the Ethics of Belief', in *Spinoza: Essays in Interpretation*, ed. Maurice Mandelbaum and E. Freeman (La Salle, 1975).

Dalbiez, R., 'Les sources scholastiques de la théorie cartésienne de l'être objectif', *Revue d'histoire de la philosophie*, 3 (1929), 464-72.

Dancy, Jonathan, *An Introduction to Contemporary Epistemology* (Oxford, 1985).

Daniélou, Jean, *Origen*, trans. W. Mitchell (London, 1955).

D'Arcy, Eric, *Conscience and its Right to Freedom* (London, 1979).

Deman, T., 'La péché philosophique', in *DTC*, vol. 12.1, cols. 255-72.

Denzinger, Henricus, *Enchiridion Symbolorum* (35th edn., Fribourg, 1973).

Descartes, René, *Philosophical Works*, trans. Elizabeth Haldane and G. R. T. Ross (New York, 1955).

Dodge, Guy, *The Political Theory of the Huguenots of the Dispersion* (New York, 1947).

Douie, Decima, *The Conflict between Seculars and the Mendicants at the University of Paris in the Thirteenth Century* (London, Aquinas Papers 23, 1954).

DTC: Vacant, Jean M. A., *et al.*, *Dictionnaire de théologie catholique* (Paris, 1903-50).

Duns Scotus, John, *God and Creatures: The Quodlibetal Questions*, trans. F. Alluntis and A. B. Wolter (Princeton, 1975).

——*Opera Omnia* (Rome, 1963).

Dworkin, Gerald, 'Non-neutral principles', *Journal of Philosophy*, 71 (1974), 491-506.

Encyclopédie, L', ed. Diderot et al. (Neufchâtel, 1765).

Evans, J. L., 'Error and the Will', *Philosophy*, 38 (1963), 136-48.

Feinberg, Joel, *Doing and Deserving* (Princeton, 1970).

Feyerabend, Paul, *Against Method* (London, 1975).

Firth, Roderick, 'Are Epistemic Concepts Reducible to Ethical Concepts?', in Alvin I. Goldman and Jaegwon Kim (eds.), *Values and Morals* (Dordrecht, 1978).

Fohr, Samuel, 'The Non-Rationality of Beliefs and Attitudes', *Personalist*, 53 (1972), 63–70.

Foot, Phillipa, *Virtues and Vices and Other Essays in Moral Philosophy* (Oxford, 1978).

Fox, James Charles, *Speeches* (London, 1815).

Fuss, Peter, 'Conscience', *Ethics*, 74 (1963–4), 111–20.

Gilson, Etienne (ed.), *The Church Speaks to the Modern World* (New York, 1954).

——*Jean Duns Scot* (Paris, 1952).

Goldstick, D., 'Immorality with a Clear Conscience', *American Philosophical Quarterly*, 17 (1980), 245–50.

Govier, Trudy, 'Belief, Values and the Will', *Dialogue* 15 (1976), 642–66.

——'Is Conscientiousness Always—or Ever—a Virtue?', *Dialogue*, 11 (1972), 241–51.

Grant, Arthur J., *The Huguenots* (London, 1934).

Grant, Brian, 'Descartes, Belief and Will', *Philosophy*, 51 (1976), 401–19.

Gratian, *Decretum*, in *Corpus Iuris Canonici*, ed. Emil Richter and Emil Friedberg (Graz, 1959).

Grotius, Hugo, *De iure belli ac pacis* (trans. F. W. Kelsey, Oxford, 1925).

Haack, Susan, 'Epistemology *with* a Knowing Subject', *Review of Metaphysics*, 33 (1979), 309–35.

Hampshire, Stuart, *Thought and Action* (London, 1959).

Hampton, Jean, 'Contracts and Choices: Does Rawls have a Social Contract Theory?', *Journal of Philosophy*, 77 (1980), 315–38.

Harent, S., 'Foi', in *DTC*, vol. 6.1, cols. 287–9.

Harris, Charles, *Duns Scotus* (Oxford, 1927).

Harrison, Archibald H. W., *The Beginnings of Arminianism* (London, 1926).

Harrison, Jonathan, 'Can I have a Duty to Believe in God?' *Philosophy*, 32 (1957), 241–52.

Hart, H. L. A., 'Are there any Natural Rights?', in Anthony Quinton (ed.), *Political Philosophy* (Oxford, 1967).

——'Bentham on Legal Rights', in Alfred Simpson (ed.), *Oxford Essays in Jurisprudence: Second Series* (Oxford, 1971).

Hempel, Carl, *Philosophy of Natural Science* (Englewood Cliffs, 1966).

Henderson, G. P., 'Censure under Control', *Ratio*, 15 (1973), 44–56.

Henriques, Ursula, *Religious Toleration in England, 1789–1833* (London, 1961).

Hoadly, Benjamin, *The Common Rights of Subjects Defended* (London, 1719).

Hobbes, Thomas, *Leviathan*, ed. C. B. Macpherson (Harmondsworth, 1968).

Holborow, L. C., 'Blame, Praise and Credit', *Aristotelian Society Proceedings*, 72 (1971–2), 85–100.

Hook, Sydney, *Heresy, Yes—Conspiracy, No* (New York, 1953).

Hooker, Richard, *Of the Laws of Ecclesiastical Polity* (London, 1907).

Hospers, John, *Human Conduct* (New York, 1961).

Hume, David, *Enquiries*, ed. L. A. Selby-Bigge and P. H. Nidditch (Oxford, 1975).

——'Of miracles', in *Enquiry Concerning Human Understanding*.

——*A Treatise of Human Nature* (London, 1911).

Hunter, J. F. M., 'Conscience', *Mind*, 72 (1963), 309–34.

Hyman, Arthur, and J. J. Walsh (eds.), *Philosophy in the Middle Ages* (Indianapolis, 1973).

Jacques, Émile, *Les Années d'exil d'Antoine Arnauld 1679–1694* (Louvain, 1976).

——'L'édition des Œuvres Complètes d'Antoine Arnauld', *Revue d'histoire ecclésiastique*, 70 (1975), 705–30.

James, E. D., 'Faith, Sincerity and Morality: Mandeville and Bayle', in *Mandeville Studies*, ed. I. Primer (The Hague, 1975).

——'Pierre Bayle on Belief and "Évidence"', *French Studies*, 27 (1973), 395–404.

Jansen, Cornelius, *Augustinus* (Louvain, 1640) (reprinted Frankfurt, 1964, 3 vols. bound as one).

Jefferson, Thomas, *Life and Select Writings*, ed. A. Koch and W. Peden (New York, 1944).

Jensen, Henning, 'Morality and Luck', *Philosophy*, 59 (1984), 323–30.

Johnson, D. M., 'A Note on Belief', *Mind*, 85 (1976), 601–2.

Jossua, Jean P., 'Pierre Bayle, précurseur des théologies modernes de la liberté religieuse', *Revue des sciences religieuses*, 39 (1965), 113–57.

Jurieu, Pierre, *Courte Revuë des maximes de morale et des principes de religion de l'auteur . . . de la Critique Générale* (1691).

Kant, Immanuel, 'An Answer to the Question: "What is Enlightenment?"', in H. Reiss (ed.), H. B. Nisbet (trans.), *Kant's Political Writings* (Cambridge, 1970).

——*Critique of Pure Reason*, trans. N. Kemp Smith (London, 1951).

——*Groundwork of the Metaphysic of Morals*, trans. H. J. Paton (New York, 1964).

——*The Metaphysical Elements of Justice*, trans. J. Ladd (Indianapolis, 1965).

——*Metaphysical Principles of Virtue*, trans. J. Ellington (New York, 1964).

——*Religion Within the Limits of Reason Alone*, trans. T. M. Greene and H. H. Hudson (New York, 1960).

Kauber, Peter and Hare, Peter H., 'The Right and the Duty to Will to Believe', *Canadian Journal of Philosophy*, 4 (1974), 327-43.

Kenner, Lionel, 'On Blaming', *Mind*, 76 (1967), 238-49.

Kilcullen, John, 'Locke on Political Obligation', *Review of Politics*, 45 (1983), 323-44.

——'Mill on Duty and Liberty', *Australasian Journal of Philosophy*, 59 (1981), 290-300.

——'Utilitarianism and Virtue', *Ethics*, 93 (1983), 451-66.

Konvitz, Milton, *First Amendment Freedoms: Selected Cases* (Ithaca, 1963).

——*Fundamental Liberties of a Free People* (Ithaca, 1957).

Kordig, Carl R., 'Pseudo-Appeals to Conscience', *Journal of Value Inquiry*, 10 (1976), 7-17.

Kornblith, Hilary, 'Beyond Foundationalism and the Coherence Theory', *Journal of Philosophy*, 67 (1980), 597-612.

——'Justified Belief and Epistemically Responsible Action', *Philosophical Review*, 92 (1983), 33-48.

Kuhn, Thomas, *The Structure of Scientific Revolutions* (Chicago, 1970).

Labrousse, Elizabeth, *Bayle*, trans. Denys Potts (Oxford, 1983).

——*Pierre Bayle* (The Hague, 1963-4), 2 vols.

Lakatos, Imre, 'Falsification and Methodology of Scientific Research Programmes', in I. Lakatos and A. Musgrave (eds.), *Criticism and the Growth of Knowledge* (Cambridge, 1970).

Laporte, Jean, *La Doctrine de Port-Royal*, (Paris, 1951).

Lecler, Joseph, *Toleration and the Reformation* (London, 1960).

Lehrer, Keith, *Knowledge* (Oxford, 1974).

Leibniz, Georg, *Discourse on Metaphysics; Correspondence with Arnauld*, trans. G. R. Montgomery (La Salle, 1957).

——*Theodicy* (London, 1952).

Lennon, Thomas, M., 'Jansenism and the *Crise pyrrhonienne*', *Journal of the History of Ideas*, 38 (1977), 297-306.

——'La logique Janséniste de la liberté', *Revue d'histoire et de philosophie religieuse*, 59 (1979), 37-44.

——'Philosophical Commentary', in Nicholas Malebranche, *The Search after Truth* (Columbus, 1980).

Levy, Leonard, *Legacy of Suppression* (Cambridge, Mass., 1960).

Ligou, Daniel, *Le protestantisme en France de 1598 à 1715* (Paris, 1968).

Locke, John, *Of the Conduct of the Understanding* in *Works* (London, 1824), vol. 2.

——*Essay Concerning Human Understanding*, ed. P. H. Nidditch (Oxford, 1975).

——*Letter Concerning Toleration*, in *Works* (London, 1824),vol. 5.

——*A Second Letter Concerning Toleration*, in *Works* (London, 1824), vol. 5.

——*Second Treatise*, in *Two Treatises of Government*, ed. P. Laslett (Cambridge, 1960).

——*A Third Letter for Toleration*, in *Works* (London, 1824), vol. 5.

——*Two Tracts of Government*, ed. P. Adams (Cambridge, 1967).

Long, Anthony, 'Freedom and Determinism in Stoic Theory of Human Action', in *Problems in Stoicism*, ed. A. A. Long (London, 1971).

Lubac, Henri de, SJ, *Augustinianism and Modern Theology*, trans. L. Sheppard (London, 1969).

Luther, Martin, *Secular Authority*, in *Works* (Philadelphia, 1915), vol. 3.

Macaulay, T. B., *Critical and Historical Essays* (London, 1907).

McCloskey, H. J., 'Liberty of Expression, its Grounds and Limits', *Inquiry*, 13 (1970), 219-37.

Magee, Brian, *Modern British Philosophy* (London, 1971).

Malebranche, Nicholas, *Traité de morale*, ed. M. Adam (Paris, 1975).

McGuire, C., 'On Conscience', *Journal of Philosophy*, 60 (1963), 253-63.

Marcuse, Herbert, 'Repressive Tolerance', in *A Critique of Pure Tolerance* (Boston, 1969).

Miel, Jan, *Pascal and Theology* (Baltimore, 1969).

Mill, James, 'The Formation of Opinions', *Westminster Review*, 6 (July 1826).

Mill, J. S., *Essays on Ethics, Religion and Society*, ed. J. Robson, in *Collected Works* (Toronto, 1969), vol. 10.

——'An Examination of Sir William Hamilton's Philosophy', in Morgenbesser and Walsh.

——*On Liberty*, ed. J. Robson, in *Collected Works* (Toronto, 1977), vol. 18.

——*Prefaces to Liberty: Selected Writings of J. S. Mill*, ed. B. Wishey (Boston, 1959).

——*Representative Government*, ed. J. Robson, in *Collected Works* (Toronto, 1977), vol. 19.

——'Sedgwick', in *Essays on Ethics*.

——'The Spirit of the Age', in J. S. Mill, *Essays on Literature and Society*, ed. J. Schneewind (New York, 1965).

——*A System of Logic*, ed. J. Robson, in *Collected Works* (Toronto, 1973), vols. 7 and 8.

——*Utilitarianism*, in *Essays on Ethics*.

Montaigne, Michel de, *Essays*, trans. John Florio (London, 1965).

More, Thomas, *Utopia*, ed. J. C. Collins (Oxford, 1904).

Morgenbesser, Sidney, and Walsh, J. J., (eds.), *Free Will* (Engelwood Cliffs, 1962).

Nagel, Thomas, 'Moral Luck', *Aristotelian Society Proceedings*, suppl. vol. 50 (1976), 115–51.

New Catholic Encyclopaedia (New York, 1967).

Nobbs, Douglas, *Theocracy and Toleration: A Study of the Disputes in Dutch Calvinism from 1600 to 1650* (Cambridge, 1938).

Nozick, Robert, *Anarchy, State and Utopia* (New York, 1974).

Oberman, Heiko, *Forerunners of the Reformation* (New York, 1966).

——*The Harvest of Medieval Theology* (Cambridge, Mass. 1963).

Ockham: see William of Ockham.

O'Hear, Anthony, 'Belief and the Will', *Philosophy*, 47 (1972), 95–111.

Orcibal, Jean, *Correspondance de Jansenius* (Louvain, 1947).

——*Louis XIV et les protestants* (Paris, 1951).

Origen, *Traité des principes*, trans. H. Crouzel and M. Simonetti (Paris, 1978).

Paine, Tom, *The Rights of Man* (Harmondsworth, 1969).

Paley, William, *Moral and Political Philosophy*, in *Works* (London, 1830), vol. 3.

Parker, Richard, 'Blame, Punishment and the Role of Results,' *American Philosophical Quarterly*, 21 (1984), 269–76.

Pascal, Blaise, *Écrits sur la grâce*, in *Œuvres complètes*, ed. J. Chevalier (Paris, 1954).

——*Les Provinciales*, ed. L. Cognet (Paris, 1965).

Peirce, Charles S., *Collected Papers*, ed. C. Hartshorne and P. Weiss (Cambridge, Mass., 1952).

——*Philosophical Writings*, ed. J. Buchler (New York, 1955).

Penelhum, Terence, *God and Skepticism* (Dordrecht, 1983).

Pennock, J. Roland, and Chapman, John W., (eds.), *Ethics, Economics and the Law* (New York, 1982).

Perkins, William, *A Discourse of Conscience* in T. W. Merrill, *William Perkins* (Niewkoop, 1966).

PL: Migne, Jacques P. (ed.), *Patrologia latina* (Paris, 1844– 64).

Pojman, Louis P., 'Belief and Will', *Religious Studies*, 14 (1978), 1–14.

Pollock, John, *Knowledge and Justification* (Princeton, 1974).

Popkin, Richard H., *The High Road to Pyrrhonism* (San Diego, 1980).

——*A History of Scepticism from Erasmus to Spinoza* (Berkeley, 1979).

——'Pierre Bayle's Place in 17th Century Scepticism', in Paul Dibon (ed.), *Pierre Bayle, le philosophe de Rotterdam* (Amsterdam, 1959).

Popper, Karl, *Conjectures and Refutations* (London, 1969).

——*Logic of Scientific Discovery* (London, 1959).

——*Objective Knowledge* (Oxford, 1972).

Price, H. H., 'Belief and Will', *Aristotelian Society Proceedings*, suppl. vol. 28 (1954).

Puaux, Frank, 'L'évolution des théories politiques du Protestantisme français pendant le règne de Louis XIV', *Bulletin de la Société de l'histoire du Protestantisme français*, 62 (1913), 386–413, 481–96.

Quinn, Warren S., 'Moral and Other Realisms: Some Initial Difficulties', in Alvin I. Goldman and Jaegwon Kim (eds.), *Values and Morals* (Dordrecht, 1978).

Raphael, David (ed.)., *British Moralists* (Oxford, 1969).

Rawls, John, *A Theory of Justice* (Oxford, 1972).

——'Justice as Reciprocity', in *Utilitarianism*, ed. S. Gorovitz (Indianapolis, 1971).

Rex, Walter, *Pascal's Provincial Letters: An Introduction* (New York, 1977).

——*Pierre Bayle and Religious Controversy* (The Hague, 1965).

Richards, David, 'International Distributive Justice', in J. R. Pennock and J. W. Chapman (eds.), *Ethics, Economics and the Law* (New York, 1982).

Richards, Norvin, 'Luck and Desert', *Mind*, 95 (1986), 198–209.

Riley, Patrick, 'General and Particular Will in the Political Thought of Pierre Bayle', *Journal of The History of Philosophy*, 24 (1986), 173–95.

Ross, W. D., *The Right and the Good* (Oxford, 1930).

Rousseau, Jean-Jacques, *The Social Contract*, trans. G. D. H. Cole (London, 1973).

Rowbotham, Arnold H., *Missionary and Mandarin: The Jesuits at the Court of China* (New York, 1966).

Sarpi, Paul, *Historie of the Councel of Trent*, trans. N. Brent (London, 1629).

Scanlon, Thomas, 'A Theory of Freedom of Expression', *Philosophy and Public Affairs*, 1 (1972), 204–26.

Schaff, Philip (ed.), *The Creeds of Christendom* (New York, 1877).

——*Select Library of the Nicene and Post-Nicene Fathers of the Christian Church: First Series* (Grand Rapids, 1969–75).

Schleyer, G. K., *Anfänge des Gallikanismus* (Berlin, 1937).

Schlossberger, Eugene, 'Why we are Responsible for our Emotions', *Mind*, 95 (1986), 37–56.

Schofield, Malcolm, Burnyeat, Myles and Barnes, Jonathan (eds.), *Doubt and Dogmatism: Studies in Hellenistic Epistmology* (Oxford, 1980).

Scotus: see Duns Scotus.

Sedgwick, Alexander, *Jansenism in Seventeenth-Century France* (Charlottesville, 1977).

Sidgwick, Henry, *Methods of Ethics* (New York, 1966).

Skinner, Quentin, *Foundations of Modern Political Thought* (Cambridge, 1978).

Snare, Frank, 'Dissolving the Moral Contract', *Philosophy*, 52 (1977), 301-12.

Spinoza, Benedict, *Works*, trans. R. Elwes (New York, 1951).

Squires, J. E. R., 'Blame', *Philosophical Quarterly*, 18 (1968), 54-60.

Stillingfleet, William, *Works* (London, 1710).

Stough, Charlotte, *Greek Scepticism* (Berkeley, 1969).

Suckiel, Ellen K., 'Adequate Evidence and the Will to Believe', *Transactions of the Peirce Society*, 15 (1979), 322-39.

Sykes, Norman, 'Benjamin Hoadly', in F. J. C. Hearnshaw (ed.), *The Social and Political Ideas of Some English Thinkers of the Augustan Age* (London, 1928).

Taylor, Jeremy, *Discourse of the Liberty of Prophesying*, in *Works*, vol. 5 (London, 1849).

——*Ductor dubitantium*, in *Works*, vol. 9 (London, 1851).

Thonnard, François J., 'Justice de Dieu et justice humaine selon Saint Augustin', *Augustinus*, 12 (1967), 387-402.

Truchet, Jacques, *La prédication de Bossuet* (Paris, 1960).

Tullock, John, *Rational Theology and Christian Philosophy in England in the 17th Century* (Edinburgh, 1874).

Unger, Peter, 'An Analysis of Factual Knowledge', *Journal of Philosophy*, 65 (1968), 157-70.

van Inwagen, Peter, *An Essay on Free Will* (Oxford, 1983).

Van Kley, Dale, *The Jansenists and the Expulsion of the Jesuits from France, 1757-1765* (New Haven, 1975).

Vidler, Alexander, *The Church in an Age of Revolution* (London, 1961).

Walker, David, *The Decline of Hell* (Chicago, 1964).

——'Origène en France', in *Courants religieux et humanisme*, (Paris, 1959).

Wellman, Carl, 'Ethical Disagreement and Objective Truth', *American Philosophical Quarterly*, 12 (1975), pp.211-21.

Wells, Norman J., 'Objective Being: Descartes and his Sources', *The Modern Schoolman*, 45 (1967-8), 49-61.

Wendel, François, *Calvin* (London, 1972).

Whiteman, Anne, 'Church and State', in *The New Cambridge Modern History* (Cambridge, 1957-79), vol. 5.

Wilcox, John T., 'Is it always right to do what you think is right?', *Journal of Value Inquiry*, 2 (1968), 95-107.

William of Ockham, *Opera plurima* (Lyon, 1495, repr. London, 1962).

——*Predestination, God's Foreknowledge and Future Contingents*, trans. Marilyn McCord Adams and Norman Kretzman (New York, 1969).

William of Sherwood, *Introduction to Logic*, trans. with an introduction and notes by Norman Kretzmann (Minneapolis, 1966).

Williams, Bernard, 'Deciding to Believe', in *Problems of the Self* (Cambridge, 1973).

——*Moral Luck* (Cambridge, 1981).

Winters, Barbara, 'Believing at Will', *Journal of Philosophy*, 76 (1979), 243–56.

Wolterstorff, Nicholas, 'Can Belief in God be Rational if it has no Foundations?', in Alvin Plantinga and N. Wolterstorff (eds.), *Faith and Rationality: Reason and Belief in God* (Notre Dame, 1983).

Woodhouse Arthur, *Puritanism and Liberty* (London, 1951).

Zeller, Eduard, *Stoics, Epicureans and Sceptics*, trans. O. J. Reichel (London, 1880).

INDEX

right action 71, 183
right of petitioning 127 n., 167 n.
rights:
    absolute 61, 127
    and duties 61-3, 114
    and liberties 62 n., 114
    implicitly claimed by actions 114
    moral 62, 63, 90-1
    natural 112-13, 114
    of conscience *see* conscience
    of truth *see* truth
    prima facie 127
    relative 61-2, 63, 66
    unjustly exercised 62-4
    vested 120
    wrongly acquired 62-3, 66
Riley, P. 74 n.
Ross, W. D. 108 n.
Rousseau, J.-J. 120 n.
Rowbotham, A. 10 n., 86 n.
ruler, function of 95, 97, 98, 99

St Bartholomew massacre 54
Saint-Cyran, Jean Duvergier de
    Hauranne, abbé de 12
salvation 9, 10, 60
    universal 10
Sanderson, W. 44 n.
Sarpi, P. 140 n.
Scanlon, T. 128 n.
scepticism 58, 59, 77, 101, 102 n.,
    115, 117, 136, 137, 140 n., 149,
    152, 169, 203
    Academic 58, 136, 170
    Pyrrhonian 58, 86 n., 136
Schaff, P. 8 n.
Schleyer, G. 11 n.
Schlossberger, E. 190 n.
scripture 24, 25, 43, 53 n., 91 n.,
    103, 104
second table 96, 98
sect 111
secundum finem 49, 51
security 122, 123, 130
Sedgwick, A. 7 n., 8 n., 11 n., 13 n.,
    14 n., 56 n.
seeming and being 76, 78, 110, 115-
    16, 152, 153
self-cultivation 182, 184, 197
self-deception 42, 44 n., 81, 82 n.,
    90 n., 127 n.
self-evidence 146
self-interest 86, 112, 122

Seneca 48
Sextus Empiricus 58, 59 n., 140 n.,
    146 n., 150 n.
Sidgwick, H. 95 n., 177 n., 196 n.,
    201 n.
sin 17, 23 n., 37, 38, 50
    formal 16, 21 n., 22, 26, 34, 38
    knowledge required for 15, 16,
    17, 18, 20, 22, 23 n., 24, 28, 30,
    32 n., 52, 53 n., 81, 82; *see also*
    thoughts; truth
    material 16, 17, 21, 22, 33, 38
    merely philosophic, possibility of
    16, 23, 29-35, 46
    moral *see* sin, philosophic
    mortal 18 n., 23 n., 29, 30, 50 n.
    philosophic 3, 15-20, 26, 27, 31,
    38, 42, 52 n., 81, 180 n.
    theological 3, 16-19, 23 n., 24 n.,
    29, 32, 49
    venial 23 n., 50
sincerity 15, 52, 79 n., 188
Skinner, Q. 11 n., 54 n.
Snare, F. 131 n.
social contract 94, 112-13, 124 n.,
    202
Socinians 103 n., 179
Socrates 59
Spinoza, B. de 141 n.
spontaneity of action 179, 201
spontaneous beliefs or thoughts 144,
    148 n., 154, 169, 196, 198, 200
Squires, J. 189 n., 194 n.
state of nature 114
Stillingfleet, W. 141 n.
Stoicism 58, 68 n., 94 n., 136, 140
Stough, C. 140 n.
subjectivism 77
Suckiel, E. 141 n.
supererogatory acts 158
suspense of judgement 58, 59, 77,
    87 n., 101, 102 n., 136, 141,
    152
suspicion of mistake 149-50, 153
Sykes, N. 15 n.

Taylor, J. 34 n., 44 n., 115 n.,
    138 n., 141 n.
temerity 87-8
temptation 94-5, 98, 99, 100, 127
Terrill, Fr 33, 34 n., 44 n.
testimony 82 n., 148 n.
theodicy 41 n.